Dictionary of Trash Behavior

Sarah Melland
Your Dating UnExpert

Published by Ripe Melland Media

This book is a work of commentary, satire, and personal opinion. Any resemblance to real persons, living or dead, dating app profiles, situationships, emotionally unavailable men, or suspiciously familiar red flags is purely coincidental… and statistically inevitable.

The content of this book is for informational and entertainment purposes only. It does not constitute medical, psychological, legal, or professional advice. The author and publisher assume no responsibility for actions taken by readers based on the material herein.

ISBN:
eBook: 978-1-969137-25-9
Paperback: 978-1-969137-24-2

Printed in the United States of America
First Edition

Table of Contents

1 Introduction

3 Core Dictionary (A–Z)

96 Clinical Terms

102 Historical / Old-School Terms

146 Acronyms & Text Culture

152 Archetypes & Roles

245 Seduction & Power Terms

277 Movies That Exhibit Trash Behavior

INTRODUCTION

If you're reading this, chances are you've lived through at least one situation that made you stop mid-text and think, *what the hell is actually happening right now.*

Maybe it was the man who texted you every day... and still somehow never asked you out.

Maybe it was the one who made you feel everything in a week... and nothing the week after.

Or maybe it was the relationship that looked completely normal on paper... but quietly drained you in real life.

This book isn't here to judge you for any of it. It's here to name it.

Because once you can name something, it stops feeling so personal... and starts becoming predictable.

I've spent years studying patterns—how people show up, how they avoid, how they take just enough to keep you there, and how easily we can confuse attention with intention. Not from a distance, but from inside it. From dating it, rationalizing it, laughing about it later, and eventually seeing it for exactly what it was.

What you're about to read is a collection of those patterns—labeled, defined, and broken down in a way that's equal parts clarity and entertainment. It's meant to be read like a conversation you'd have with your friends after two drinks... the kind where everything suddenly makes sense and everyone starts saying, *wait... that happened to me too.*

You can read it straight through, jump around, or send screenshots to your group chat like evidence.

Because let's be honest—half the power of understanding this behavior is recognizing it in real time... and the other half is being able to say:

Oh. That's what that was.

And once you see it clearly, you don't unsee it.

A

Abs-olutely Not (Shirtless Profile Guy) /abs-ə-ˈlü-t-lē nɒt/ A man whose entire personality is his torso and nothing else. Synonyms: shirtless spammer, gym mirror philosopher, thirst trapper. Antonyms: substance, personality, effort. Savage Sentence: The Abs-olutely Not profile had six angles of his chest and zero evidence of a personality. UnExpert Advice: If all he offers is abs, that's all you're getting.

Access Without Title /ˈak-ˌses wi-ˈthout ˈtī-təl/ Full girlfriend privileges... with zero commitment. Synonyms: benefits without labels, unpaid emotional labor, undefined access Antonyms: commitment, clarity, defined relationship Savage Sentence: He access-without-titled her into giving everything for nothing. UnExpert Advice: If he won't define it, don't give it everything.

Adultery /ə-ˈdəl-tə-rē/ Engaging in sexual relationships outside of a committed marriage. Synonyms: cheating, infidelity, marital betrayal Antonyms: fidelity, loyalty, commitment Savage Sentence: She didn't steal your man, she inherited a liability with a history of adultery. UnExpert Advice: If they justify it once, they'll justify it again.

Affair (Emotional or Physical) /ə-ˈfer/ A secret romantic or sexual connection outside a committed relationship, often involving emotional or physical betrayal. Synonyms: side relationship, hidden intimacy, betrayal bond Antonyms: exclusivity, transparency, loyalty Savage Sentence: An affair is just cheating that thinks it sounds romantic. UnExpert Advice: If it needs to be hidden, it shouldn't exist.

Affection Rationing /ə-ˈfek-shən ˈra-shə-niŋ/ Gives love in tiny doses... to control your behavior. Synonyms: affection control, emotional withholding, love restriction Antonyms: consistency, generosity, emotional availability Savage Sentence: If you feel addicted to their attention, you're probably dealing with affection rationing. UnExpert Advice: If love feels controlled, it's not love.

Affordating /ə-ˈfȯr-ˌdā-tiŋ/ Low-effort, low-investment dating disguised as being "chill" or "practical." Synonyms: bare minimum dating, low-effort courting, budget bonding Antonyms: intentional dating, thoughtful effort, real investment Savage Sentence: Affordating is doing the bare minimum and calling it a vibe. UnExpert Advice: Cheap isn't the problem. The lack of effort is. Learn the difference.

Algorithmic Validation Addiction /ˌal-gə-ˈri-thmik va-lə-ˈdā-shən ə-ˈdik-shən/ Prioritizing likes, views, and online attention over real-life emotional connection. Synonyms: clout chasing, attention dependency, social media validation loop Antonyms: presence, real connection, emotional availability Savage Sentence: Algorithmic validation addiction is why everything feels performative and nothing feels real. UnExpert Advice: If you feel like you're competing with strangers online, you're not in a relationship. You're in a casting call.

Alimony /ˈa-lə-ˌmō-nē/ Court-ordered financial support paid to an ex-spouse after separation or divorce. Synonyms: spousal support, financial tie, post-relationship obligation Antonyms: financial independence, clean break Savage Sentence: Alimony is the monthly reminder that bad decisions come with subscriptions. UnExpert Advice: Some endings aren't clean. Just make sure they're understood.

Almost Accountability /ˈôl-mōst ə-ˌkoun-tə-ˈbi-lə-tē/ "I'm sorry you feel that way." No ownership. Just vibes. Synonyms: fake apology, responsibility dodge, blame deflection Antonyms: ownership, real apology, accountability Savage Sentence: He almost-accountability'd his way out of every conversation. UnExpert Advice: An apology without ownership is just manipulation in polite wording.

Almost Guy /ˈôl-mōst gī/ Almost calls. Almost commits. Almost chooses you. Almost wastes your time. Synonyms: almost-there man, near-miss relationship, potential without delivery Antonyms: decisive partner, full effort, real commitment Savage Sentence: He almost-guyed his way through something that never fully existed. UnExpert Advice: Almost is not a relationship. It's a delay tactic.

The "Almost Text" King /ðə ˈôl-mōst tekst kiŋ/ Types... deletes... disappears... reappears three days later like nothing happened. Synonyms: hesitation texter, inconsistency communicator, delay specialist Antonyms: direct communication, consistency, intention Savage Sentence: The "Almost Text" King is effort stuck in draft mode. UnExpert Advice: Consistency beats potential every time.

Almost Griever /ˈôl-mōst ˈgrē-vər/ Mourns something that was never fully real... like it was. Synonyms: unrealized loss, imagined grief, incomplete attachment Antonyms: closure, clarity, acceptance Savage Sentence: She almost grieved something that never fully existed. UnExpert Advice: Let go of what never fully was.

Alpha (Dating Context) /ˈal-fə/ A self-proclaimed dominant personality, often masking insecurity with control, ego, or performative masculinity. Synonyms: faux-dominant, ego performer, podcast alpha Antonyms: grounded confidence, emotional intelligence, secure masculinity Savage Sentence: If he has to tell you he's the alpha, he's already not. UnExpert Advice: Real power is quiet. If it feels forced, it's a performance.

Alpha Widow /ˈal-fə ˈwi-dō/ A woman who remains emotionally attached to a high-value ex who never committed, comparing all future partners to him and sabotaging new relationships. Synonyms: ex-obsessed, comparison trapper, past-locked Antonyms: emotional closure, presence, forward movement Savage Sentence: No one can compete with a fantasy that never had to work in real life like an alpha widow can. UnExpert Advice: If you're still emotionally somewhere else, don't pretend to be available here.

Antiversary /ˌan-tə-ˈvər-sə-rē/ The anniversary of a breakup, betrayal, or relationship trauma that is revisited or obsessed over instead of released. Synonyms: breakup anniversary, trauma loop, emotional timestamp Antonyms: closure, healing, release Savage Sentence: You didn't move on, you just scheduled your pain with an antiversary hoping it would make you feel better. UnExpert Advice: Healing doesn't need a yearly reminder.

Approach Anxiety /ə-ˈprōch aŋ-ˈzī-ə-tē/ The fear of initiating conversation with someone attractive, often leading to avoidance and reliance on apps instead of real-world interaction. Synonyms: social hesitation, fear of rejection, initiation block Antonyms: confidence, action, social courage Savage Sentence: He approach-anxietied himself into staying invisible. UnExpert Advice: Confidence isn't natural. It's practiced.

Attachmencycle /ə-ˈtach-mən-ˌsī-kəl/ You detach → he returns → you reattach → repeat until insanity. Synonyms: attachment loop, emotional relapse cycle, on-off pattern Antonyms: detachment, closure, emotional freedom Savage Sentence: She attachmencycled her way back into the same outcome. UnExpert Advice: If the pattern repeats, the ending won't change.

Attachment Hallucination /ə-ˈtach-mənt hə-ˌlü-sə-ˈnā-shən/ Feels a deep bond... that doesn't actually exist. Mistakes minimal effort for deep interest.

Synonyms: imagined connection, illusion bond, false signal reading, attention misinterpretation Antonyms: real connection, mutual interest, clarity, discernment Savage Sentence: One message and suddenly you think he cares, you are in an attachment hallucination loop. UnExpert Advice: Interest is shown consistently, not occasionally.

Attention Leasing /ə-ˈten-shən ˈlē-siŋ/ He borrows your time, energy, and attention… with no intention of ever owning up. Synonyms: temporary access agreement, emotional renting, noncommittal usage Antonyms: investment, commitment, ownership of actions Savage Sentence: He attention leased you like a rental car. Drives it hard, returns it empty, and disappears. UnExpert Advice: If he's not investing, revoke access. You're not a free resource.

Attention Whore / Attention Seeker /ə-ˈten-shən hōr/ Someone who craves constant validation through flirting, posting, or drama—prioritizing attention over real connection. Synonyms: validation addict, thirst trapper, drama generator Antonyms: self-worth, grounded attention, intentional connection Savage Sentence: She attention-whored her way into constant noise and zero depth. UnExpert Advice: If they need the crowd, they'll never choose just you.

Attentionorexic /ə-ˌten-shə-ˈnôr-ek-sik/ Starves you of attention… then binges it when he's bored. Synonyms: attention restrictor, intermittent engager, emotional binge cycle Antonyms: consistency, steady attention, reliability Savage Sentence: He disappears for days, then floods you with attention like it resets everything. It doesn't, he's just attentionorexic. UnExpert Advice: Consistency matters more than intensity spikes.

Attentionship /ə-ˈten-shən-ˌship/ He doesn't want you… he wants access to your attention. Synonyms: attention-based connection, ego feeding dynamic, validation loop Antonyms: real relationship, mutual interest, emotional connection Savage Sentence: He attentionshipped his way into staying relevant without commitment. UnExpert Advice: Attention is not affection. Don't confuse the two.

Attention Starvation Mode /ə-ˈten-shən ˌstär-ˈvā-shən mōd/ So deprived of attention that anything feels like love. Synonyms: attention deprivation, affection hunger, validation desperation Antonyms: fulfillment, self-worth, emotional abundance Savage Sentence: When you're starved, crumbs feel like a feast. That's the problem, you are in attention starvation mode. Girl, eat. UnExpert Advice: Fill your own life so you're not desperate for someone else's attention.

Audacity Syndrome /ô-ˈda-sə-tē ˈsin-ˌdrōm/ When he brings nothing to the table... but still has high standards for you. Synonyms: inflated ego disorder, delusion complex, entitlement epidemic Antonyms: self-awareness, humility, equal standards Savage Sentence: The way he has requirements with zero qualifications should be studied and peer reviewed as audacity syndrome. UnExpert Advice: If he expects more than he offers, let him go find someone equally delusional.

Audition Mode Forever /ô-ˈdi-shən mōd fər-ˈe-vər/ You keep trying to prove your worth... for a role that was never open. Synonyms: endless proving, approval chasing, performance dating Antonyms: being chosen, mutual effort, secure connection Savage Sentence: You're performing for a man who already decided you weren't the lead. Keep being in audition mode forever, sis. UnExpert Advice: You don't audition for someone who's meant to choose you.

Aura (Dating Context) /ˈȯr-ə/ The unspoken energy or vibe someone gives off that instantly attracts—or repels. Synonyms: vibe, presence, energy, magnetism Antonyms: awkwardness, try-hard energy, cringe behavior Savage Sentence: You didn't lose feelings—you watched his aura disappear in real time. UnExpert Advice: Attraction isn't always logical. But losing it? Usually is.

B

B (or "b") /bē/ A casual, noncommittal term of endearment used early in flirting to create familiarity without intention. Synonyms: vague pet name, low-effort affection, placeholder term Antonyms: intentional language, defined interest, real labels Savage Sentence: If everyone is "b," no one is special. UnExpert Advice: Pet names without intention are just placeholders for effort.

Baby Mama Drama / Baby Daddy Drama /ˈbā-bē ˈmä-mə ˈdrä-mə/ • /ˈbā-bē ˈda-dē ˈdrä-mə/ Ongoing chaos with a co-parent or ex that spills into new relationships, often involving conflict, money, or emotional baggage. Synonyms: co-parent chaos, ex entanglement, baggage overload. Antonyms: healthy co-parenting, boundaries, emotional stability. Savage Sentence: You thought you were dating him... but you're actually in a relationship with his unresolved past of Baby mama drama. UnExpert Advice: If the chaos isn't contained, it becomes yours. Choose accordingly.

Back Burner /bak ˈbər-nər/ Keeping someone as a secondary option—maintaining minimal contact to preserve access while prioritizing others. Synonyms: backup option, emotional reserve, safety net. Antonyms: priority, commitment, full attention. Savage Sentence: He gave you the Back Burner and showed you just enough attention to keep you there. UnExpert Advice: If you feel like an option, stop acting like one.

Bad Pancake /bad pan-kāk/ The first person you date after a serious breakup—used as emotional practice but rarely meant to last. Synonyms: rebound trial, emotional warm-up, practice relationship. Antonyms: intentional partner, healed connection, readiness Savage Sentence: You weren't the one—you were the bad pancake. UnExpert Advice: If they're fresh out of something serious, don't expect something serious.

Bae /bā/ Originally "Before Anyone Else," now often used loosely or ironically to label undefined or non-exclusive relationships. Synonyms: fake title, ironic label, situationship nickname Antonyms: real partner, defined relationship, exclusivity Savage Sentence: He called her his bae in private... and "just a friend" in public. UnExpert Advice: If the title is unclear, the relationship is too.

Banksying /ˈbänk-sē-iŋ/ Using cryptic, artistic, or vague romantic gestures instead of clear communication or commitment. Synonyms: performative romance, poetic avoidance, emotional ghost art Antonyms: direct communication, clarity, intentional effort He banksy'd you with poems instead of giving you a real answer. UnExpert Advice: If you have to decode it, it's not love. It's deflection.

Bare Minimum Bandit /ber ˈmi-nə-məm ˈban-dɪt/ A man who does the absolute least... and still expects applause, loyalty, and sex. Synonyms: effort thief, low-effort legend, participation trophy seeker Antonyms: overdeliverer, intentional partner, grown man Savage Sentence: He texts "good morning" and thinks he deserves a standing ovation and your body. The delusion is athletic with this bare minimum bandit. UnExpert Advice: If the bar is in hell and he still trips over it, stop lowering yourself to meet him.

Bare Minimum Love Language /ber ˈmi-nə-məm ləv ˈlaŋ-gwij/ His version of love is replying... eventually. Synonyms: delayed response affection, minimal effort communication, crumbs as care Antonyms: active love, presence, effort Bare Minimum Love Language is effort at its lowest setting. Savage Sentence: If replying is his version of love, the relationship is already underperforming. UnExpert Advice: Love is shown consistently, not occasionally.

Bare Minimum Addiction /ber ˈmi-nə-məm ə-ˈdik-shən/ Gets hooked on the smallest effort like it's heroin. Synonyms: crumb addiction, minimal effort dependency, attention craving Antonyms: standards, consistency, full effort Savage Sentence: One decent moment and suddenly you're hooked again with bare minimum addiction. UnExpert Advice: Don't get addicted to what should be standard.

Bare Minimum Beggar /ber ˈmi-nə-məm ˈbe-gər/ Accepts crumbs... then thanks him for the meal. Synonyms: low-standard accepter, gratitude for nothing, crumb collector Antonyms: standards, self-worth, expectation of effort Savage Sentence: You're thanking him for doing the absolute least. That's the problem. Stop being a bare minimum beggar. UnExpert Advice: Stop rewarding behavior you don't want repeated.

Bare Minimum Gratitude /ber ˈmi-nə-məm ˈgra-tə-ˌtüd/ He texts "good morning" once... and suddenly he's husband material. Synonyms: low-effort praise, inflated appreciation, minimal effort worship Antonyms: standards, discernment, expectation of consistency Savage Sentence: She bare minimum gratituded his behavior into something meaningful. UnExpert Advice: Consistency matters more than isolated moments.

Bareminimumism /ˈber ˈmi-nə-mə-ˌni-zəm/ Does one thing right... and thinks he deserves lifelong loyalty. Synonyms: effort exaggeration, minimalism in action, overvalued behavior Antonyms: consistency, sustained effort, reliability Savage Sentence: He did one decent thing and now acts like he's been a great man ever since with one bareminimumism gesture. UnExpert Advice: One moment doesn't define someone. Patterns do.

Barely There Boyfriend /ˈber-lē ther ˈboi-ˌfrend/ Technically exists... emotionally unavailable, physically inconsistent, spiritually missing. Synonyms: part-time partner, ghost with benefits, low-presence male Antonyms: present partner, consistent man, fully available Savage Sentence: Your barely there boyfriend shows up like a Wi-Fi signal in a basement. UnExpert Advice: If you feel alone in a relationship, you already are.

Beige Flag (or Pink Flag) /bāzh flag/ • /piŋk flag/ Mildly off-putting or odd behaviors that aren't dealbreakers but make you pause. Synonyms: soft warning, minor ick, low-level turn-off. Antonyms: green flag, strong attraction, aligned behavior. Savage Sentence: A Beige Flag is the quiet "hmm..." you can't ignore. UnExpert Advice: Small things don't stay small. Pay attention early.

Benching /ˈben-chiŋ/ Keeping you on standby while they explore other options... then subbing you in when they're bored. Synonyms: backup plan energy, roster management, emotional substitute. Antonyms: prioritization, exclusivity, respect. Savage Sentence: Benching looks real cute until you realize you've been clapping for a man who never even put you in the game. UnExpert Advice: You are not the bench. You are the game. Act like it.

Beta (Dating Context) /ˈbā-tə/ A label often used to describe someone as passive, lacking confidence, or overly accommodating—sometimes inaccurately or unfairly. Synonyms: passive partner, approval-seeker, low-assertion energy. Antonyms: assertive, confident, self-assured. Savage Sentence: You called him Beta the second you realized you could walk all over him. UnExpert Advice: Kind is good. Passive is not. Learn the difference.

Bio of Demands (Don't-Want Girl/Guy) /ˈbī-ō əv di-ˈmands/ A profile made entirely of complaints and disqualifications instead of actual personality. Synonyms: negativity list, anti-attraction bio, resentment résumé. Antonyms: inviting profile, self-expression, positivity. Savage Sentence: The Bio of Demands had more rules than personality and somehow still expected attraction. UnExpert Advice: If it reads like a warning label, believe it.

Blizzard Buddy /ˈbli-zərd ˈbə-dē/ A temporary partner chosen for convenience during a storm or isolating event, built on circumstance, not substance.

Synonyms: seasonal fling, convenience partner, situational hookup. Antonyms: intentional relationship, lasting connection, genuine compatibility. Savage Sentence: You called him your Blizzard Buddy, he called it something to do until life went back to normal. UnExpert Advice: If it only works in isolation, it won't survive real life.

Blurface Bandit /ˈblər-ˌfās ˈban-dət/ Uses blurry, outdated, or strategically bad photos to hide current reality. Synonyms: pixel fraud, nostalgia catfisher, low-res liar. Antonyms: clear photos, honesty, present-day reality. Savage Sentence: The Blurface Bandit showed up looking nothing like his profile and acted surprised you noticed. UnExpert Advice: If it's blurry, it's intentional.

Body Count /ˈbä-dē kount/ The number of someone's past sexual partners, often used in dating conversations. Synonyms: sexual history, partner count. Antonyms: privacy, irrelevance, maturity. Savage Sentence: He kept bringing up your Body Count like it mattered, and you kept forgetting he has nothing else to offer. UnExpert Advice: Anyone using your past to shame you doesn't deserve your future.

Boomerang (Relationship Version) /ˈbü-mə-ˌraŋ/ An ex who repeatedly comes back for attention, sex, or comfort, only to disappear again. Synonyms: repeat offender, emotional recycler, zombie on steroids. Antonyms: closure, consistency, emotional availability. Savage Sentence: You keep answering that Boomerang like the ending is going to change this time. UnExpert Advice: If they keep coming back without changing, stop being available.

Booty Call /ˈbü-tē kȯl/ A late-night message or invite purely for sex, with no emotional intention or follow-through. Synonyms: late-night link, hookup call, no-strings invite. Antonyms: planned date, emotional connection, intentional intimacy. Savage Sentence: If he only texts you at night, you are not dating, you are a Booty Call. UnExpert Advice: If they only show up at night, they're not part of your life.

Boundaryphobia /ˈboun-dər-ē ˈfō-bē-ə/ Afraid to set boundaries because she doesn't want to lose him. Synonyms: boundary fear, people-pleasing, conflict avoidance. Antonyms: assertiveness, self-respect, clarity. Savage Sentence: Your Boundaryphobia has you tolerating things you would tell your best friend to leave over. UnExpert Advice: If setting a boundary makes them leave, let them.

Boxoflies Syndrome /ˈbäks-əv-ˌlīz ˈsin-ˌdrōm/ Keeping memories, letters, and fake love, knowing it wasn't real. Synonyms: nostalgia trap, emotional evidence hoarding, illusion storage. Antonyms: release, truth, acceptance.

Savage Sentence: You are in Boxoflies Syndrome if you are still holding onto moments that never turned into anything real. UnExpert Advice: If it wasn't real then, it's not real now.

Breadcrumb Cousins (OnlyFans Energy Variant) /ˈbred-ˌkrəm ˈkə-zənz/ A next-level version of breadcrumbing where the person strategically alternates between tiny effort and high-engagement bursts to keep you hooked long-term. Synonyms: intermittent reinforcement king, drip-feed dater, attention yo-yo Antonyms: consistency, steady effort, clear intention Savage Sentence: The Breadcrumb Cousins kept you confused—one day it was paragraphs and plans, the next it was silence and a meme. UnExpert Advice: Inconsistency is not mystery—it's a pattern. Stop trying to decode it and start responding to it.

Breadcrumbing /ˈbredˌkrəm-bɪŋ/ Giving you just enough attention to keep you interested… but never enough to actually move forward. Synonyms: emotional rationing, minimum effort flirting, string-along strategy. Antonyms: consistency, effort, actual interest. Savage Sentence: He breadcrumbed you for months and you called it potential. UnExpert Advice: If it feels like scraps, it is. You're not a bird. Stop pecking at crumbs.

Break /ə brāk/ A vague pause in a relationship where one person explores other options while keeping the other emotionally available. Synonyms: soft breakup, option testing, emotional limbo. Antonyms: clear ending, commitment, defined boundaries. Savage Sentence: He asked for a Break and you stayed loyal like it was still a relationship. UnExpert Advice: If it's not clear, it's not safe. Choose clarity.

Breakup Performance /ˈbrāk-ˌəp pər-ˈfôr-məns/ Acting unbothered publicly… losing your mind privately. Synonyms: fake composure, emotional masking, public illusion. Antonyms: authenticity, emotional processing, honesty. Savage Sentence: You're deep in Breakup Performance if your feed says thriving and your nights say otherwise. UnExpert Advice: You don't have to look okay to actually become okay.

Broke-narc /ˈbrōk-närk/ Has the ego of a billionaire and the bank account of a DoorDash driver. Synonyms: inflated ego, delusion spender, zero-asset king. Antonyms: humility, self-awareness, actual success. Savage Sentence: You dated a Broke-narc who talked like luxury and lived like overdraft. UnExpert Advice: Confidence is attractive. Delusion is expensive. Know the difference.

C

Cannonballing /ˈka-nən-ˌbȯ-liŋ/ Jumping into intense emotions, intimacy, or sex immediately, skipping the natural build and pacing of connection. Synonyms: emotional rushing, fast-forward intimacy, instant intensity. Antonyms: slow burn, intentional pacing, emotional buildup. Savage Sentence: He cannonballed you into something intense and left you holding feelings he never planned to keep. UnExpert Advice: Fast doesn't mean real. It usually means temporary.

Care Package Clownery /ker-ˈpa-kij ˈklau-nə-rē/ Bringing gifts, snacks, apologies to a man who already rejected you. Synonyms: overgiving, rejection denial, effort misplacement. Antonyms: self-respect, boundaries, emotional withdrawal. Savage Sentence: You pulled care package clownery and showed up giving more to someone who already gave you nothing. UnExpert Advice: Don't invest where you've already been declined.

Carfishing Bro /kär-ˌfi-shiŋ brō/ Uses cars, rentals, or borrowed luxury to signal status instead of substance. Synonyms: vehicle flexer, lease-life liar, driveway performer. Antonyms: authenticity, grounded lifestyle, real success. Savage Sentence: The Carfishing Bro posed harder with the car than he ever did with a real personality. UnExpert Advice: If the car is the highlight, so is the emptiness.

Casual-Only Crusader /ˈka-zhə-wəl ˈōn-lē krü-ˌsā-dər/ Says "looking for something casual" but still expects consistency, attention, and emotional access. Synonyms: commitment dodger, low-effort dater, benefit collector. Antonyms: intentional dating, commitment, clarity. Savage Sentence: The Casual-Only Crusader wanted girlfriend energy while offering absolutely nothing in return. UnExpert Advice: If it's labeled casual, treat it casually—or don't engage at all.

Catching Print /ˈka-chiŋ print/ Scanning a man's pants to assess size based on visible outline, reducing attraction to a physical guess before interaction. Synonyms: bulge-checking, visual screening, surface-level judging. Antonyms: connection-based attraction, curiosity, actual conversation. Savage Sentence:

You caught his print and decided everything before he even opened his mouth. UnExpert Advice: If attraction starts and ends at anatomy, don't expect anything deeper to follow.

Catfishing / Kittenfishing /ˈkat-ˌfi-shiŋ/ • /ˈki-tən-ˌfi-shiŋ/ Misrepresenting yourself online through fake or heavily altered photos, with kittenfishing being the subtler version. Synonyms: digital deception, profile fraud, filtered reality. Antonyms: authenticity, transparency, real presentation. Savage Sentence: He kittenfished you just enough to get the date and hoped you wouldn't notice the difference. UnExpert Advice: If they start with deception, it doesn't get more honest later.

Celebrity Clinger /sə-ˈle-brə-tē ˈkliŋ-ər/ Name-drops or posts photos with famous people to manufacture relevance. Synonyms: clout chaser, fame leech, status borrower. Antonyms: self-made identity, authenticity, independence. Savage Sentence: The Celebrity Clinger made one random encounter sound like a lifelong friendship. UnExpert Advice: If they need someone else's fame, they don't have their own.

Chalance /ˈcha-ləns/ The intentional choice to show effort, interest, and clarity instead of pretending not to care. Synonyms: intentional effort, direct energy, clear pursuit. Antonyms: nonchalance, playing it cool, emotional games. Savage Sentence: He chalance'd you hard in the beginning and then disappeared when it was time to maintain it. UnExpert Advice: If the energy isn't consistent, it was never real.

Cheating (Physical, Emotional, Micro-cheating) /ˈchē-tiŋ/ Violating agreed relationship boundaries through physical or emotional intimacy with someone else, including subtle betrayals like secret flirting or hidden connections. Synonyms: infidelity, betrayal, boundary breaking. Antonyms: loyalty, exclusivity, trust. Savage Sentence: He micro-cheated you long before you ever had proof of anything bigger. UnExpert Advice: If it has to be hidden, it's already crossing a line.

Chemistry Confusion /ˈke-mə-strē kən-ˈfyü-zhən/ Mistakes emotional instability for a "spark." Synonyms: chaos attraction, intensity illusion, unstable chemistry. Antonyms: compatibility, stability, real connection. Savage Sentence: You called it Chemistry Confusion when you kept going back to something that only felt good because it was inconsistent. UnExpert Advice: Real chemistry feels calm, not chaotic.

Chill Girl Complex /ˈchil-ˌgərl ˈkäm-pleks/ Proud of "not asking for anything"... while slowly being treated like nothing. Synonyms: low-expectation identity, silent sufferer, needs suppression. Antonyms: standards, communication, self-worth. Savage Sentence: You played the Chill Girl Complex so well he never once thought you needed more. UnExpert Advice: If you ask for nothing, you will receive exactly that.

Chokehold /ˈchōk-ˌhōld/ When someone has an intense emotional or psychological grip on you, often without earning it. Synonyms: emotional grip, obsessive pull, mental takeover. Antonyms: detachment, clarity, emotional control. Savage Sentence: You're in a Chokehold over a man who did the bare minimum and somehow made it feel like everything. UnExpert Advice: Intensity isn't always earned. Sometimes it's just projection.

Clarity Avoidance Addiction /ˈkler-ə-tē ə-ˈvoi-dəns ə-ˈdik-shən/ Avoids asking questions... because she knows the answer will hurt. Synonyms: truth avoidance, question suppression, fear-based silence. Antonyms: directness, courage, honesty. Savage Sentence: You stayed quiet with Clarity Avoidance Addiction because hearing the truth out loud would have ended it. UnExpert Advice: The answer you're avoiding is usually the one you need.

Clarity Starvation /ˈkler-ə-tē ˌstär-ˈvā-shən/ You're starving for answers... and he's feeding you confusion crumbs. Synonyms: answer deprivation, confusion feeding, emotional starvation. Antonyms: clarity, transparency, communication. Savage Sentence: You're in Clarity Starvation if you're rereading texts trying to find answers he never gave. UnExpert Advice: If you have to guess, it's already a no.

Clarityphobia /ˌkler-ə-tē-ˈfō-bē-ə/ Terrified of defining anything... but very comfortable wasting your time. Synonyms: definition avoidance, label fear, commitment hesitation. Antonyms: directness, clarity, decisiveness. Savage Sentence: You're dealing with Clarityphobia if every time you ask what this is, he suddenly needs more time. UnExpert Advice: If he won't define it, don't stay in it.

Clingstitution /kliŋ-stə-ˈtü-shən/ Should be admitted for excessive texting, overanalyzing, and emotional spiraling. Synonyms: emotional overload, attachment spiral, overthinking crisis. Antonyms: calm, detachment, emotional regulation. Savage Sentence: You hit full Clingstitution when you sent the text, deleted it, rewrote it, and still felt worse after. UnExpert Advice: If it makes you anxious, it's not secure.

Cloaking /ˈklō-kiŋ/ Standing someone up and then immediately blocking them on all platforms, erasing access without explanation. Synonyms: vanish blocking, ghosting extreme, digital disappearance. Antonyms: accountability, communication, basic respect. Savage Sentence: He pulled Cloaking on you and acted like disappearing was easier than being honest. UnExpert Advice: Closure isn't always given. Sometimes it's shown through behavior.

Closure Addiction /ˈklō-zhər ə-ˈdik-shən/ Needs one more explanation... from someone who already showed you. Synonyms: answer chasing, explanation dependency, closure loop. Antonyms: acceptance, finality, self-closure. Savage Sentence: You kept going back with Closure Addiction even after his actions already gave you the answer. UnExpert Advice: The answer is already in their actions.

Closure Chaser /ˈklō-zhər-ˌchā-sər/ Needs one more conversation... that turns into 17 more. Synonyms: explanation addict, conversation loop, closure seeker. Antonyms: acceptance, detachment, finality. Savage Sentence: You turned into a closure chaser the moment you believed one more talk would change anything. UnExpert Advice: Closure is something you give yourself, not something you beg for.

Closure Resurrection /ˈklō-zhər ˌre-zə-ˈrek-shən/ Reappearing under the guise of "closure" to regain access, attention, or emotional control. Synonyms: fake closure, emotional re-entry, access revival. Antonyms: real closure, finality, emotional release. Savage Sentence: He pulled a Closure Resurrection and suddenly needed "closure" right when you were finally moving on. UnExpert Advice: Dead things don't need conversations.

Clout Chasing (in Romance) /klout ˈchā-siŋ/ Using a relationship, or the appearance of one, for attention, followers, or social media gain. Synonyms: attention dating, performative relationship, content coupling. Antonyms: privacy, genuine connection, authenticity. Savage Sentence: He clout-chased you the second your relationship started getting him more attention than you. UnExpert Advice: If it feels staged, it probably is.

Clownattachment /klaun ə-ˈtach-mənt/ Gets emotionally attached to inconsistent behavior. Synonyms: chaos attachment, inconsistency bonding, unstable connection. Antonyms: stability, consistency, emotional security. Savage Sentence: You developed Clownattachment to someone who only showed up when it suited them. UnExpert Advice: If it's inconsistent, it's not worth attaching to.

Clown Contract /klaun ˈkän-ˌtrakt/ The invisible agreement where you keep showing up and he keeps disappointing you. Synonyms: self-betrayal agreement, unpaid emotional labor contract, circus participation. Antonyms: boundaries, self-respect, walking away. Savage Sentence: You stayed in a

Clown Contract where you kept giving and he kept proving you shouldn't. UnExpert Advice: If the only thing consistent is disappointment, cancel the contract.

Clownfidence /ˈklaun-fə-dən(t)s/ Has the confidence of a man who has never once been self-aware. Synonyms: delusion confidence, ego inflation, blind self-belief. Antonyms: self-awareness, grounded confidence, humility. Savage Sentence: He walked in with full Clownfidence like confidence alone was enough to impress you. UnExpert Advice: Confidence without self-awareness is just noise.

Cock Tease / Prick Tease /käk tēz/ • /prik tēz/ Leading someone on sexually or flirtatiously without intention to follow through, often for attention or control. Synonyms: sexual baiting, attention teasing, ego feeding. Antonyms: clarity, mutual intention, honest boundaries. Savage Sentence: She pulled a Cock Tease and kept him hooked without ever intending to follow through. UnExpert Advice: Mixed signals are usually intentional. Act accordingly.

Commitmency /kə-ˈmit-mən-sē/ Severely lacking the ability to choose you... but not lacking access to you. Synonyms: commitment deficiency, choice avoidance, access addiction. Antonyms: decisiveness, commitment, intentional choice. Savage Sentence: You're dealing with Commitmency if he won't choose you but still expects full access to you. UnExpert Advice: If he can't commit, he shouldn't have access.

Commitphobe-ian /kə-ˈmit-ˌfō-bē-ən/ Has a long, detailed history of almost relationships... and zero accountability for any of them. Synonyms: commitment historian, pattern repeater, excuse archivist. Antonyms: growth, accountability, commitment. Savage Sentence: You found a Commitphobe-ian if every ex is "crazy" and he somehow learned nothing from any of it. UnExpert Advice: If every ex is "the problem," you're looking at the common denominator.

Confidence Catfish /ˈkän-fə-dən(t)s ˈkat-ˌfish/ Acts confident at first... turns out it was ego, insecurity, and audacity in a trench coat. Synonyms: false confidence, ego disguise, insecure performer. Antonyms: real confidence, grounded self-worth, authenticity. Savage Sentence: He pulled a Confidence Catfish and had you thinking he was secure until the mask slipped. UnExpert Advice: Real confidence is calm. Ego is loud. Learn the difference early.

Confusionbond /kən-ˈfyü-zhən-ˌbänd/ You mistake inconsistency for connection. Synonyms: chaos attachment, mixed-signal bond, unstable connection. Antonyms: clarity, emotional safety, consistency. Savage

Sentence: You built a whole Confusionbond with someone who never gave you anything steady. UnExpert Advice: If it feels confusing, it's not a bond. It's a pattern.

Confusionship /kən-ˈfyü-zhən-ˌship/ You're not dating... you're decoding. Synonyms: mixed signal mess, emotional puzzle, unclear dynamic. Antonyms: clarity, directness, defined relationship. Savage Sentence: You're in a Confusionship if you're rereading texts like they're clues instead of just living your life. UnExpert Advice: Clarity should not feel like a luxury.

Convenience Chemistry /kən-ˈvēn-yəns ˈke-mə-strē/ It feels like a spark... but really it's just proximity and availability. Synonyms: situational spark, proximity attraction, timing illusion. Antonyms: real compatibility, depth, intentional connection. Savage Sentence: You called it Convenience Chemistry when it only worked because you were both available at the same time. UnExpert Advice: Just because it's easy doesn't mean it's right.

Convenience King /kən-ˈvēn-yəns kiŋ/ Only dates you when it's easy for him. The second it requires effort, gone. Synonyms: low-effort ruler, situational boyfriend, when-it-works-for-me energy. Antonyms: consistency, effort, reliability. Savage Sentence: You're dealing with a Convenience King if he disappears the second things require real effort. UnExpert Advice: If you're only an option when it's convenient, make yourself unavailable.

Consistency Cosplay /kən-ˈsi-stən-sē ˈkäs-ˌplā/ Acts consistent for a week or two... just long enough to hook you. Synonyms: temporary effort, bait behavior, short-term reliability. Antonyms: real consistency, long-term effort, stability. Savage Sentence: He pulled Consistency Cosplay and had you thinking he changed when he was just buying time. UnExpert Advice: Consistency is proven over time, not demonstrated in bursts.

Cookie Jarring /ˈku̇-kē ˈjär-iŋ/ Keeping someone as a backup option while pursuing others, offering just enough attention to keep them interested. Synonyms: backup dating, emotional hoarding, option stacking. Antonyms: exclusivity, focus, intentional dating. Savage Sentence: You got Cookie Jarred the moment he kept you close while chasing someone else. UnExpert Advice: If you feel like a backup, stop playing the role.

Coolgirling /ˈkül-ˌgər-liŋ/ Acting low maintenance, chill, and "not like other girls"... while suppressing every real need. Synonyms: chill performance, low-maintenance act, approval masking. Antonyms: authenticity, expression, self-honoring. Savage Sentence: You coolgirled your way through everything and ended up with someone who thought you didn't need anything at all. UnExpert Advice: The right person won't punish you for having needs.

Copy-Paste Casanova /ˈkä-pē pāst ˌka-sə-ˈnō-və/ Sends the same long, overly polished message to every match. Synonyms: script swiper, mass messenger, template charmer. Antonyms: genuine interest, personalized effort. Savage Sentence: The Copy-Paste Casanova sent a novel that somehow felt like it wasn't written for you at all. UnExpert Advice: If it sounds rehearsed, it probably is.

Cougar /ˈkü-gər/ An older woman pursuing younger men, often for casual or sexual relationships. Synonyms: age-gap dater, experienced pursuer. Antonyms: balanced dynamic, mutual stage alignment. Savage Sentence: She cougared him for the attention and called it empowerment when it was really validation. UnExpert Advice: Age gaps aren't the issue, intentions are.

Crazy Ex ("She's Crazy") /ˈkrā-zē eks/ A dismissive label used to discredit a former partner's emotional reaction, often to avoid accountability. Synonyms: blame shifting, narrative control, emotional dismissal. Antonyms: accountability, self-awareness, honesty. Savage Sentence: He pulled the Crazy Ex line and expected you not to notice the pattern. UnExpert Advice: Pay attention to patterns, not labels.

Crymaxing /ˈkrī-ˌmak-siŋ/ Turns one situation into a full emotional breakdown production. Synonyms: emotional escalation, dramatic release, overwhelm response. Antonyms: regulation, grounding, calm processing. Savage Sentence: You crymaxed the situation and turned something small into something that consumed you. UnExpert Advice: Feel your emotions, but don't let them run the entire show.

Crypto Prophet /ˈkrip-tō ˈprä-fət/ Talks about crypto like it's a personality, a religion, and a retirement plan. Synonyms: blockchain bro, investment evangelist, digital dream seller. Antonyms: grounded earner, realistic planner, actual stability. Savage Sentence: The Crypto Prophet promised future millions while asking you to split dinner. UnExpert Advice: If it's all future wealth, check the present reality.

Cuck / Cuckold /kək/ A dynamic where one partner allows or derives from their partner's involvement with others, trash when it's one-sided or used to disguise betrayal. Synonyms: unequal openness, forced dynamic, disguised infidelity. Antonyms: mutual consent, balanced boundaries, respect. Savage Sentence: He called it a Cuck dynamic while you sat there uncomfortable and expected to accept it. UnExpert Advice: Consent isn't silence, it's clarity from both sides.

Cuffing Season /ˈkə-fiŋ ˈsē-zən/ The time of year when people seek temporary relationships to avoid being alone during colder months or holidays. Synonyms: seasonal dating, temporary pairing, winter attachment. Antonyms: long-term commitment, intentional partnership. Savage Sentence: He cuffed you for the season and uncuffed you the moment it got warm again. UnExpert Advice: If it only works in one season, it's not built to last.

Cushioning /ˈku-shə-niŋ/ Keeping multiple romantic backups "just in case" so they're never alone if something falls apart. Synonyms: emotional insurance policy, safety net flirting, commitment hedging. Antonyms: loyalty, focus, emotional maturity. Savage Sentence: You got cushioned the second he kept you close while lining up other options. UnExpert Advice: If someone needs backups, let them lose access to the main option too.

Cut-Out Casualty /kət-ˈau̇t ˈka-zhə-wəl-tē/ Clearly cropped an ex out of photos instead of taking new ones. Synonyms: lazy dater, recycled pics guy, breakup editor. Antonyms: fresh photos, effort, intentional dating. Savage Sentence: The Cut-Out Casualty left just enough of her arm in the photo to tell you everything you needed to know. UnExpert Advice: If they won't update photos, they won't update effort.

Cyberflashing /ˈsī-bər-ˌfla-shiŋ/ Sending unsolicited explicit images, usually sexual, without consent. Synonyms: digital flashing, unsolicited nudes, online harassment. Antonyms: consent, respect, basic decency. Savage Sentence: He cyberflashed you like that was supposed to impress you instead of immediately ending the conversation. UnExpert Advice: Block, don't respond. Attention is exactly what they want.

D

Daddy Issues Dating /ˈda-dē ˈi-sho͞oz ˈdā-tiŋ/ Choosing emotionally unavailable, older, or authority-figure-like men because they trigger familiar childhood wounds instead of healthy partnership. Synonyms: father-wound shopping, unresolved attachment dating, safety-through-familiar-pain. Antonyms: secure attachment dating, healed partnering, conscious choice. Savage Sentence: You daddy-issues-dated your way into another man who felt just like home and treated you the same way. UnExpert Advice: Heal the wound. Stop casting men in roles they never auditioned for.

Date Ghosting /dāt ˈgō-stiŋ/ Disappearing after several dates once the other person starts showing real interest or expectations. Synonyms: post-investment vanishing, slow-fade exit, hope-then-ghost. Antonyms: honest communication, respectful closure, adult follow-through. Savage Sentence: He date ghosted you right when you started thinking it might actually go somewhere. UnExpert Advice: If they vanish right when things get real, they were never planning to stay.

Debt Dumper /det ˈdəm-pər/ Someone who offloads their financial, emotional, or literal baggage onto you once they sense you care. Synonyms: responsibility evacuator, problem transferrer, walking liability. Antonyms: self-sufficient partner, equal contributor, accountable adult. Savage Sentence: You dated a Debt Dumper who showed up empty and somehow left you paying for everything. UnExpert Advice: Love is not a nonprofit. Don't become their emergency fund.

Deflection King /di-ˈflek-shən kiŋ/ Master at turning every concern, boundary, or question back on you so he never has to own anything. Synonyms: blame shifter, accountability dodger, conversation terrorist. Antonyms: ownership, self-reflection, emotional maturity. Savage Sentence: You told a Deflection King how you felt and ended up apologizing by the end of the conversation. UnExpert Advice: If every problem becomes your fault, you're dating a mirror with commitment issues.

Delayed Disrespect /di-ˈlād ˌdis-rə-ˈspekt/ Everything seems fine... until one day you realize he's been disrespecting you the entire time. Synonyms: slow-burn disrespect, subtle erosion, delayed clarity. Antonyms: respect, awareness, immediate clarity. Savage Sentence: You're dealing with Delayed Disrespect when you look back and realize none of it was actually okay. UnExpert Advice: If something feels off early, it probably is. Don't wait for proof to validate your intuition.

Delulu /də-ˈlü-lü/ The state of being deeply delusional about a situationship or low-effort man, convinced it's "different this time" despite evidence. Synonyms: fantasy fixation, hope overdose, reality rejection, copium maximum. Antonyms: radical acceptance, pattern recognition, grounded discernment. Savage Sentence: You went full Delulu turning bare minimum attention into a love story. UnExpert Advice: Delulu isn't cute past 25. If the facts and your feelings don't match, trust the facts.

Delulu Dating /də-ˈlü-lü ˈdā-tiŋ/ When you ignore every red flag because you like the idea of him more than the reality. Synonyms: fantasy fixation, red flag blindness, imagination over information. Antonyms: clarity, discernment, reality check. Savage Sentence: You Delulu Dated him straight through every red flag like they were just part of the aesthetic. UnExpert Advice: Date what's in front of you, not what could exist if he suddenly became a different person.

Delulunarc /də-ˈlü-lü-närk/ Truly believes he's the prize with absolutely no evidence. Synonyms: delusion king, self-appointed legend, confidence without cause. Antonyms: self-awareness, humility, earned confidence. Savage Sentence: He showed up with full Delulunarc energy and expected you to be impressed by confidence alone. UnExpert Advice: Confidence is attractive. Delusion without substance is a warning sign.

Deluluvictim /də-ˈlü-lü-ˌvik-təm/ Knows exactly what he's doing but still acts shocked every time. Synonyms: fake innocence, selective awareness, performative confusion. Antonyms: accountability, honesty, self-awareness. Savage Sentence: He played the Deluluvictim so well you almost forgot he caused the entire situation. UnExpert Advice: If someone keeps acting confused, it's usually strategic.

Delusiondependence /də-ˈlü-zhən di-ˈpen-dən(t)s/ Needs the fantasy to survive... because the reality is too obvious. Synonyms: illusion reliance, fantasy attachment, reality avoidance. Antonyms: acceptance, clarity, truth. Savage Sentence: You're deep in Delusiondependence when you see exactly what's happening and still choose the version that feels better. UnExpert Advice: Reality hurts once. Delusion hurts repeatedly.

Delusionloophole /də-ˈlü-zhən ˈlüp-ˌhōl/ Finds ONE good moment... to justify 50 bad ones. Synonyms: selective optimism, excuse anchor, moment overvaluer. Antonyms: pattern recognition, realism, discernment. Savage Sentence: You used a Delusionloophole to turn one decent moment into a reason to ignore everything else. UnExpert Advice: Patterns matter more than moments.

Delusionmaintenance /də-ˈlü-zhən ˈmān-tə-nəns/ Constantly rewriting reality to make it make sense. Synonyms: narrative rewriting, illusion upkeep, reality editing. Antonyms: truth, acceptance, clarity. Savage Sentence: You're doing Delusionmaintenance if you have to keep explaining his behavior just to feel okay staying. UnExpert Advice: If it needs constant explaining, it's not right.

Delusionship /də-ˈlü-zhən-ˌship/ You think you're building something... he thinks you're passing time. Synonyms: one-sided belief, imagined relationship, misaligned reality. Antonyms: shared vision, mutual intention, clarity. Savage Sentence: You're in a Delusionship if you're planning a future and he's just filling space. UnExpert Advice: Make sure you're both in the same story.

Dick Appointment /dik ə-ˌpȯint-mənt/ Treating sex like a scheduled service with zero emotional follow-up or relationship intent. Synonyms: scheduled booty, transactional intimacy, orgasm logistics. Antonyms: mutual desire, integrated intimacy, connected sex. Savage Sentence: You set your schedule around a Dick Appointment and called it a relationship. UnExpert Advice: If the only consistent thing is his dick, that's not consistency.

Dick Pic /dik pik/ An unsolicited or poorly timed photo of a penis, usually sent with zero context, charm, or consent. Synonyms: visual harassment, low-effort nudes, digital flashing. Savage Sentence: He sent a Dick Pic like that was supposed to start a conversation instead of ending it. UnExpert Advice: Block. Do not respond. Do not "be nice about it." Attention is the only currency these men trade in.

- **Unsolicited Dick Pic** /ˌən-sə-ˈli-sə-təd dik pik/ Randomly sending genital photos to someone who never asked and likely never wanted to see it. Savage Sentence: He sent an Unsolicited Dick Pic in the middle of the day like that was a normal adult decision. UnExpert Advice: Block. Do not respond. Do not "be nice about it." Attention is the only currency these men trade in.

- **Recycled Dick Pic** /ˈrē-ˌsī-kəld dik pik/ Sending the same dick pic to multiple people or the same person again like it's a reusable attachment. Savage Sentence: He hit you with a Recycled Dick Pic like you wouldn't notice it's part of a group chat tour. UnExpert Advice: If he can't even take a new one, he definitely can't offer anything new.

Digital Boyfriend /ˈdi-jə-təl ˈboi-ˌfrend/ A man who exists mostly through texts, memes, and voice notes but is physically and emotionally absent. Synonyms: phone fiancé, pixel partner, app-based almost-relationship. Antonyms: in-real-life presence, full-spectrum partner, tangible effort. Savage Sentence: You've got a Digital Boyfriend if all you have is messages and no real-life plans. UnExpert Advice: If he only shows up in your notifications, he's not showing up in your life.

The Disappearing Act Deluxe /ðə ˌdi-sə-ˈpir-iŋ akt di-ˈləks/ Doesn't ghost all at once... just slowly removes himself until you question if you imagined him. Synonyms: slow vanish premium, phased exit strategy, subtle ghosting. Antonyms: direct ending, clear communication, presence. Savage Sentence: He pulled the Disappearing Act Deluxe and had you questioning yourself instead of his behavior. UnExpert Advice: If someone slowly disappears, don't chase clarity. Accept the exit.

Discount Dick /ˈdis-kau̇nt dik/ Low-effort, low-value sexual access that somehow still costs you self-respect, time, and emotional energy. Synonyms: bargain-bin benefits, participation-trophy penis, cheap thrill tax. Antonyms: high-value intimacy, reciprocal desire, earned access. Savage Sentence: You gave access to Discount Dick and still ended up paying the highest price. UnExpert Advice: Stop giving premium pussy to discount behavior.

Divorce Baiter /di-ˈvȯrs ˈbā-tər/ Married or almost-married person who flirts, dates, or builds emotional connections while keeping the spouse as a safety net. Synonyms: marital sampler, wedding-ring shopper, side-piece scout. Antonyms: separated, divorced, ethically available. Savage Sentence: You entertained a Divorce Baiter who called himself single while still fully married. UnExpert Advice: If they're not legally and emotionally free, they're not free.

Doormat / Doormatting / Doormatism /ˈdôr-mət-ˌi-zəm/ Letting him walk all over you... then asking if his feet hurt. Synonyms: self-abandonment, boundary collapse, over-accommodation. Antonyms: self-respect, boundaries, assertiveness. Savage Sentence: You stayed in Doormatism so long he stopped seeing you as someone he had to respect. UnExpert Advice: If you don't stand up for yourself, no one else will.

Double Life /ˈdə-bəl līf/ Living two separate romantic or personal lives simultaneously... often maintaining a committed relationship while secretly acting single elsewhere. Synonyms: secret relationship, parallel dating, hidden partner syndrome. Antonyms: honesty, transparency, integrity. Savage Sentence: He lived a Double Life and somehow had you believing you were the only one. UnExpert Advice: If something feels hidden, it usually is. Truth doesn't require secrecy.

Double Text (Double Texting) /ˈdə-bəl tekst/ Sending a second or third message before the other person has replied, often driven by anxiety while the recipient is low-effort or fading. Synonyms: reply chasing, anxiety spam, dignity erosion via iMessage. Antonyms: self-control, graceful withdrawal, one-and-done texting. Savage Sentence: You double-texted him for days straight while he ignored you like you never hit send. UnExpert Advice: One text is interest. Two or more is auditioning for a role they already rejected. Send it once and let silence speak.

Double Text Denial /ˈdə-bəl tekst di-ˈnī-əl/ Refusing to accept silence or minimal replies, so you send more anyway. Synonyms: reply chasing, dignity erosion via iMessage, desperation loop. Antonyms: graceful withdrawal, self-respect, one-and-done texting. Savage Sentence: You're in Double Text Denial if you keep texting like he didn't already answer you with silence. UnExpert Advice: Double texting doesn't create interest. It reveals desperation.

Drama-Free Disclaimer /ˈdrä-mə frē di-ˈsklā-mər/ Claims "no drama" in the bio while being the common denominator of every chaotic situation. Synonyms: chaos magnet, projection king/queen, accountability avoider. Antonyms: emotional stability, self-awareness, maturity. Savage Sentence: The Drama-Free Disclaimer sounded peaceful until you realized they were the source of every problem. UnExpert Advice: If they have to announce it, it's not true.

Dry Begging /drī ˈbe-giŋ/ Subtly hinting for attention, affection, or effort instead of asking directly or walking away. Synonyms: passive thirst, hint-dropping, emotional panhandling. Antonyms: direct communication, self-sufficiency, standards. Savage Sentence: You were dry begging for effort from someone who already showed you they weren't giving any. UnExpert Advice: Stop begging for bare minimum. Either ask clearly or leave.

Dry Dating / Sober Dating /drī ˈdā-tiŋ • ˈsō-bər ˈdā-tiŋ/ Intentionally dating without alcohol to build clearer, more authentic connections, often revealing the reality of the dynamic. Synonyms: clear-headed courting, substance-free romance, reality dating. Antonyms: drunk dialing, liquid courage dating, blackout bonding. Savage Sentence: You tried dry dating and realized there was nothing there once the drinks were gone. UnExpert Advice: If the vibe dies without drinks, the vibe was never real.

Dry Texting /drī ˈtekst-iŋ/ One-word, emoji-only, or delayed low-effort replies that signal disinterest. Synonyms: conversational starvation, breadcrumb texting, minimum viable response. Antonyms: engaged texting, enthusiastic communication, reciprocal effort. Savage Sentence: You kept replying to dry texting like it was going to turn into an actual conversation. UnExpert Advice: Dry texting isn't busy. It's a polite fade. Match the energy and exit the chat.

E

E-Girl / E-Boy Energy /ē-gərl • ē-boi ˈe-nər-jē/ Performative internet aesthetic flirting with filters, curated vibes, and zero real substance or emotional availability. Synonyms: aesthetic-only attraction, digital cosplay dating, vibe merchant, filter-flirting. Antonyms: authentic presence, substance-driven connection, real-life energy. Savage Sentence: You fell for E-boy energy and ended up dating a personality that only existed on a screen. UnExpert Advice: If the whole vibe is curated for the camera but crumbles in person, you didn't meet a person. You met content.

Echo Ghosting /ˈe-kō ˈgō-stiŋ/ Replying to stories, liking old photos, or watching everything while ignoring real communication and plans. Synonyms: digital haunting, low-effort lurking, silent orbiting. Antonyms: direct communication, consistent effort, real presence. Savage Sentence: He echo-ghosted you by watching everything you posted while ignoring every message you sent. UnExpert Advice: If he's only active in your highlights but silent in your DMs, he's not interested, he's just keeping the option warm.

Effortapologist /ˈe-fərt ə-ˈpä-lə-jist/ Defends his lack of effort like it's reasonable. Synonyms: effort defender, behavior excuser, low-standard protector. Antonyms: accountability, expectation, standards. Savage Sentence: You turned into an Effortapologist the moment you started explaining why his lack of effort "makes sense." UnExpert Advice: Stop defending behavior that doesn't meet your standards.

Effortastrophe /ə-ˈfər-tə-ˌsträ-fē/ When even basic effort feels like a natural disaster to him. Synonyms: effort meltdown, minimal effort crisis, basic task avoidance. Antonyms: initiative, consistency, reliability. Savage Sentence: Asking him to plan one date turned into a full Effortastrophe like you asked for something unreasonable. UnExpert Advice: If basic effort is too much for him, he's not enough for you.

Effort Inflation /ˈe-fərt in-ˈflā-shən/ When he does one nice thing and expects it to carry him for months. Synonyms: one-time effort hype, overvalued gesture, bare minimum bonus. Antonyms: consistency, ongoing effort, reliability. Savage Sentence: He pulled Effort Inflation and expected one decent date to excuse everything that came after. UnExpert Advice: Consistency matters more than one grand gesture.

Effort Reversal /ˈe-fərt ri-ˈvər-səl/ Starts strong, then slowly hands the relationship over to you. Synonyms: effort drop-off, bait-and-switch energy, responsibility transfer. Antonyms: sustained effort, mutual investment, consistency. Savage Sentence: He hit you with Effort Reversal so smoothly you didn't realize you were doing everything. UnExpert Advice: If you're carrying it alone, it's not a relationship.

Effort Sponge /ˈe-fərt spənj/ Absorbs all your planning, energy, and emotional labor while giving nothing back. Synonyms: one-way battery, effort vampire, relationship freeloader. Antonyms: mutual investment, reciprocal effort, self-starter. Savage Sentence: You dated an Effort Sponge and wondered why you felt drained all the time. UnExpert Advice: Match effort or walk away.

Effortlesshole /ˈe-fərt-ləs-hōl/ Proud of how little he tries, like it's a personality trait. Synonyms: low-effort menace, bare minimum bro, apathy enthusiast. Antonyms: intentional partner, effort-driven, engaged. Savage Sentence: He showed up as an Effortlesshole and still expected to be taken seriously. UnExpert Advice: If effort feels optional to him, make access optional for you.

Effortphobic /ˈe-fərt-ˌfō-bik/ Allergic to planning, consistency, and basic decency. Synonyms: effort avoider, planning allergic, consistency rejecter. Antonyms: initiative, reliability, effort. Savage Sentence: He's Effortphobic if planning something simple feels like a burden but having access to you doesn't. UnExpert Advice: If effort is too much for him, he's not enough for you.

Ego Baiting /ˈē-gō ˈbā-tiŋ/ Giving you attention just to feel desired, not because they actually want you. Synonyms: validation fishing, attention drip, ego refill strategy. Antonyms: genuine interest, intentional pursuit, emotional honesty. Savage Sentence: He ego baited you just enough to keep you interested while never actually choosing you. UnExpert Advice: If the attention feels empty, it is.

Ego Farming /ˈē-gō ˈfär-miŋ/ Collecting women for validation like it's a personality trait. Synonyms: validation hoarding, attention collector, emotional influencer. Antonyms: depth, connection, actual interest. Savage Sentence: He ego farmed his way through women and still needed more to feel important. UnExpert Advice: You are not a stat. Remove yourself from the scoreboard.

Ego-nomics /ˈē-gō ˈnä-miks/ Everything revolves around his ego and you're the one paying the price. Synonyms: ego economy, self-centered system, one-sided investment. Antonyms: balance, reciprocity, mutual benefit. Savage Sentence: You invested everything into his ego-nomics and got nothing back but depletion. UnExpert Advice: If you're the only one paying emotionally, exit the system.

Ego Preservation Mode /ˈē-gō ˌpre-zər-ˈvā-shən mōd/ Avoids accountability and rewrites reality to protect their self-image. Synonyms: accountability allergy, self-image defense system, blame deflection shield. Antonyms: ownership, humility, self-reflection. Savage Sentence: He switched into Ego Preservation Mode and somehow made your feelings the problem. UnExpert Advice: Real grown people can say "I was wrong."

Ego-sexual /ˈē-gō ˈsek-shə-wəl/ Attracted to attention, admiration, and validation, not you. Synonyms: validation addict, attention lover, ego-driven dater. Antonyms: genuine attraction, emotional connection, real interest. Savage Sentence: He was ego-sexual from the start and needed attention more than he ever needed you. UnExpert Advice: If the connection feels shallow, it is.

Egoverload /ˈē-gō-ˌō-vər-ˌlōd/ Too much ego, not enough substance. Synonyms: inflated self-image, overconfidence disorder, empty hype. Antonyms: substance, humility, grounded confidence. Savage Sentence: He walked in with full egoverload and nothing real to back it up. UnExpert Advice: Pay attention to what someone backs up, not what they project.

Emotional Airbnb /ə-ˈmō-shə-nəl ˈer-ˌbē-ˌen-bē/ He stays just long enough to feel something, then checks out and leaves the mess. Synonyms: temporary intimacy, emotional short-term stay, mess-and-leave behavior. Antonyms: stability, accountability, long-term presence. Savage Sentence: You hosted an Emotional Airbnb and he left you cleaning up feelings he never planned to keep. UnExpert Advice: If he treats you like a temporary stay, stop offering permanent access.

Emotional Blackmail /i-ˈmō-shə-nəl ˈblak-ˌmāl/ Using guilt, tears, or threats to keep you from leaving or holding boundaries. Synonyms: guilt tripping, emotional extortion, pity play. Antonyms: healthy boundaries, accountability, adult communication. Savage Sentence: He pulled Emotional Blackmail and suddenly you felt guilty for wanting basic respect. UnExpert Advice: Love is not a hostage situation.

Emotional Booty Call /ə-ˈmō-shə-nəl ˈbü-tē kôl/ He doesn't want sex, he wants comfort and validation when he's low. Synonyms: emotional late-night text, comfort collector, validation grab. Antonyms: mutual support, balanced connection, real intimacy. Savage Sentence: He emotional-booty-called you every time he felt low and disappeared the second he felt better. UnExpert Advice: You are not emergency emotional support.

Emotional Hoarder /ə-ˈmō-shə-nəl ˈhôr-dər/ Keeps memories, texts, and pain long after it should've been released. Synonyms: memory hoarder, attachment keeper, emotional clutter. Antonyms: release, detachment, letting go. Savage Sentence: You stayed an Emotional Hoarder, holding onto moments that kept hurting you every time you revisited them. UnExpert Advice: If it hurts to revisit, it's time to release it.

Emotional Hoovering /i-ˈmō-shə-nəl ˈhu̇-və-riŋ/ An ex pulls you back in the moment you start healing. Synonyms: vacuum ex, pull-back maneuver, attachment hoover. Antonyms: clean break, no-contact peace, genuine closure. Savage Sentence: He emotional-hoovered you right when you were finally moving on and expected access like nothing happened. UnExpert Advice: Block and keep the boundary.

Emotional Overdraft /i-ˈmō-shə-nəl ˈō-vər-ˌdraft/ You keep giving long after you're empty. Synonyms: emotional bankruptcy, one-sided overgiving, resentment investment. Antonyms: balance, self-care, mutual support. Savage Sentence: You ran into Emotional Overdraft trying to give to someone who never deposited anything back. UnExpert Advice: Stop pouring into people who don't pour into you.

Emotional Pick-Me /i-ˈmō-shə-nəl pik mē/ Bends over backwards for male approval and puts other women down to get it. Synonyms: male-pleaser, internalized cool girl, self-deprecating chaser. Antonyms: self-respect, authenticity, standards. Savage Sentence: You went Emotional Pick-Me trying to stand out to a man who never valued you. UnExpert Advice: The right man won't need you to compete.

Emotional Ping-Pong /ə-ˈmō-shə-nəl ˈpiŋ-ˌpäŋ/ Hot, cold, interested, distant, repeat. Synonyms: emotional whiplash, inconsistency cycle, push-pull pattern. Antonyms: stability, consistency, emotional safety. Savage Sentence: He kept you in Emotional Ping-Pong until you were exhausted trying to keep up. UnExpert Advice: Peace is not boring, it's healthy.

Emotional Placeholder /ə-ˈmō-shə-nəl ˈplās-ˌhōl-dər/ You're not the one, you're just filling space until he finds her. Synonyms: temporary girlfriend, interim option, emotional standby. Antonyms: chosen partner, priority, intentional relationship. Savage Sentence: You stayed an Emotional Placeholder while he waited for someone he actually wanted. UnExpert Advice: If you feel like a pause, leave.

Emotional Recycling /ə-ˈmō-shə-nəl rē-ˈsī-kliŋ/ Repeating the same type of relationship with different people. Synonyms: pattern repetition, type addiction, cycle dating. Antonyms: growth, change, awareness. Savage Sentence: You're in Emotional Recycling if every new person feels different but ends the same. UnExpert Advice: Change the pattern, not the person.

Emotional Self-Betrayal /ə-ˈmō-shə-nəl self-bə-ˈtrā-əl/ Ignoring your intuition over and over again. Synonyms: self-override, intuition dismissal, internal betrayal. Antonyms: self-trust, alignment, intuition. Savage Sentence: You committed Emotional Self-Betrayal the moment you ignored what you knew from the start. UnExpert Advice: Listen to yourself sooner.

Emotional Self-Harm /ə-ˈmō-shə-nəl self-härm/ Going back even though you know how it ends. Synonyms: self-inflicted pain, emotional relapse, repeated damage. Antonyms: healing, self-protection, growth. Savage Sentence: You emotionally self-harmed every time you went back knowing exactly what would happen. UnExpert Advice: Awareness should break the cycle.

Emotional Slot Machine /i-ˈmō-shə-nəl slät mə-ˈshēn/ Random bursts of attention that keep you hooked. Synonyms: intermittent reinforcement, hot-cold casino, crumb dispenser. Antonyms: consistent care, steady love, reliable partner. Savage Sentence: You stayed at the Emotional Slot Machine hoping the next pull would finally pay off. UnExpert Advice: Stop playing games where the odds are never in your favor.

Emotionalillusionism /ə-ˈmō-shə-nəl i-ˈlü-zhə-ˌni-zəm/ Turns inconsistency into "depth." Synonyms: chaos romanticizing, instability reframing, illusion building. Antonyms: clarity, emotional stability, truth. Savage Sentence: You emotionalillusionismed confusion into something meaningful just to make it make sense. UnExpert Advice: Depth feels stable, not confusing.

Emotionally Bankrupt /ə-ˈmō-shə-nə-lē ˈbaŋ-krəpt/ Has nothing to give... but still applying for a relationship loan. Synonyms: emotionally empty, unavailable partner, depleted connection. Antonyms: emotionally available, generous, present. Savage Sentence: You're dealing with someone emotionally bankrupt asking for more than they've ever deposited. UnExpert Advice: If someone has nothing to give, stop expecting something.

Emotionallygoner /ə-ˈmō-shə-nə-lē ˈgô-nər/ Physically present, texting sometimes... but emotionally, mentally? Gone. Synonyms: absent presence, checked-out partner, hollow connection. Antonyms: emotional availability, presence, engagement. Savage Sentence: You're talking to someone emotionallygoner and still wondering why nothing is landing. UnExpert Advice: Presence is more than proximity.

Emotionallyparasitic /ə-ˈmō-shə-nə-lē ˌper-ə-ˈsi-tik/ Feeds off your energy, empathy, and attention... leaves you drained and confused. Synonyms: emotional leech, energy drainer, empathy exploiter. Antonyms: mutual support, balanced connection, emotional reciprocity. Savage Sentence: You stayed with someone emotionallyparasitic until there was nothing left of you to give. UnExpert Advice: If it constantly drains you, it's not meant for you.

Emotionallystitious /ə-ˌmō-shə-nə-lē-ˈsti-shəs/ Acts like commitment is bad luck and vulnerability will ruin everything. Synonyms: commitment avoider, vulnerability phobic, emotional skeptic. Antonyms: openness, trust, emotional security. Savage Sentence: He's emotionallystitious and treats real connection like it's something to avoid, not build. UnExpert Advice: If someone fears connection, they're not ready for it.

Endless Talking Stage /ˈen-dləs ˈtȯ-kiŋ ˈstāj/ Months of deep conversations, memes, and "getting to know you" with zero movement toward real dates or commitment. Synonyms: textationship, prolonged audition, situationship limbo. Antonyms: intentional dating, clear progression, defined relationship. Savage Sentence: You stayed in the Endless Talking Stage while he kept you entertained and never actually showed up. UnExpert Advice: If it's all talk and no traction after a few weeks, you're not dating.

Energy Vampire /ˈe-nər-jē ˈvam-ˌpī(-ə)r/ Drains your emotional, mental, and physical energy while offering nothing back. Synonyms: emotional leech, battery killer, soul sucker. Antonyms: energizing partner, mutual support, life-giver. Savage Sentence: You spent time with an Energy Vampire and left every interaction feeling worse than when you arrived. UnExpert Advice: Pay attention to how you feel after, not just how they act during.

Entitled Ex /in-ˈtī-təld eks/ An ex who still expects access, attention, or emotional support after the relationship ends. Synonyms: leftover landlord, post-breakup squatter, nostalgia narcissist. Antonyms: respectful closure, clean break, self-sufficient ex. Savage Sentence: Your Entitled Ex still expected access to you like the breakup was just a suggestion. UnExpert Advice: The relationship ended. So did your access.

Escalation Phobia /ˌes-kə-ˈlā-shən ˈfō-bē-ə/ Afraid of defining the relationship or taking any next step while still wanting all the benefits. Synonyms: commitment allergy, label fear, progression paralysis. Antonyms: clear intention, healthy progression, decisive action. Savage Sentence: He had Escalation Phobia and kept you right where you were while avoiding every next step. UnExpert Advice: If they fear progress, stop letting them stay.

Everything But /ˈev-rē-thiŋ bət/ Does everything that looks like a relationship except actually commit or define it. Synonyms: situationship deluxe, almost-relationship, commitment dodger special. Antonyms: defined relationship, full commitment, clarity. Savage Sentence: You accepted Everything But and called it something real when it never actually was. UnExpert Advice: "Everything but" is still nothing.

Exaholism /eks-ˈä-hə-ˌli-zəm/ Addicted to checking, stalking, texting, and emotionally relapsing with an ex. Synonyms: ex addiction, emotional relapse, attachment loop. Antonyms: detachment, healing, moving on. Savage Sentence: You fell into Exaholism and kept reopening something that was already closed. UnExpert Advice: Breaking the habit is harder than breaking the attachment, but it's necessary.

Excuseologist /ik-ˌskyüz-ˈä-lə-jist/ Constantly explains away obvious behavior with excuses. Synonyms: justification expert, behavior defender, reality rewriter. Antonyms: honesty, clarity, acceptance. Savage Sentence: You turned into an Excuseologist trying to make his lack of effort sound reasonable. UnExpert Advice: If you have to keep explaining it, it's already clear.

F

Fade Out /fād out/ Gradually reducing communication until the connection dies without being addressed. Synonyms: slow ghost, soft vanishing, silent exit strategy. Antonyms: honest conversation, clear closure, respectful ending. Savage Sentence: He did a full Fade Out and had you staring at your phone like something was coming when it already ended. UnExpert Advice: A fade out is still a breakup.

Fake Closure /fāk ˈklō-zhər/ A conversation that sounds mature but avoids real accountability. Synonyms: polite discard, scripted goodbye, illusion of maturity. Antonyms: real accountability, clean break, honest ending. Savage Sentence: He gave you Fake Closure and somehow left you more confused than before the call even started. UnExpert Advice: If it feels like damage control, it's not closure.

Fake Name Energy /fāk nām ˈe-nər-jē/ Uses a fake name to hide identity or double life. Synonyms: alias dater, identity dodger, secret profile. Antonyms: transparency, honesty, real identity. Savage Sentence: The Fake Name Energy made sense the second his story stopped adding up. UnExpert Advice: If they're hiding the basics, assume they're hiding everything.

Fantasy Attachment or Fantasy Fixation /ˈfan-tə-sē ə-ˈtaCH-mənt/ • /ˈfan-tə-sē fik-ˈsā-shən/ Attached to who he could be, not who he is. Synonyms: potential addiction, imaginary partner syndrome, projection attachment. Antonyms: reality-based connection, clarity, acceptance. Savage Sentence: You built a whole Fantasy Attachment and got attached to someone who never actually existed. UnExpert Advice: Fall in love with behavior, not potential.

Fantasy Man Checklist /ˈfan-tə-sē man ˈchek-ˌlist/ A rigid list of unrealistic traits and requirements that no real person could consistently meet. Synonyms: perfection filter, unrealistic standards, projection dating. Antonyms: flexibility, real connection, human expectations. Savage Sentence: The Fantasy Man Checklist eliminated everyone before anyone even had a chance to be real. UnExpert Advice: If no one qualifies, the problem isn't everyone else.

Filter Fraud (Male Version) /ˈfil-tər fród/ Photos that create a completely different person than reality. Synonyms: catfishing lite, angle abuse, expectation deception. Antonyms: authentic photos, accurate representation, no surprises. Savage Sentence: The Filter Fraud showed up and you immediately knew the profile was doing all the work. UnExpert Advice: If the photos look engineered, assume the reality is too.

Filterella (Female Version) /ˌfil-tə-ˈrel-ə/ A woman who heavily filters and edits her appearance into a completely different person. Synonyms: angle queen, curated illusionist, catfish adjacent. Antonyms: authentic presentation, realness, accuracy. Savage Sentence: She went full Filterella and the in-person reveal had you doing a double take. UnExpert Advice: Meet in natural light early.

Fitness Personality Disorder (Gym Bro Syndrome) /ˈfit-nəs ˌpər-sə-ˈna-lə-tē dis-ˈór-dər/ A man whose entire identity revolves around the gym and nothing else. Synonyms: protein philosopher, mirror addict, rep counter romantic. Antonyms: balanced personality, depth, emotional availability. Savage Sentence: The Fitness Personality Disorder profile had routines, macros, and zero emotional range. UnExpert Advice: Muscles don't replace personality.

Fizzled / Slow Fade /ˈfi-zəld • slō fād/ Gradual death of a connection with no real conversation or closure. Synonyms: slow ghost, soft vanishing, diminishing replies. Antonyms: direct communication, honest ending, respectful closure. Savage Sentence: It fizzled into a Slow Fade and you kept checking your phone like something was still alive. UnExpert Advice: A slow fade is still rejection.

Flaky /ˈflā-kē/ Constantly cancels, reschedules, or disappears before plans. Synonyms: unreliable energy, vaporware dating, commitment-phobic behavior. Antonyms: consistency, reliability, respect. Savage Sentence: He was so Flaky you started assuming plans weren't real until he actually showed up. UnExpert Advice: Flaky isn't busy, it's low priority.

Floodlighting /ˈfləd-ˌlī-tiŋ/ Dumping intense personal trauma too early. Synonyms: trauma dumping, emotional overshare, instant therapy session. Antonyms: paced vulnerability, healthy boundaries, gradual disclosure. Savage Sentence: He floodlighted you so hard you knew his entire life story before you even knew if you liked him. UnExpert Advice: Vulnerability is earned.

Fluent in Nothing (Sarcasm Guy) /ˈflü-ənt in ˈnə-thiŋ/ Claims "fluent in sarcasm" to mask lack of personality. Synonyms: dry humor crutch, personality substitute, effort dodger. Antonyms: wit, actual humor, engaging personality. Savage Sentence: The Fluent in Nothing bio warned you early that effort wouldn't be included. UnExpert Advice: If sarcasm is the personality, expect immaturity.

Four Ps /fȯr pēz/ Warning about high-chaos professions. Synonyms: profession red flags, ego-heavy jobs, high-drama careers. Antonyms: stability, availability, balance. Savage Sentence: You ignored the Four Ps and ended up dating chaos with a job title. UnExpert Advice: Date the lifestyle, not the uniform.

Fragile Ego /ˈfra-jəl ˈē-gō/ Crumbles or lashes out when not validated. Synonyms: praise-dependent, criticism allergic, ego on glass. Antonyms: secure confidence, resilience, self-awareness. Savage Sentence: His Fragile Ego couldn't handle one honest comment without turning it into a full issue. UnExpert Advice: Never date someone who needs constant applause.

Freak Matching /frēk ˈma-chiŋ/ Bonding over chaos instead of compatibility. Synonyms: chaos bonding, toxic alignment, unstable pairing. Antonyms: healthy compatibility, value alignment, stability. Savage Sentence: The Freak Matching felt exciting until you realized it was just mutual dysfunction. UnExpert Advice: Shared chaos is not compatibility.

Freckling /ˈfre-kə-liŋ/ A seasonal fling that disappears when life gets real. Synonyms: summer romance, temporary situationship, seasonal attachment. Antonyms: consistency, long-term effort, stability. Savage Sentence: He freckled you all summer and disappeared the second real life started. UnExpert Advice: If it's seasonal, it's temporary.

Friendzone /ˈfrend-zōn/ One wants more, the other keeps it platonic while benefiting emotionally. Synonyms: emotional placeholder, romantic rejection parking lot. Antonyms: mutual interest, clarity, reciprocity. Savage Sentence: You sat in the Friendzone hoping it would change while he stayed comfortable exactly where it was. UnExpert Advice: The friendzone is not a waiting room.

Fuckboy /ˈfək-ˌbȯi/ Master of mixed signals and low effort. Synonyms: walking red flag, situational lover, commitment allergic. Antonyms: consistent partner, emotionally available, grown man. Savage Sentence: He showed you he was a Fuckboy and you still tried to make him the exception. UnExpert Advice: Believe behavior.

Fuckcockery /ˈfək-kä-kə-rē/ High effort in bed, zero effort everywhere else. Synonyms: bedroom-only personality, selective effort syndrome. Antonyms: consistency, effort, partnership. Savage Sentence: The Fuckcockery was unmatched until you realized that's the only place he showed up. UnExpert Advice: No full access without full presence.

Future Faking /ˈfyü-chər ˈfā-kiŋ/ Talking about a future they never intend to build. Synonyms: empty promises, illusion planning. Antonyms: follow-through, action, integrity. Savage Sentence: He future faked a whole life with you and couldn't even follow through on a simple plan. UnExpert Advice: Believe the present, not the promises.

G

Gaslighting /ˈgas-ˌlī-tiŋ/ Twisting reality so you question your own memory, feelings, or sanity. Synonyms: reality distortion, mental gymnastics, blame shifting olympics. Antonyms: truth, validation, accountability. Savage Sentence: You're being gaslit if you walk into a conversation confident and leave questioning your own memory. UnExpert Advice: Trust the version of reality you lived, not the one they're trying to rewrite.

- **Gaslightinator** /ˈgas-ˌlī-tə-ˌnā-tər/ The advanced model who does it so smoothly you don't realize what's happening until you're already doubting everything.
- **Gaslightortion** /ˌgas-ˌlī-tôr-ˈshən/ Gaslighting taken so far you end up apologizing for things you didn't do.
- **Gaslightzilla** /ˌgas-ˌlī(t)-ˈzil-ə/ Full-scale destruction of your reality with zero hesitation and maximum confidence.

Ghost Profile Husband /gōst ˈprō-ˌfīl ˈhə-zbənd/ No photos, vague bio, and suspiciously private... because he's absolutely married. Synonyms: hidden husband, secret swiper, double-life dater. Antonyms: transparency, single status, openness. Savage Sentence: The Ghost Profile Husband had no photos and somehow even less availability. UnExpert Advice: If he's invisible, there's a reason.

Ghosting /ˈgō-stiŋ/ Suddenly disappearing with zero explanation after consistent communication, dates, or even a relationship. Synonyms: digital vanishing, silent exit, nuclear fade. Antonyms: honest conversation, respectful closure, basic decency. Savage Sentence: You got ghosted the second he decided disappearing was easier than acting like an adult. UnExpert Advice: Ghosting isn't mysterious. It's cowardice with a Wi-Fi connection. Don't chase ghosts.

- **Ghostationship** /ˈgōs-tə-ˌlā-shən-ˌship/ A relationship that ends without warning or explanation, like it never existed.
- **Ghostcycle** /ˈgōst-ˌsī-kəl/ The pattern of disappearing and reappearing over and over.

- **Ghostdependency** /ˈgōst-di-ˌpen-dən-sē/ Only shows up when he needs attention and disappears when you do.
- **Ghostscripted** /ˈgōst-ˌskrip-təd/ Disappears right when things get real... like he's following a predictable playbook.
- **Ghostwhisperer** /ˈgōst-ˌhwis-pər-ər/ Knows exactly how to disappear... and then reappear just softly enough to pull you back in.

Ghostlighting /ˈgōstˌlītɪŋ/ When someone ghosts you... then comes back acting like you're crazy for noticing they disappeared. Synonyms: selective amnesia king, vanish-and-deny, delusion dealer. Antonyms: accountability, basic decency, emotional continuity. Savage Sentence: He ghostlighted you and tried to act like the silence never happened while you were sitting there with the receipts. UnExpert Advice: If someone rewrites reality after disappearing, block them and let them stay gone.

Glow-up Era /ˈglō-ˌəp ˈer-ə/ The phase of intense self-improvement after a breakup, often used as revenge while avoiding real healing. Synonyms: post-breakup glow, revenge glow-up, main character renovation. Antonyms: genuine healing, quiet growth, internal work. Savage Sentence: She entered her Glow-up Era looking incredible and still texting the same man who caused the breakdown. UnExpert Advice: A glow-up without healing just upgrades the same patterns.

Goblin Mode Dating /ˈgä-blin mōd ˈdā-tiŋ/ Embracing chaotic, low-effort dating and calling it "authentic" or "healing." Synonyms: hot mess matching, chaos cosplay, unhinged situationship era. Antonyms: intentional growth, accountability, healthy standards. Savage Sentence: She went full Goblin Mode Dating and kept waking up in situations she wouldn't even claim in daylight. UnExpert Advice: Chaos isn't healing. It's avoidance.

- **Goblinitmacy (Goblintimacy)** /ˌgäb-lin-ˈti-mə-sē/ Chaotic, messy, low-effort intimacy disguised as "real connection."

Gold Digger /ˈgōld ˌdi-gər/ Someone who dates primarily for money, lifestyle, or financial gain. Synonyms: lifestyle shopper, transactional romantic, sponsored partner. Antonyms: self-sufficient, mutual investment, genuine affection. Savage Sentence: She wasn't dating him, she was gold digging the lifestyle and tolerating the personality. UnExpert Advice: Wanting stability is normal. Pretending exploitation is love is not.

Golden Boy Syndrome /ˈgōl-dən bȯi ˈsin-drōm/ Believes he deserves special treatment while offering minimal effort. Synonyms: main character complex, unearned entitlement, participation trophy king. Antonyms: humility, earned confidence, self-awareness. Savage Sentence: He had Golden Boy Syndrome and expected praise for doing the bare minimum. UnExpert Advice: Stop rewarding mediocrity.

Gooning /ˈgü-niŋ/ Obsessively fixating on someone or their content in a way that replaces real connection. Synonyms: porn-brain fixation, obsessive scrolling, fantasy attachment. Antonyms: healthy desire, present intimacy, balanced attraction. Savage Sentence: He was gooning over her online while barely acknowledging her in real life. UnExpert Advice: If the fantasy matters more than the person, it's not connection.

Grand Gesture Guy /grand ˈjes-chər gī/ Uses big romantic acts to distract from consistent lack of effort. Synonyms: spectacle over substance, fireworks without foundation, reset button romantic. Antonyms: steady effort, reliability, consistency. Savage Sentence: He pulled the Grand Gesture Guy move and thought flowers erased weeks of disappearing. UnExpert Advice: Big moments don't fix consistent absence.

Gray Rocking /grā ˈrä-kiŋ/ Becoming emotionally unresponsive to make yourself uninteresting to a toxic person. Synonyms: detachment strategy, emotional shutdown, boredom defense. Antonyms: emotional engagement, vulnerability, connection. Savage Sentence: She started gray rocking him and suddenly he had nothing to work with. UnExpert Advice: Sometimes the power move is becoming unavailable.

Green Flag /grēn flag/ A positive sign of emotional health, effort, or compatibility. Synonyms: healthy indicator, positive trait, compatibility marker. Antonyms: red flag, warning sign, dealbreaker. Savage Sentence: You called it a Green Flag and ignored everything else that clearly wasn't. UnExpert Advice: One green flag doesn't cancel ten red ones.

Green Flag Chaser /grēn flag ˈchā-sər/ Overhypes basic decency while ignoring major red flags. Synonyms: bare minimum enthusiast, hope merchant, delusion olympian. Antonyms: discernment, standards, pattern recognition. Savage Sentence: You became a Green Flag Chaser celebrating "he texted back" like it meant something. UnExpert Advice: Basic effort is not exceptional.

Grooming (Dating Context) /ˈgrüm-iŋ/ Building trust and emotional dependency with the intent to control or exploit. Synonyms: slow manipulation, trust harvesting, predatory patience. Antonyms: healthy connection, transparency, mutual respect. Savage Sentence: What felt like care turned into grooming once you realized it was all about control. UnExpert Advice: If it isolates you or accelerates too fast, step back.

Group Chat Energy /grüp chat ˈe-nər-jē/ Treating dating like a performance for friends instead of taking it seriously. Synonyms: locker room mentality, broadcast dating, ego entertainment. Antonyms: private respect, genuine interest, emotional maturity. Savage Sentence: He had full Group Chat Energy and turned your conversations into content. UnExpert Advice: If you're being shared, you're not being respected.

Group Photo Gambler /grüp ˈfō-tō ˈgam-blər/ Only posts group photos so you can't tell which one he is. Synonyms: identity hider, friend camouflage, mystery match. Antonyms: clear identity, solo photos, confidence. Savage Sentence: The Group Photo Gambler made you play "spot the red flag" before the first message. UnExpert Advice: If you have to guess, pass.

Groundhogging /ˈground-ˌhä-giŋ/ Repeatedly dating the same toxic type expecting different results. Synonyms: type addiction, pattern repetition, same-man-different-face. Antonyms: growth, awareness, intentional change. Savage Sentence: You're groundhogging if every new guy feels different but ends the exact same way. UnExpert Advice: Change the pattern or repeat the outcome.

Guilt Tripping /gilt ˈtrip-iŋ/ Using shame or emotion to manipulate you into staying or giving more. Synonyms: emotional blackmail, pity play, obligation weaponization. Antonyms: accountability, boundaries, direct communication. Savage Sentence: He started guilt tripping the second you stopped tolerating his behavior. UnExpert Advice: Guilt is not a reason to stay.

H

Habitual Almost /hə-ˈbi-chə-wəl ˈȯl-ˌmōst/ Master of the "almost relationship"—almost commits, almost plans, almost chooses you... forever. Synonyms: professional almost-guy, eternal maybe man, progress pretender. Antonyms: decisive partner, full commitment, clear intention. Savage Sentence: You kept waiting for it to become real, but Habitual Almost made sure you lived in "almost" the entire time. UnExpert Advice: Almost is a lifestyle, not a phase. Exit the waiting room.

Harbinger (Heart Harbinger) /ˈhär-bin-jər/ The early sign of what's coming—subtle behaviors that quietly predict the entire relationship pattern before it fully unfolds. Synonyms: warning sign, pattern preview, emotional forecast. Antonyms: surprise outcome, unexpected shift, healthy progression. Savage Sentence: You ignored the little things, but the Harbinger told you exactly how this would end from the beginning. UnExpert Advice: The beginning always hints at the ending—pay attention sooner.

Hard Launch /härd lônch/ Officially posting your partner clearly on social media to confirm the relationship publicly. Synonyms: public claim, official reveal, social confirmation. Antonyms: pocketing, secrecy, hidden relationship. Savage Sentence: You were ready for a Hard Launch while he was still acting like you were a soft draft. UnExpert Advice: If it's not mutual, it's not real.

Hatfishing /ˈhat-ˌfi-shiŋ/ Hiding hair loss or appearance by always wearing a hat to create a misleading impression. Synonyms: appearance deception, style masking, visual misrepresentation. Antonyms: authenticity, transparency, honesty. Savage Sentence: The chemistry changed the second Hatfishing had nowhere left to hide. UnExpert Advice: If it disappears in real life, it wasn't real to begin with.

Haunting / Zombieing /ˈhȯn-tiŋ • ˈzäm-bē-iŋ/ Ghosting someone, then reappearing later acting normal without accountability. Synonyms: zombie texting, resurfacing ghost, undead reentry. Antonyms: closure, consistency, self-awareness. Savage Sentence: He vanished completely, then came back

Haunting like you were supposed to forget everything. UnExpert Advice: If they disappeared once, they'll do it again.

Healing Era Cosplay /ˈhē-liŋ ˈer-ə ˈkäz-ˌplā/ Claiming personal growth while repeating the same toxic behaviors with new people. Synonyms: fake healing, performative growth, rebranded toxicity. Antonyms: real growth, accountability, change. Savage Sentence: The captions said growth, but Healing Era Cosplay kept producing the exact same results. UnExpert Advice: Growth shows in patterns, not captions.

Heightfishing /ˈhīt-ˌfi-shiŋ/ Misrepresenting height, typically exaggerating to appear taller than reality. Synonyms: profile lying, physical exaggeration, stat inflation. Antonyms: honesty, accuracy, transparency. Savage Sentence: He said six feet, but Heightfishing made the truth very obvious the second he stood up. UnExpert Advice: If they lie about something obvious, imagine what else they'll lie about.

Hidden Roster /ˈhid-ən ˈrä-stər/ Keeping you thinking you're the main option while maintaining multiple backups. Synonyms: secret roster management, main-character delusion feeder, quiet rotation. Antonyms: transparency, exclusivity, respect. Savage Sentence: You thought you were chosen, but Hidden Roster energy had you competing without even knowing it. UnExpert Advice: If they're vague about options, assume there are many.

High-Value Hypocrite /hī-ˈval-(ˌ)yü ˈhī-pə-ˌkrit/ Preaches standards and self-worth while acting in complete contradiction to them. Synonyms: walking contradiction, selective standards king/queen, performative values. Antonyms: congruence, integrity, self-aware standards. Savage Sentence: The High-Value Hypocrite demanded excellence while delivering the bare minimum and calling it boundaries. UnExpert Advice: Watch behavior, not branding.

Hobosexual /ˈhō-bō-ˌsek-shə-wəl/ Someone who enters relationships primarily for housing, financial stability, or convenience. Synonyms: opportunist dater, survival partner, dependent lover. Antonyms: independent partner, self-sufficient individual, equal contributor. Savage Sentence: The feelings escalated fast, but Hobosexual motives needed a place to land more than a person to love. UnExpert Advice: Fast attachment often comes with hidden needs.

Hookup Culture (Trash Angle) /ˈhu̇k-ˌəp ˈkəl-chər/ Casual sex normalized to avoid real connection, often leaving emotional fallout. Synonyms: casual sex culture, non-commitment dating, surface-level intimacy. Antonyms:

intentional dating, emotional connection, commitment. Savage Sentence: It felt modern and free, but Hookup Culture kept recycling people without ever building anything real. UnExpert Advice: If it avoids connection, it creates confusion.

Hookup Hopscotch /ˈhu̇-ˌkäp ˈhäp-ˌskäch/ Jumping from one casual situation to the next while avoiding real connection. Synonyms: serial casualist, situationship tourist, commitment dodger's playbook. Antonyms: intentional dating, emotional investment, monogamous focus. Savage Sentence: It looked like freedom, but Hookup Hopscotch kept you moving without ever arriving anywhere. UnExpert Advice: If every connection is temporary, the pattern isn't accidental.

Honeymoon Hijacker /ˈhən-ē-ˌmün ˈhī-ˌjak-ər/ Creates intense early "forever" energy to lock you in, then drops to minimal effort once you're invested. Synonyms: love-bomb runner, intensity baiter, false future faker. Antonyms: slow burn, consistent pacing, earned intimacy. Savage Sentence: He honeymoon-hijacked you with soulmate energy early, then disappeared the second consistency was expected. UnExpert Advice: If it feels too perfect too fast, it's usually a hijacking, not a honeymoon.

Hoovering /ˈhü-və-riŋ/ Pulling an ex back into a toxic cycle after a breakup through manipulation or sudden attention. Synonyms: emotional vacuuming, toxic return, cycle reentry. Antonyms: closure, detachment, finality. Savage Sentence: Just when you moved on, Hoovering showed up to pull you right back in. UnExpert Advice: The cycle only continues if you let it.

Hope Override System /hōp ˈō-vər-ˌrīd ˈsi-stəm/ Ignoring logic and evidence in favor of hopeful thinking. Synonyms: denial loop, optimism bias, emotional override. Antonyms: clarity, logic, discernment. Savage Sentence: You saw every red flag clearly, but the Hope Override System convinced you to stay anyway. UnExpert Advice: Hope without evidence is self-sabotage.

Hopeaddiction /hōp ə-ˈdik-shən/ Staying because "maybe" feels better than accepting "no." Synonyms: possibility fixation, hope dependency, denial attachment. Antonyms: acceptance, closure, reality. Savage Sentence: You stayed in Hopeaddiction, turning crumbs into possibility while ignoring a very clear answer. UnExpert Advice: If it's not a clear yes, it's already a no.

Hot and Cold /hät ənd kōld/ Alternating between intense affection and sudden distance to create emotional instability. Synonyms: push-pull dynamic, inconsistency, emotional whiplash. Antonyms: consistency, stability, secure attachment. Savage Sentence: It felt intense one day and distant the next, and

Hot and Cold kept you chasing something that never stayed. UnExpert Advice: Consistency is the standard, not the bonus.

Hovering /ˈhə-vər-iŋ/ Lurking through views, likes, and passive engagement without direct communication or effort. Synonyms: passive orbiter, digital loiterer, low-effort lurker. Antonyms: direct communicator, intentional pursuer. Savage Sentence: He never reached out, but Hovering kept him just present enough to stay in your head. UnExpert Advice: Views and likes are not interest—they're placeholders.

I

Ick /ik/ A sudden, visceral turn-off triggered by a small behavior that instantly shifts attraction. Synonyms: instant turn-off, attraction killer, cringe trigger. Antonyms: attraction, intrigue, appeal. Savage Sentence: It was going fine until the Ick hit and suddenly everything about him felt wrong. UnExpert Advice: Don't negotiate with the Ick—your body already decided.

Ick Accumulator (Ick Spiral) /ik ə-ˈkyü-myü-ˌlā-tər • ik ˈspī-rəl/ When small turn-offs build over time until attraction completely collapses. Synonyms: attraction erosion, delayed dealbreaker, post-ick regret. Antonyms: sustained attraction, compatibility, alignment. Savage Sentence: You ignored the early signs, and the Ick Accumulator turned mild annoyance into full-blown repulsion. UnExpert Advice: Honor the Ick early—it compounds fast.

Ideal Lover (Archetype) /ī-ˈdi-(ə-)l ˈlə-vər/ Mirrors your deepest desires and fantasies to create the illusion of perfect compatibility. Synonyms: fantasy match, projection partner, tailored illusion. Antonyms: authentic partner, reality-based connection, grounded compatibility. Savage Sentence: It felt like destiny, but the Ideal Lover was just reflecting everything you wanted to see. UnExpert Advice: If it feels too perfect, check if it's actually real.

Inconsistencium (Inconsistent King/Queen) /ˌin-kən-ˈsi-stən(t)-sē-əm/ Alternates between intense presence and complete absence, creating emotional instability. Synonyms: hot-cold champion, effort yo-yo, pattern dodger. Antonyms: consistency, reliability, steady presence. Savage Sentence: You kept adjusting to the highs and lows, but Inconsistencium made sure you never felt secure. UnExpert Advice: Inconsistency isn't complex—it's incompatible.

Influencer-in-Disguise /ˈin-flü-ən-sər in dis-ˈgīz/ Uses a dating profile to build followers, brand image, or attention instead of forming real connections. Synonyms: clout chaser, content collector, validation marketer. Antonyms: genuine dater, connection-focused, private individual. Savage Sentence: The Influencer-in-Disguise matched with you just to gain a follower, not a relationship. UnExpert Advice: If it feels like marketing, it is.

Interest Inflation Scheme /ˈin-trəst in-ˈflā-shən skēm/ Shows exaggerated interest early, then dramatically pulls back once you're invested. Synonyms: false intensity, overpromise underdeliver, bait-and-switch interest. Antonyms: consistent effort, steady interest, genuine pacing. Savage Sentence: The energy was loud in the beginning, but the Interest Inflation Scheme couldn't sustain what it started. UnExpert Advice: Don't trust early intensity without consistency.

Intermittent Reinforcement (Intermittent Reinforcer) /ˌin-tər-ˈmit-ənt ˌrē-ən-ˈfȯr-smənt/ Gives unpredictable bursts of attention that create addictive emotional attachment. Synonyms: crumb dating, variable reward trap, hot-cold conditioning. Antonyms: consistent care, steady investment, reliable love. Savage Sentence: The highs felt incredible, but Intermittent Reinforcement kept you addicted to scraps. UnExpert Advice: Unpredictability is what hooks you—not what sustains you.

Intimacy Acceleration Trap /ˈin-tə-mə-sē ək-ˌsel-ə-ˈrā-shən trap/ Rushes emotional or physical closeness to create a false sense of connection. Synonyms: forced bonding, rushed intimacy, false closeness. Antonyms: natural pacing, earned intimacy, emotional progression. Savage Sentence: It felt deep fast, but the Intimacy Acceleration Trap skipped everything real. UnExpert Advice: Real connection doesn't need to sprint.

Intimacyfraud /ˈin-tə-mə-sē ˌfrôd/ Fakes emotional depth just long enough to gain access, then disappears. Synonyms: fake vulnerability, emotional scam, depth illusion. Antonyms: genuine intimacy, authenticity, real connection. Savage Sentence: You opened up fully, but Intimacyfraud was already planning the exit. UnExpert Advice: Real intimacy is consistent, not strategic.

Instantship (Instant Boyfriend/Girlfriend) /ˈin-stənt-ˌship/ Acts like a full relationship exists almost immediately without real foundation. Synonyms: premature commitment, love-bomb lite, speedrun relationship. Antonyms: slow intentional pacing, earned closeness, grounded connection. Savage Sentence: It felt exciting at first, but Instantship made expectations grow faster than reality could support. UnExpert Advice: Fast starts usually skip real substance.

Intuition Override /ˌin-tü-ˈi-shən ˈō-vər-ˌrīd/ Ignoring your gut instinct because the truth is inconvenient. Synonyms: instinct denial, gut suppression, emotional override. Antonyms: intuition, alignment, self-trust. Savage Sentence: You felt it immediately, but Intuition Override convinced you to stay anyway. UnExpert Advice: Your intuition speaks first—trust it sooner.

Investment Imbalance /in-ˈvest-mənt ˌim-ˈba-lən(t)s/ One person invests heavily while the other contributes minimal effort but expects full benefits. Synonyms: one-sided effort, emotional labor overload, uneven investment. Antonyms: reciprocity, balance, mutual effort. Savage Sentence: You gave everything, and Investment Imbalance made sure they gave just enough to keep you there. UnExpert Advice: Match effort with reality, not hope.

Isolation Game (Isolator) /ˈī-sə-ˌlā-tər/ Gradually separates you from your support system to increase dependency. Synonyms: dependency engineering, social cutoff, control tactic. Antonyms: supportive partnership, independence, healthy boundaries. Savage Sentence: It didn't happen all at once, but the Isolation Game slowly made your world revolve around them. UnExpert Advice: Anyone who limits your world isn't expanding your life.

J/K

J-Guy (J-Name Theory) /ˈjā-gī/ The belief that men with names starting with "J" are disproportionately chaotic, non-committal, or toxic. Synonyms: J-curse, name red flag, Justin/Jason/Jordan warning. Antonyms: name neutrality, unbiased dating. Savage Sentence: She laughed off the pattern until the third J-Guy in a row pulled the exact same disappearing act. UnExpert Advice: It's not the letter—it's the pattern. But if the pattern keeps repeating... start paying attention.

Jawlineblindness /ˈjô-ˌlīn ˈblīn(d)-nəs/ Ignoring every red flag because he's attractive. Synonyms: attraction bias, looks over logic, physical distraction. Antonyms: discernment, awareness, standards. Savage Sentence: You let Jawlineblindness carry the whole situation while his behavior was quietly failing every test. UnExpert Advice: Looks don't compensate for behavior.

Jump Scare (Jump Scare Boyfriend) /ˈjəmp ˈsker/ The sudden personality shift once they feel secure—sweet turns cold, effort disappears, mask drops. Synonyms: mask slip, personality 180, post-love-bomb reveal. Antonyms: consistency, steady character, emotional stability. Savage Sentence: It felt perfect until the Jump Scare hit and the version of him you liked completely vanished. UnExpert Advice: The real person is who shows up after the switch.

Just Ask Lazybones /jəst ask ˈlā-zē-ˌbōnz/ Uses "just ask" instead of writing an actual bio. Synonyms: zero-effort bio, conversational freeloader, blank slate dater. Antonyms: thoughtful bio, intentional effort. Savage Sentence: The Just Ask Lazybones expected curiosity without giving you a single reason to be curious. UnExpert Advice: If they won't try here, they won't try later.

Justification Junkie /ˌjəs-tə-fə-ˈkā-shən ˈjəŋ-kē/ Constantly creates excuses to avoid accountability for bad behavior. Synonyms: excuseologist, rationalization addict, blame alchemist. Antonyms: ownership, honesty, self-awareness. Savage Sentence: He justification-junkied every red flag into something "understandable" until nothing made sense anymore. UnExpert Advice: If everything has an excuse, nothing gets fixed.

"K" Responder /ˈkā ri-ˈspän-dər/ The one-letter texter who gives minimal effort while expecting full engagement. Synonyms: conversational corpse, effort assassin, low-energy communicator. Antonyms: engaged texter, enthusiastic communicator. Savage Sentence: Three "K" responses later, the K Responder still expected you to carry the entire conversation. UnExpert Advice: Match the energy, then lower it.

Keeping Score /ˈkēp-iŋ skȯr/ Tracking effort, favors, or actions to use as leverage later. Synonyms: emotional accountant, tit-for-tat trap, resentment ledger. Antonyms: generosity, mutual giving, no-strings support. Savage Sentence: Every interaction turned into currency because Keeping Score made sure nothing was ever freely given. UnExpert Advice: If everything is tracked, nothing is genuine.

King Baby /kiŋ ˈbā-bē/ An emotionally immature adult who expects to be taken care of while offering little in return. Synonyms: man-child deluxe, emotional infant, entitlement machine. Antonyms: emotional adult, equal partner, self-sufficient individual. Savage Sentence: The King Baby expected patience, nurturing, and understanding while contributing absolutely nothing back. UnExpert Advice: If he needs parenting, he's not ready for partnership.

Kittenfishing /ˈki-tən-ˌfi-shiŋ/ Subtle online deception using curated images or slightly altered truths. Synonyms: soft catfishing, filtered fraud, polished illusion. Antonyms: authenticity, honesty, accurate presentation. Savage Sentence: The profile looked flawless, but Kittenfishing made the real-life version feel like a completely different person. UnExpert Advice: Expect the in-person version to be the least filtered one.

Klownery /ˈklau̇-nə-rē/ Absurd, chaotic, or self-sabotaging behavior someone expects you to tolerate. Synonyms: circus behavior, dating chaos, emotional nonsense. Antonyms: maturity, stability, self-respect. Savage Sentence: The situation kept getting worse, but Klownery made it feel like you were stuck in a show you didn't sign up for. UnExpert Advice: If it feels ridiculous, it is—leave the circus.

L

Last Minute Larry /last ˈmi-nət ˈler-ē/ Only makes plans at the last possible second and expects you to be available. Synonyms: flaky king, convenience planner, zero-notice texter. Antonyms: intentional dating, respectful planning, consistency. Savage Sentence: You rearranged your whole night for him once, and Last Minute Larry made sure it became a habit. UnExpert Advice: If he plans last minute, treat him like one.

Leaf Test /lēf test/ Watching how someone treats low-stakes things (plants, service staff, small responsibilities) to predict how they'll treat you. Synonyms: character test, entitlement detector, behavior tell. Antonyms: empathy, awareness, respect. Savage Sentence: He failed the Leaf Test in small ways long before he failed you in big ones. UnExpert Advice: How they treat what doesn't matter to them is exactly how they'll treat you later.

Leading On /ˈlē-diŋ ȯn/ Giving just enough attention and hope to keep access without real intention. Synonyms: stringing along, false hope merchant, emotional placeholder tactic. Antonyms: clarity, honesty, direct intention. Savage Sentence: You kept waiting for clarity, but Leading On made sure you stayed confused just enough to stay. UnExpert Advice: Mixed signals are not confusion—they're strategy.

Left on Read /left ȯn red/ Reading messages and choosing not to respond as a control or avoidance tactic. Synonyms: digital disrespect, silent dismissal, read-and-ignore. Antonyms: communication, respect, responsiveness. Savage Sentence: You saw the read receipt, and Left on Read said everything he didn't bother to. UnExpert Advice: Silence after attention is a message—believe it.

Lie Loop /lī lüp/ A pattern of small lies that stack over time until trust is completely eroded. Synonyms: deception cycle, truth erosion, layered lying. Antonyms: honesty, transparency, integrity. Savage Sentence: Each lie felt small, but the Lie Loop made the truth impossible to find. UnExpert Advice: Repeated small lies equal one big reality.

Limerence /ˈli-mə-rən(t)s/ Obsessive, fantasy-driven infatuation that overrides logic and amplifies emotional attachment. Synonyms: emotional addiction, obsessive crush, fantasy bonding. Antonyms: grounded love, secure attachment, clarity. Savage Sentence: You thought it was real, but Limerence had you building a relationship in your head that never existed. UnExpert Advice: If it feels consuming, it's not love—it's limerence.

Lithosexual / Akoisexual /ˌli-thō-ˈsek-shə-wəl/ Experiences attraction but loses interest when it's reciprocated. Synonyms: chase addict, unreciprocated attraction, situationship enabler. Antonyms: mutual desire, emotional availability, secure connection. Savage Sentence: It felt intense at first, but Lithosexual energy disappeared the second things became real. UnExpert Advice: If they only want you when you're unavailable, they don't want you—they want the chase.

Long Game Ghost /lȯŋ gām gōst/ Invests time, effort, and emotional depth only to disappear later without explanation. Synonyms: delayed ghoster, patient manipulator, slow-burn vanisher. Antonyms: consistency, follow-through, emotional integrity. Savage Sentence: You trusted the time invested, but the Long Game Ghost proved that effort doesn't always mean intention. UnExpert Advice: Time doesn't equal sincerity—patterns do.

Love Bombing /ˈləv ˌbäm-iŋ/ Over-the-top affection early on designed to hook you fast before the mask slips. Synonyms: emotional fireworks, intensity illusion, fast-track fantasy. Antonyms: steady connection, healthy pacing, genuine interest. Savage Sentence: You got pulled into Love Bombing and mistook intensity for something real before it disappeared. UnExpert Advice: Real love builds. It doesn't explode on impact.

- **Lovebombshell** /ˈləv-ˌbäm-ˌshel/ Comes in hot, overwhelming, then leaves you dealing with the aftermath alone.

Love Haze /ləv hāz/ Early infatuation fog that makes red flags feel like personality quirks. Synonyms: honeymoon blindness, chemistry delusion, attraction fog. Antonyms: discernment, clarity, awareness. Savage Sentence: You ignored everything because Love Haze made the wrong things feel right. UnExpert Advice: The haze always lifts—don't commit before it does.

Low Effort Loop /lō ˈe-fərt lüp/ You lower your standards, he lowers his effort, and the cycle keeps shrinking you. Synonyms: downward spiral dating, self-worth erosion cycle, effort collapse. Antonyms: standards, boundaries, upward growth. Savage Sentence: You stayed in the Low Effort Loop and watched your standards drop every time he gave you less. UnExpert Advice: Raise your standards once and the cycle breaks.

Lowefforticus /lō-ˈe-fər-ti-kəs/ Walks around like a king but contributes nothing. Synonyms: entitled minimalist, ego emperor, zero-effort ruler. Antonyms: contributing partner, grounded man, equal effort. Savage Sentence: He showed up as Lowefforticus and still expected treatment he never earned. UnExpert Advice: If he wants more, he needs to do more.

Luxury Broke /ˈlək-shə-rē brōk/ Projects high standards and expensive taste without the means or contribution to match. Synonyms: lifestyle faker, aesthetic rich, reality broke. Antonyms: financial stability, grounded lifestyle, authenticity. Savage Sentence: The lifestyle looked expensive, but Luxury Broke made sure you paid the difference. UnExpert Advice: If they can't match the standard, they'll expect you to.

M

Main Character Syndrome /mān ˈka-rək-tər ˈsin-drōm/ Treating your partner like a side character while everything revolves around your needs, feelings, and narrative. Synonyms: emotional spotlight hog, one-person show dater, delulu lead role. Antonyms: mutual partnership, empathy, shared focus. Savage Sentence: The relationship felt one-sided because Main Character Syndrome made sure everything revolved around them. UnExpert Advice: If there's only one main character, you're not in a relationship—you're in a storyline.

Manipulationship /mə-ˌnip-yə-ˈlā-shən-ˌship/ Everything feels like a relationship until you realize it's just control in disguise. Synonyms: control dynamic, emotional strategy, power imbalance. Antonyms: mutual respect, partnership, equality. Savage Sentence: You were in a Manipulationship thinking it was love while every outcome kept working in his favor. UnExpert Advice: If the power isn't equal, it's not a relationship.

Mansplaining /ˈman-ˌsplā-niŋ/ Explaining something in a condescending way, especially when you already know more about it. Synonyms: patronizing lecture, fake expertise, confidence overload. Antonyms: mutual respect, listening, humility. Savage Sentence: He mansplained your own experience to you and still expected you to be impressed. UnExpert Advice: Confidence without awareness is just arrogance.

Manspreading (Dating Context) /ˈman-ˌspred-iŋ/ Taking up emotional, conversational, or physical space without consideration for the other person. Synonyms: emotional hogging, space dominance, attention monopolizer. Antonyms: awareness, balance, consideration. Savage Sentence: The entire dynamic felt suffocating because Manspreading left no room for you to exist in it. UnExpert Advice: If there's no space for you, there's no relationship.

Married & Matching /ˈmer-ēd ənd ˈma-chiŋ/ Actively on dating apps while fully in a relationship or marriage. Synonyms: double-lifer, cheating swiper, secret spouse. Antonyms: single, honest, available. Savage Sentence: The

Married & Matching profile had availability online but nowhere else. UnExpert Advice: If they hide you, they have something to lose.

Marriage Material Cosplay /ˈmer-ij mə-ˈtir-ē-əl ˈkäz-ˌplā/ Acting like a serious, long-term partner while delivering zero real substance. Synonyms: performative partner, illusion builder, future faker lite. Antonyms: genuine commitment, real effort, follow-through. Savage Sentence: It looked promising at first, but Marriage Material Cosplay couldn't hold up in reality. UnExpert Advice: If it's all talk, it's all temporary.

Mask Slip /mask slip/ The moment the charming, "perfect" version drops and the real person shows up. Synonyms: true colors reveal, personality shift, post-honeymoon reality. Antonyms: consistency, authenticity, alignment. Savage Sentence: Everything felt effortless until the Mask Slip revealed a completely different person. UnExpert Advice: The real version always shows—just not immediately.

Memorymasochist /ˈmem-ə-rē ˈma-sə-kist/ Re-reads old messages just to hurt herself again. Synonyms: pain revisiter, nostalgia addict, emotional self-saboteur. Antonyms: detachment, healing, release. Savage Sentence: You went full Memorymasochist reopening messages that only remind you why it ended. UnExpert Advice: If it hurts every time, stop revisiting it.

Micro-Cheating /ˈmī-krō ˈchē-tiŋ/ Small, deniable boundary violations that slowly erode trust. Synonyms: gray-area betrayal, sneaky intimacy, emotional cheating lite. Antonyms: loyalty, transparency, clear boundaries. Savage Sentence: It seemed harmless at first, but Micro-Cheating kept crossing lines just enough to break trust. UnExpert Advice: If it feels off, it's not small—it's a pattern.

Micro-Dosing Affection /ˈmī-krō ˌdō-siŋ ə-ˈfek-shən/ Tiny hits of attention spaced out just enough to keep you hooked. Synonyms: affection rationing, emotional drip feed, intermittent reinforcement. Antonyms: consistency, full presence, steady care. Savage Sentence: You stayed on Micro-Dosing Affection waiting for the next hit instead of noticing how little you were actually getting. UnExpert Advice: If it feels like withdrawal between texts, it's not love.

Micro-mance /ˈmī-krō mans/ Small gestures of affection that can be meaningful—or manipulative when used as bare minimum to keep someone attached. Synonyms: breadcrumb romance, minimal effort affection, emotional drip. Antonyms: real effort, consistency, intentional love. Savage Sentence: The Micro-mance felt sweet at first, until it became the only thing you were getting. UnExpert Advice: Small gestures should add to effort, not replace it.

Mixed Signal Olympics /mikst ˈsig-nəl ō-ˈlim-piks/ Saying one thing and doing the complete opposite. Synonyms: contradiction champion, confusion athlete, inconsistency expert. Antonyms: alignment, clarity, consistency. Savage Sentence: You sat through the Mixed Signal Olympics trying to decode behavior that was already telling you everything. UnExpert Advice: Believe behavior, not promises.

Mommy Issues Dater /ˈmä-mē ˈi-shüz ˈdā-tər/ Seeks a partner to emotionally parent, regulate, and carry them. Synonyms: man-child magnet, emotional dependent, surrogate seeker. Antonyms: emotional adult, self-sufficient partner, equal contributor. Savage Sentence: The relationship shifted fast because the Mommy Issues Dater needed support more than partnership. UnExpert Advice: If they need parenting, they're not ready for partnership.

Monkey Barring /ˈməŋ-kē ˈbär-iŋ/ Keeping multiple options active while transitioning from one person to another. Synonyms: overlap dating, safety-net behavior, backup planner. Antonyms: exclusivity, honesty, clean transitions. Savage Sentence: The timeline didn't add up because Monkey Barring made sure there was never a gap. UnExpert Advice: If there's always someone else, you're never the choice.

Monkey Branching /ˈməŋ-kē ˈbranch-iŋ/ Swinging from one partner to the next without ever being alone. Synonyms: serial overlapper, branch hopper, pre-breakup shopper. Antonyms: independence, clean break, self-awareness. Savage Sentence: The transition felt seamless because Monkey Branching made sure you were replaced before you were gone. UnExpert Advice: If they can't be alone, they're not choosing you.

Moving the Goalposts /ˈmüv-iŋ ðə ˈgōl-ˌpōsts/ Constantly changing expectations so you can never meet them. Synonyms: shifting standards, expectation trap, satisfaction sabotage. Antonyms: clarity, fairness, consistency. Savage Sentence: No matter what you did, Moving the Goalposts made sure it was never enough. UnExpert Advice: If you can't win, stop playing.

Mugging Off /ˈmə-giŋ ȯf/ Being openly disrespected or played while the other person acts like it's nothing. Synonyms: blatant disrespect, getting played, public embarrassment. Antonyms: respect, consideration, integrity. Savage Sentence: It felt obvious to everyone else because Mugging Off doesn't even try to hide it. UnExpert Advice: If it's blatant, don't tolerate it.

Mutual Delusion /ˈmyü-chə-wəl di-ˈlü-zhən/ Both people pretending something casual or undefined is deeper than it actually is. Synonyms: shared illusion, situationship fantasy, denial agreement. Antonyms: clarity, honesty, reality. Savage Sentence: It felt meaningful, but Mutual Delusion kept both of you avoiding the truth. UnExpert Advice: If no one defines it, no one benefits from it.

N

Narcissicarry /ˌnär-sə-sə-ˈker-ē/ You carry the entire relationship while he carries the audacity. Synonyms: one-sided effort, emotional labor overload, imbalance dynamic. Antonyms: mutual effort, shared responsibility, balance. Savage Sentence: You kept Narcissicarrying the whole situation while he contributed nothing and still acted like the prize. UnExpert Advice: If you're carrying it alone, put it down.

- **Narcissiship** /ˌnär-sə-ˈsi-ˌship/ A relationship where only one person exists and it's not you. Savage Sentence: You were in a Narcissiship where your needs didn't even make the conversation.
- **Narcissituationship** /ˌnär-sə-ˈsi-chə-ˌwā-shən-ˌship/ Keeps you confused, attached, and emotionally invested without ever choosing you. Savage Sentence: You stayed in a Narcissituationship giving everything while he refused to even define it.

Narcissicharm /ˌnär-sə-sə-ˈchärm/ Charming at first, calculated the entire time. Synonyms: strategic charm, calculated charisma, manipulative appeal. Antonyms: genuine warmth, authenticity, real connection. Savage Sentence: You fell for Narcissicharm and didn't realize the script was written before you even showed up. UnExpert Advice: Fast charm often comes with slow consequences.

- **Narcissipulation** /ˌnär-sə-ˌsi-pyə-ˈlā-shən/ Twists everything just enough to keep you hooked and confused. Savage Sentence: You were stuck in Narcissipulation trying to make sense of something that was designed not to make sense.
- **Narcissistication** /ˌnär-sə-ˌsi-stə-ˈkā-shən/ Disguises toxic behavior as "standards" or "boundaries." Savage Sentence: He used Narcissistication to make control sound like self-respect and expected you to agree.

Narcissicide /ˌnär-sə-ˈsi-ˌsīd/ Slowly destroys your confidence while convincing you it's your fault. Synonyms: confidence erosion, emotional destruction, identity breakdown. Antonyms: empowerment, support, emotional safety. Savage Sentence: You didn't just lose confidence,

Narcissicide chipped it away until you barely recognized yourself. UnExpert Advice: If you feel smaller around someone, leave before you disappear.

- **Narcissisolation** /ˌnär-sə-sə-ˈsō-lā-shən/ Slowly pulls you away from your reality, your people, and your instincts. Savage Sentence: You didn't notice the Narcissisolation until your world got smaller and his control got bigger.

Narcissidelusion /ˌnär-sə-sə-di-ˈlü-zhən/ Believes he's the prize while actively being the problem. Synonyms: self-inflated illusion, delusion of greatness, blind ego. Antonyms: self-awareness, accountability, grounded reality. Savage Sentence: He moved through life in Narcissidelusion acting like the catch while sabotaging everything around him. UnExpert Advice: If his self-image doesn't match his behavior, believe the behavior.

- **Narcissisick** /ˌnär-sə-sə-ˈsik/ So deeply self-obsessed it's honestly a condition. Savage Sentence: Every conversation with him turned into Narcissisick behavior where somehow everything circled back to him.
- **Narciseximon** /ˈnär-sə-ˌsek-sə-ˌmän/ Needs constant attention, validation, and an audience but gives nothing back. Savage Sentence: You dealt with a Narciseximon who treated your attention like oxygen and gave nothing back but exhaustion.
- **Narcisexual** /ˌnär-sə-ˈsek-shə-wəl/ Only shows interest when it benefits his ego or gets him access. Savage Sentence: He was fully Narcisexual and only showed up when it benefited him.

Narcissillusion /ˌnär-sə-ˈsil-ü-zhən/ Creates a perfect image at first, then slowly reveals the chaos behind it. Synonyms: false perfection, illusion builder, curated persona. Antonyms: authenticity, transparency, real character. Savage Sentence: The Narcissillusion held up just long enough for you to believe it before everything started slipping. UnExpert Advice: Pay attention to consistency, not first impressions.

Negging /ˈne-giŋ/ Backhanded compliments designed to lower your confidence so you seek their approval. Synonyms: insult flirtation, confidence undermining, pickup artist tactic. Antonyms: genuine compliments, secure attraction, respect. Savage Sentence: The "compliment" felt off because Negging always leaves you questioning yourself instead of feeling good. UnExpert Advice: If it lowers you, it's not flirting—it's manipulation.

New Supply /nü ˈsə-ˌplī/ The next person someone jumps to for validation and attention after draining you. Synonyms: replacement fuel, ego refill, next target. Antonyms: genuine connection, mutual relationship, emotional depth. Savage Sentence: The timeline made sense once you realized New Supply was already lined up before you were gone. UnExpert Advice: It's not about them being better—it's about them being available.

Nice Guy™ /nīs gī/ Uses basic decency as leverage and feels entitled to attraction or a relationship because of it. Synonyms: transactional nice, covert entitlement, approval seeker. Antonyms: genuine kindness, no-strings behavior, emotional maturity. Savage Sentence: The switch was instant because Nice Guy™ only stays nice when he's getting what he wants. UnExpert Advice: Kindness isn't currency—you don't owe attraction in return.

"Not Ready" Guy /nät ˈre-dē gī/ Claims he's not ready for a relationship while still expecting full access to you. Synonyms: commitment dodger, timing excuse king, situationship specialist. Antonyms: clear intention, emotional availability, readiness. Savage Sentence: The Not Ready Guy kept you close enough for benefits but far enough to avoid responsibility. UnExpert Advice: If he's not ready, step back—not closer.

Non-Responder /ˌnän-ri-ˈspän-dər/ Consistently avoids replying while still engaging passively (views, likes, lurking). Synonyms: silent ghost, digital avoider, low-effort communicator. Antonyms: responsiveness, effort, communication. Savage Sentence: The pattern was obvious because the Non-Responder had time for everything except actually replying. UnExpert Advice: If they wanted to respond, they would.

Normalization Trap /ˌnȯr-mə-lə-ˈzā-shən trap/ Gradually accepting worse behavior until disrespect feels normal. Synonyms: red flag desensitization, slow erosion, boiling frog dating. Antonyms: strong boundaries, awareness, standards. Savage Sentence: It didn't happen all at once, but the Normalization Trap made unacceptable behavior feel routine. UnExpert Advice: If it wouldn't be okay in the beginning, it's not okay now.

No Reciprocity Rule /nō ˌre-sə-ˈprä-sə-tē rül/ A one-sided dynamic where effort, attention, and care are never returned equally. Synonyms: one-way street, emotional imbalance, uneven investment. Antonyms: mutual effort, balance, reciprocity. Savage Sentence: The No Reciprocity Rule made sure you gave everything while receiving almost nothing back. UnExpert Advice: If it's not mutual, it's not sustainable.

Nostalgia Bombing /nä-ˈstal-jə ˈbäm-iŋ/ Using past memories and good moments to pull you back in or avoid accountability. Synonyms: memory manipulation, emotional time machine, past leverage. Antonyms: present accountability, forward movement, growth. Savage Sentence: Just when you were moving on, Nostalgia Bombing pulled you back into something that hadn't changed. UnExpert Advice: The past felt good—but it didn't last for a reason.

- **Nostalgia Manipulation** /nä-ˈstal-jə mə-ˌni-pyə-ˈlā-shən/ Bringing up old memories to soften you, distract you, or regain control. Savage Sentence: The conversation shifted fast because Nostalgia Manipulation replaced accountability with "remember when."

Nuclear Discard /ˈnü-klē-ər di-ˈskärd/ A sudden, harsh, and often cruel ending with no warning or closure. Synonyms: brutal cutoff, emotional detonation, hard discard. Antonyms: respectful ending, closure, communication. Savage Sentence: It ended instantly because Nuclear Discard leaves nothing to repair or understand. UnExpert Advice: When it ends like that, don't chase clarity—protect your peace.

"Nunya" Boundary Invader /ˈnən-yə ˈbau̇n-dər-ē in-ˈvā-dər/ Asks intrusive, inappropriate questions disguised as interest. Synonyms: nosy interrogator, boundary pusher, disguised curiosity. Antonyms: respect, awareness, appropriate interest. Savage Sentence: It felt uncomfortable because the "Nunya" Boundary Invader kept crossing lines under the excuse of getting to know you. UnExpert Advice: Curiosity without respect is just intrusion.

O

Oblivious Dumper /ə-ˈbli-vē-əs ˈdəm-pər/ Ends things with little to no awareness of the emotional impact because they were never as invested. Synonyms: casual discarder, low-empathy ghost, detached ender. Antonyms: respectful closure, emotional awareness, accountability. Savage Sentence: The Oblivious Dumper walked away like it was nothing while you were still processing everything. UnExpert Advice: Their indifference is your closure.

On-Again-Off-Again /ˌȯn-ə-ˌgen-ˌȯf-ə-ˌgen/ A repeating cycle of breaking up and reconnecting that prevents real progress. Synonyms: emotional boomerang, breakup loop, commitment cycle. Antonyms: clean break, forward movement, growth. Savage Sentence: The On-Again-Off-Again pattern kept resetting instead of fixing anything. UnExpert Advice: If it keeps ending, it's not meant to keep going.

One Foot Out /wən fu̇t out/ Staying partially invested while keeping an easy exit available. Synonyms: half-in dater, escape planner, low-commitment energy. Antonyms: full presence, emotional investment, decisiveness. Savage Sentence: The connection never felt secure because One Foot Out made sure it never fully settled. UnExpert Advice: If they're not all in, don't meet them halfway.

OnlyFans Energy /ˈōn-lē fanz ˈe-nər-jē/ Giving just enough content, attention, or access to keep someone subscribed... while keeping the real version behind a paywall (or never delivering it at all). Synonyms: pay-to-play affection, teaser attention, subscription flirting Antonyms: full access, genuine availability, real connection Savage Sentence: He hit you with full OnlyFans Energy—constant previews, zero real access, and somehow you were still paying with your time. UnExpert Advice: If it always feels like you're waiting for more that never comes, you're not dating—you're subscribed.

Opencasting /ˈō-pən-ˌka-stiŋ/ Broadcasting availability while juggling multiple people as ongoing options. Synonyms: roster broadcasting, parallel dating, open auditioning. Antonyms: exclusivity, intentional dating, focus. Savage

Sentence: It felt personal until Opencasting made it clear you were just one of many. UnExpert Advice: If it feels like an audition, don't perform.

Open-Minded Mirage /ˈō-pən ˈmīn-dəd mə-ˈräzh/ Uses "open-minded" as a vague cover for unclear intentions. Synonyms: ambiguity king, undefined dater, soft manipulator. Antonyms: clarity, intention, honesty. Savage Sentence: The Open-Minded Mirage sounded flexible but delivered absolutely no direction. UnExpert Advice: Vague is rarely innocent.

Optionality King /ˌäp-shə-ˈna-lə-tē kiŋ/ Keeps multiple options active to avoid ever fully choosing one person. Synonyms: roster manager, options addict, non-exclusive champion. Antonyms: decisiveness, exclusivity, intentional partner. Savage Sentence: The Optionality King kept you close enough to stay while never choosing you completely. UnExpert Advice: If they need options, they're not ready to choose.

Orbiting /ˈôr-bə-tiŋ/ Watches everything you post but never actually communicates or shows up. Synonyms: digital lurking, ego surveillance, commitment-phobic fan club. Antonyms: direct communication, intentional dating, grown man behavior. Savage Sentence: He's been Orbiting your life like a fan while doing absolutely nothing to be part of it. UnExpert Advice: Viewers are not contenders.

Overfunctioner /ˌō-vər-ˈfəŋk-shə-nər/ Takes on the majority of emotional labor, planning, and effort in the relationship. Synonyms: relationship martyr, emotional carrier, unpaid project manager. Antonyms: reciprocity, balance, shared effort. Savage Sentence: The Overfunctioner kept everything running while the other person contributed almost nothing. UnExpert Advice: If you're doing it all, you're doing too much.

Overpromiser /ˌō-vər-ˈprä-mi-sər/ Makes big promises about the future but rarely follows through with action. Synonyms: future faker, words-over-actions, empty planner. Antonyms: consistency, follow-through, integrity. Savage Sentence: The Overpromiser made the future sound amazing while the present stayed disappointing. UnExpert Advice: Watch what they do, not what they say.

Overunderstander /ˈō-vər-ˌən-dər-ˌstan-dər/ Understands him so deeply she ignores how he actually treats her. Synonyms: over-empathizer, excuse amplifier, empathy overload. Antonyms: discernment, boundaries, self-protection. Savage Sentence: You turned into an Overunderstander and explained away behavior you should've walked away from. UnExpert Advice: Understanding someone doesn't mean accepting everything from them.

P

Paperclipping /ˈpā-pər-ˌkli-piŋ/ Disappears, then randomly pops back up like nothing happened. Synonyms: pop-up nuisance, emotional boomerang, "u up?" specialist. Antonyms: closure, consistency, self-awareness. Savage Sentence: He tried Paperclipping you with a "hey stranger" like you forgot exactly why he became a stranger. UnExpert Advice: You are not a recycling bin for unfinished men.

Pattern Amnesia /ˈpa-tərn am-ˈnē-zhə/ Forgetting someone's repeated toxic behavior the second they reappear with attention. Synonyms: selective memory, hope blindness, red flag amnesia. Antonyms: pattern recognition, boundaries, reality acceptance. Savage Sentence: The moment he texted "I miss you," Pattern Amnesia erased every reason you walked away. UnExpert Advice: Patterns don't change because your feelings do.

Pen Pal /pen pal/ A connection that exists almost entirely through texting with no real-life progression. Synonyms: digital relationship, textationship deluxe, keyboard romance. Antonyms: real-life effort, presence, intentional dating. Savage Sentence: You built a whole connection, but Pen Pal energy never translated into anything real. UnExpert Advice: If it lives in your phone, it's not living in your life.

Performance Dater /pər-ˈfȯr-mən(t)s ˈdā-tər/ Treats dating like a performance, showing a curated version instead of their real self. Synonyms: mask dater, approval performer, curated connection. Antonyms: authenticity, vulnerability, real presence. Savage Sentence: It felt perfect at first, but Performance Dating made sure none of it was sustainable. UnExpert Advice: If it feels too polished, it's probably not real.

Pet Name Dispenser /pet nām di-ˈspen-sər/ Uses "babe," "baby," or "love" immediately and indiscriminately with everyone. Synonyms: generic charmer, mass affection user, emotional shortcut taker. Antonyms: intentional language, earned intimacy, genuine connection. Savage Sentence: The Pet Name Dispenser called you "baby" before even remembering your actual name. UnExpert Advice: If it's used on everyone, it means nothing to anyone.

Pickmeisha /ˈpik-mē-shə/ Bends, shrinks, and performs just to be chosen. Synonyms: approval chaser, self-abandoner, validation seeker. Antonyms: self-worth, authenticity, confidence. Savage Sentence: You went full Pickmeisha and still weren't chosen after doing everything to be liked. UnExpert Advice: The right person doesn't require you to shrink.

- **Pickmesis** /ˈpik-mē-ˌsis/ Loses her personality the moment a man shows interest.
- **Pickmeparalysis** /ˈpik-mē pə-ˈra-lə-səs/ Too afraid to leave even when she's unhappy.
- **Pickmeperformance** /ˈpik-mē pər-ˈfôr-məns/ Pretends to be "chill" while suppressing real needs.
- **Pickmesurvivalmode** /ˈpik-mē sər-ˈvī-vəl mōd/ Operates from fear of losing him instead of self-worth.

Player /ˈplā-ər/ Juggles multiple romantic interests through charm, deception, and omission to maintain access and ego. Synonyms: roster king, commitment avoider, emotional multitasker. Antonyms: intentional partner, honest communicator, exclusivity. Savage Sentence: The Player kept everything just vague enough to deny while still benefiting from all of it. UnExpert Advice: If clarity makes them uncomfortable, it's intentional.

Pocketing /ˈpä-kə-tiŋ/ Keeps you hidden from their life while still benefiting from you. Synonyms: undercover dating, hidden asset, private but not respected. Antonyms: public acknowledgment, inclusion, real relationship. Savage Sentence: You got pocketed so hard no one in his life even knew you existed. UnExpert Advice: If he can't show you, he doesn't deserve you.

Political Personality Profile /pə-ˈli-ti-kəl ˌpər-sə-ˈna-lə-tē ˈprō-ˌfīl/ Makes political beliefs their entire identity in a dating bio. Synonyms: ideology-first dater, debate bait, identity over personality. Antonyms: balanced identity, openness, multidimensional personality. Savage Sentence: The Political Personality Profile told you their stance on everything except who they actually are. UnExpert Advice: If it replaces personality, it limits connection.

Post-Intimacy Personality Shift /pōst ˈin-tə-mə-sē pər-sə-ˈna-lə-tē shift/ A noticeable change in behavior immediately after intimacy. Synonyms: post-sex switch, emotional withdrawal, intimacy drop-off. Antonyms: consistency, emotional integration, genuine connection. Savage Sentence: The energy changed instantly because Post-Intimacy Personality Shift revealed who they actually were. UnExpert Advice: Who they are after matters more than who they were before.

Post-Nut Clarity /pōst nət ˈkla-rə-tē/ The sudden loss of interest or emotional shift after physical release. Synonyms: clarity crash, post-sex withdrawal, temporary desire collapse. Antonyms: consistent desire, emotional connection, stability. Savage Sentence: Everything shifted the second Post-Nut Clarity hit and the effort disappeared with it. UnExpert Advice: Pay attention to behavior after, not words before.

Potential Projection Disorder /pə-ˈten(t)-shəl prə-ˈjek-shən dis-ˈȯr-dər/ Falling in love with who someone *could be* instead of who they actually are. Synonyms: fantasy attachment, future-based illusion, projection dating. Antonyms: reality-based connection, clarity, acceptance. Savage Sentence: Potential Projection Disorder had you investing in a version of them that didn't exist. UnExpert Advice: Potential is not a personality.

Potentialpsychosis /pə-ˈten(t)-shəl sī-ˈkō-səs/ Believes in who he could be more than who he consistently is. Synonyms: potential obsession, fantasy attachment, reality avoidance. Antonyms: acceptance, clarity, present awareness. Savage Sentence: You stayed in Potentialpsychosis defending a version of him that never actually showed up. UnExpert Advice: Potential is not a personality.

Potentialwife Syndrome /pə-ˈten(t)-shəl wīf ˈsin-ˌdrōm/ Acts like a wife for a man who hasn't even made her his girlfriend. Synonyms: premature commitment, unclaimed devotion, role overextension. Antonyms: boundaries, pacing, earned commitment. Savage Sentence: You slipped into Potentialwife Syndrome giving everything to someone who hadn't even chosen you. UnExpert Advice: Don't give full access without full commitment.

Proximity Ghost /präk-ˈsi-mə-tē gōst/ Only shows up when it's convenient or physically easy, then disappears otherwise. Synonyms: situational dater, convenience lover, location-based effort. Antonyms: consistency, intentional presence, reliability. Savage Sentence: The connection only existed in person because Proximity Ghost disappeared the moment effort was required. UnExpert Advice: Convenience is not commitment.

Psychotexting /ˈsī-kō-ˌtek-stiŋ/ Writing, deleting, rewriting, and overanalyzing texts before sending. Synonyms: text spiral, overthinking messaging, anxiety texting. Antonyms: calm communication, clarity, restraint. Savage Sentence: You went full Psychotexting turning one message into a full emotional event. UnExpert Advice: If it feels chaotic to send, pause before you hit send.

Pump and Dump /pəmp ən dəmp/ Pursues aggressively for sex, then disappears or loses interest immediately after. Synonyms: conquest chaser, hit-it-and-quit-it, post-intimacy ghost. Antonyms: mutual desire, respect, emotional consistency. Savage Sentence: The effort vanished overnight because Pump and Dump was always the goal. UnExpert Advice: If the energy dies after intimacy, it was never about you.

Push-Pull /pu̇sh pu̇l/ Alternates between closeness and distance to create emotional instability and attachment. Synonyms: hot-cold dynamic, emotional yo-yo, intermittent reinforcement. Antonyms: consistency, stability, emotional safety. Savage Sentence: Push-Pull kept you chasing a connection that never stayed the same long enough to trust. UnExpert Advice: Instability is not chemistry—it's manipulation.

Q

Quality Time Thief /ˈkwä-lə-tē tīm thēf/ Takes your time, attention, and emotional energy without reciprocating meaningful effort. Synonyms: time waster, attention taker, one-sided engager. Antonyms: reciprocity, mutual presence, balanced investment. Savage Sentence: The Quality Time Thief kept taking hours of your life without ever giving you anything real back. UnExpert Advice: Your time is valuable—don't spend it where it's not respected.

Question Dodger /ˈkwes-chən ˈdä-jər/ Avoids direct questions about intentions, exclusivity, or the future through deflection or vagueness. Synonyms: clarity avoider, deflection expert, commitment dodger. Antonyms: direct communicator, transparency, accountability. Savage Sentence: The Question Dodger turned every serious conversation into a joke, a distraction, or a disappearing act. UnExpert Advice: If they won't answer, that *is* the answer.

Quick Fade /kwik fād/ Rapid drop in effort and interest once things start becoming real or require consistency. Synonyms: interest evaporation, sudden slowdown, post-honeymoon drop-off. Antonyms: consistency, sustained effort, intentional dating. Savage Sentence: The Quick Fade showed up right when things needed to get real—and suddenly the effort was gone. UnExpert Advice: If the energy disappears when expectations appear, it was never solid.

Quicksand Relationship /ˈkwik-ˌsand ri-ˈlā-shən-ˌship/ A dynamic where the more effort you put in, the more stuck and drained you become. Synonyms: effort trap, emotional sinkhole, self-betrayal loop. Antonyms: healthy dynamic, supportive partnership, mutual growth. Savage Sentence: The Quicksand Relationship pulled you deeper every time you tried to fix what was never stable. UnExpert Advice: The harder you try shouldn't be what makes it worse—walk away instead.

Quiet Quitting /ˈkwī-ət ˈkwi-tiŋ/ Emotionally checking out while staying physically in the relationship and doing the bare minimum. Synonyms: stealth fade, emotional retirement, silent detachment, internal ghosting. Antonyms: direct communication, clean break, mutual effort. Savage Sentence: The Quiet

Quitting had you doing all the work while they slowly disappeared right in front of you. UnExpert Advice: If they're present but not participating, the relationship is already over.

R

Ratcheting (Ratchety Behavior) /ˈra-chə-tiŋ/ Loud, chaotic, classless drama that turns dating into a full-blown spectacle. Synonyms: messy chaos, public drama, reality-TV behavior. Antonyms: composure, emotional control, respect. Savage Sentence: The date went from drinks to Ratcheting in under ten minutes and suddenly everyone in the restaurant was involved. UnExpert Advice: If it feels like a show, don't stay for the episode.

Reactive Abuse /rē-ˈak-tiv ə-ˈbyüs/ When someone provokes you until you react, then uses your reaction against you. Synonyms: victim flipping, blame shifting, provoked reaction trap. Antonyms: accountability, emotional safety. Savage Sentence: Reactive Abuse made your reaction the focus while their behavior went ignored. UnExpert Advice: Don't let someone rewrite the story using your breaking point.

Reality Bending Lite /rē-ˈa-lə-tē ben-diŋ līt/ Subtly reframing situations so you question your reactions without full-blown gaslighting. Synonyms: soft manipulation, narrative twisting, perception shifting. Antonyms: clarity, honesty, direct communication. Savage Sentence: The Reality Bending Lite left you second-guessing yourself after conversations that should've been simple. UnExpert Advice: Confusion is often the strategy.

Reality Gap /rē-ˈa-lə-tē gap/ The disconnect between what someone *says* and what they consistently *does* over time. Synonyms: words vs actions gap, illusion disconnect, behavior mismatch. Antonyms: alignment, integrity, consistency. Savage Sentence: The Reality Gap kept you holding onto what he said while completely ignoring what he showed you. UnExpert Advice: When words and actions don't match, believe the actions every time.

Realityresistance /rē-ˈa-lə-tē ri-ˈzis-təns/ Knows the truth but actively avoids accepting it. Synonyms: truth avoidance, denial state, resistance to clarity. Antonyms: acceptance, awareness, truth. Savage Sentence: You're in Realityresistance seeing everything clearly and still choosing not to accept it. UnExpert Advice: Acceptance is where change starts.

Rebound /ˈrē-ˌbaund/ Jumping into a new relationship immediately after a breakup to avoid processing pain. Synonyms: distraction romance, emotional placeholder, post-breakup filler. Antonyms: intentional healing, self-reflection, clean single time. Savage Sentence: The Rebound felt intense because it was built on unresolved feelings, not real connection. UnExpert Advice: You can't heal by replacing—only by processing.

- **Reboundery** /ri-ˈbaund-ər-ē/ Jumps into something new just to avoid feeling anything old. Savage Sentence: You went straight into Reboundery and carried all the same emotions into someone new.

Rebrand Relationship /rē-ˈbrand ri-ˈlā-shən-ˌship/ He treats the next woman better using everything he learned from failing you. Synonyms: upgraded behavior elsewhere, lesson applied too late, personal growth theft. Antonyms: consistency, accountability with you, growth in real time. Savage Sentence: You watched a full Rebrand Relationship happen while he suddenly became the man he couldn't be for you. UnExpert Advice: You weren't the failure, you were the lesson.

Recreational Use Only /ˌre-krē-ˈā-shə-nəl yüs ˈōn-lē/ Someone a person dates, hooks up with, or keeps around strictly for fun, convenience, or temporary enjoyment—while already knowing they would never consider them for a serious, long-term relationship. Synonyms: placeholder pleasure, temporary access pass, situationship slot, non-serious option. Antonyms: long-term partner, intentional choice, marriage-minded. Savage Sentence: He treated you as Recreational Use Only—full access when it was fun, zero consideration when it came to anything real. UnExpert Advice: If someone's actions don't match long-term energy, believe them—you're not being "developed," you're being used for the experience.

Recyclationship /rē-ˈsī-kəl-ˌlā-shən-ˌship/ Same patterns, same behavior, just a different person. Synonyms: pattern repeat, recycled chaos, same story different face. Antonyms: growth, change, accountability. Savage Sentence: He's in another Recyclationship running the exact same script with a new audience. UnExpert Advice: If the pattern doesn't change, neither does the outcome.

Red Flag /red flag/ A clear warning sign in behavior, communication, or patterns that signals future problems. Synonyms: warning sign, dealbreaker indicator, behavioral alert. Antonyms: green flag, healthy trait, aligned behavior. Savage Sentence: You saw the Red Flag early and still stayed long enough to watch it turn into a full situation. UnExpert Advice: Red flags don't become green with time. They become patterns.

- **Redflagnesia** /red-flag-ˈnē-zhə/ Forgetting everything the second he gives attention again.
- **Redflagcollector** /red-flag kə-ˈlek-tər/ Sees every issue and keeps dating him anyway.
- **Redflagdenialism** /red-flag di-ˈnī-ə-liz-əm/ Knows it's bad and stays anyway.
- **Redflagdesensitization** /red-flag di-ˌsen(t)-sə-tə-ˈzā-shən/ Gets used to behavior that should never be normal.
- **Redflagrationalization** /red-flag ˌra-shə-nə-lə-ˈzā-shən/ Explains away obvious disrespect.
- **Redflagromance** /red-flag-rō-ˈmans/ Confuses chaos for passion.
- **Redflagromantic** /red-flag-rō-ˈman-tik/ Sees toxicity and calls it love.

Red Herring Relationship /red ˈher-iŋ ri-ˈlā-shən-ˌship/ A relationship that distracts you from deeper issues or personal growth. Synonyms: avoidance romance, distraction dynamic, emotional decoy. Antonyms: aligned connection, growth partnership. Savage Sentence: The Red Herring Relationship kept your focus on them instead of what actually needed attention. UnExpert Advice: Distraction feels easier than growth—but it costs more.

Rejectionaddiction /ri-ˈjek-shən ə-ˈdik-shən/ Keeps going back trying to win someone who already didn't choose you. Synonyms: approval chasing, validation addiction, rejection loop. Antonyms: self-worth, acceptance, walking away. Savage Sentence: You stayed in Rejectionaddiction trying harder for someone who already gave you the answer. UnExpert Advice: Stop auditioning for someone who didn't pick you.

- **Rejectionromanticism** /ri-ˈjek-shən rō-ˈman-tə-ˌsi-zəm/ Gets rejected and becomes more attached.

Relationship Anorexic /ri-ˈlā-shən-ˌship ˌa-nə-ˈrek-sik/ Withholds effort, attention, and intimacy while still expecting the relationship to function. Synonyms: emotional starvation, bare minimum partner, effort restrictor. Antonyms: nourishment, emotional availability, investment. Savage Sentence: The Relationship Anorexic gave just enough to keep it alive while slowly starving everything that made it real. UnExpert Advice: You can't sustain a relationship on crumbs.

Rescationship /ˈres-kyü-ˌlā-shən-ˌship/ You're not choosing him, you're trying to be saved by him. Synonyms: dependency dynamic, rescue fantasy, savior attachment. Antonyms: independence, self-reliance, equal partnership.

Savage Sentence: You fell into a Rescationship looking for rescue instead of building something real. UnExpert Advice: Save yourself first.

Resentment Collector /ri-ˈzent-mənt kə-ˈlek-tər/ Quietly keeps score of every slight, disappointment, or unmet expectation to use later. Synonyms: emotional hoarder, silent scorekeeper, grievance saver. Antonyms: communication, release, resolution. Savage Sentence: The Resentment Collector stayed quiet in the moment but came back later with a full list of everything you "did wrong." UnExpert Advice: Unspoken resentment doesn't disappear—it compounds.

The Return Policy Man /ðə ri-ˈtərn ˈpä-lə-sē man/ Leaves whenever he wants and comes back expecting full access again. Synonyms: revolving door man, no-consequence king, boomerang behavior. Antonyms: boundaries, accountability, permanence. Savage Sentence: He pulled Return Policy Man behavior and expected to come back like nothing expired. UnExpert Advice: Access revoked should stay revoked.

Reverse Catfishing /ri-ˈvərs ˈkat-ˌfi-shiŋ/ Using worse photos or info so the real-life version exceeds expectations. Synonyms: inverted catfish, lowball reveal, surprise upgrade tactic. Antonyms: accurate representation, authenticity, transparency. Savage Sentence: The Reverse Catfishing worked because the real-life version felt like an upgrade you didn't expect. UnExpert Advice: Even when it "works," deception is still deception.

Revolving Door Relationship /ri-ˈväl-viŋ dȯr ri-ˈlā-shən-ˌship/ Repeatedly letting the same person back in without real change or growth. Synonyms: boomerang romance, ex recycling, endless second chances. Antonyms: boundaries, closure, forward movement. Savage Sentence: The Revolving Door Relationship kept reopening what should've stayed closed. UnExpert Advice: Closure only works if you keep it closed.

Right Person Wrong Time Excuse /rīt ˈpər-sən rȯŋ tīm ik-ˈskyüs/ A comforting explanation used to avoid admitting incompatibility or lack of effort. Synonyms: timing delusion, soft rejection, future-faking logic. Antonyms: accountability, honest incompatibility. Savage Sentence: The Right Person Wrong Time Excuse sounded hopeful but never changed the outcome. UnExpert Advice: If it were right, it wouldn't require perfect timing.

Roster Dating /ˈrä-stər ˈdā-tiŋ/ Maintaining multiple casual connections at once to avoid investment in any one person. Synonyms: parallel dating, option stacking, casual rotation. Antonyms: exclusivity, intentional focus, emotional investment. Savage Sentence: Roster Dating kept everyone just interested enough while no one actually got anything real. UnExpert Advice: If everyone's an option, no one's a priority—including you.

Roster Recycling /ˈrä-stər ˌrē-ˈsī-kliŋ/ Repeating cycles with the same people instead of moving forward. Synonyms: recycled roster, comfort dating, pattern repetition. Antonyms: growth, new connections, pattern-breaking. Savage Sentence: Roster Recycling kept the same stories playing with different timestamps. UnExpert Advice: If nothing changes, neither will the outcome.

Rotational Attachment System /rō-ˈtā-shə-nəl ə-ˈta-chmənt ˈsi-stəm/ Cycling through people to avoid emotional responsibility or depth. Synonyms: rotation dating, attachment avoidance system, emotional evasion loop. Antonyms: commitment, depth, emotional accountability. Savage Sentence: The Rotational Attachment System made it clear you weren't chosen—you were scheduled. UnExpert Advice: If it feels like a system, don't become part of it.

Rubber Banding /ˈrəb-ər ban-diŋ/ Extreme push-pull dynamic with intense closeness followed by sudden withdrawal. Synonyms: emotional slingshot, intensity crash, hot-cold extreme. Antonyms: consistency, stability, emotional safety. Savage Sentence: The connection kept snapping because Rubber Banding pulled you in hard just to fling you right back out. UnExpert Advice: If it keeps snapping back, stop holding onto it.

Rumination /ˌrü-mə-ˈnā-shən/ Obsessively replaying conversations and scenarios trying to find answers or change outcomes. Synonyms: mental looping, overthinking addiction, emotional replay. Antonyms: acceptance, detachment, forward focus. Savage Sentence: Rumination had you rereading everything while the reality stayed exactly the same. UnExpert Advice: If you need to overanalyze it, you already have your answer.

Rusting /ˈrə-stiŋ/ Being out of the dating scene so long that your skills come back awkward, clumsy, or desperate. Synonyms: dating regression, social rust, awkward re-entry. Antonyms: confidence, ease, social fluency. Savage Sentence: The Rusting showed when basic conversations turned into overthinking and oversharing. UnExpert Advice: Awkward is fixable—desperation isn't. Slow down.

S

Sapiosexual /ˌsā-pē-ō-ˈsek-shə-wəl/ Claims attraction to intelligence but often uses it to justify emotional unavailability or endless talking with no action. Synonyms: intellectualizer, deep-talk dater, conversation addict. Antonyms: emotional availability, action-based connection, real intimacy. Savage Sentence: The Sapiosexual kept the conversation stimulating while the relationship went absolutely nowhere. UnExpert Advice: Intelligence is attractive—avoidance disguised as depth is not.

Savior Complex /ˈsā-vyər ˈkäm-pleks/ Believing you can fix or heal someone through love and effort. Synonyms: fixer mindset, rescuer delusion, project dating. Antonyms: boundaries, mutual growth, self-responsibility. Savage Sentence: The Savior Complex had you doing all the work while they stayed exactly the same. UnExpert Advice: You can support someone—you can't save them.

Selective Amnesia King /sə-ˈlek-tiv ˌam-ˈnē-zhə kiŋ/ Forgets what he said, what he promised, and what he did but remembers exactly how to come back. Synonyms: convenient forgetter, memory manipulator, promise evaporator. Antonyms: accountability, follow-through, integrity. Savage Sentence: He pulled Selective Amnesia King and acted brand new about promises you both know he made. UnExpert Advice: If his memory only fails when it benefits him, it's not forgetfulness.

Selective Depth Disorder /sə-ˈlek-tiv depth dis-ˈȯr-dər/ Can go deep on random topics but avoids anything real about the relationship. Synonyms: intellectual deflector, depth dodger, emotional avoider. Antonyms: clarity, emotional honesty, direct communication. Savage Sentence: Selective Depth Disorder had you discussing the universe while still having no idea where you stood. UnExpert Advice: Depth without direction is distraction.

Self-Abandonment Loop /self-ə-ˈban-dən-mənt lüp/ Repeatedly chooses him over herself and ends up hurt every time. Synonyms: self-betrayal cycle, identity loss loop, emotional repetition. Antonyms: self-alignment, boundaries, self-trust. Savage Sentence: You stayed in the Self-abandonment loop choosing him again while knowing exactly how it ends. UnExpert Advice: The pattern doesn't break until you choose yourself differently.

- **Selfabandonmentship** /self-ə-ˈban-dən-mənt-ˌship/ A relationship where you lose yourself just to keep him.

Self-Employed-ish /self im-ˈploid-ish/ Claims to be self-employed but lacks consistency, structure, or actual income. Synonyms: vague hustler, unemployed rebrand, instability spinner. Antonyms: stable income, clear career, grounded work. Savage Sentence: The Self-Employed-ish lifestyle sounded impressive until you realized nothing was actually consistent. UnExpert Advice: Ask what they *do*, not what they *call it*.

Self-Respect Amnesia /self-ri-ˈspekt ˌam-ˈnē-zhə/ Forgets who she is every time he reappears. Synonyms: identity lapse, boundary loss, self-forgetting. Antonyms: self-awareness, grounding, standards. Savage Sentence: You went into self-respect amnesia and let one message erase everything you already decided. UnExpert Advice: If your standards disappear that fast, they weren't solid yet.

- **Self-Respect Deficit** /self-ri-ˈspekt ˈde-fə-sət/ Knows better but still chooses worse.

Self-Worth Outsourcing /self-wərth ˈout-ˌsôr-siŋ/ Lets a man's attention determine her value. Synonyms: external validation, worth dependency, approval reliance. Antonyms: self-worth, confidence, internal validation. Savage Sentence: You slipped into self-worth outsourcing and let his attention decide how you felt about yourself. UnExpert Advice: Your value isn't determined by who chooses you.

Shelf Life /shelf līf/ An unspoken expiration date placed on a connection from the start. Synonyms: temporary placement, seasonal partner, built-in ending. Antonyms: long-term intention, sustained effort. Savage Sentence: The Shelf Life showed up when everything started fading right on schedule. UnExpert Advice: If it feels temporary, don't treat it like it's permanent.

Shrekking /ˈshrek-iŋ/ Dating someone you perceive as "below you" to maintain control or feel superior. Synonyms: power-dating, ego pairing, control dynamic. Antonyms: equal partnership, genuine attraction, mutual respect. Savage Sentence: The Shrekking strategy backfired when the person you underestimated walked away first. UnExpert Advice: If you need a power imbalance to feel secure, it's not connection.

Side Piece / Side Chick / Side Dude /sīd pēs/ A hidden secondary partner kept secret while someone maintains a primary relationship. Synonyms: affair partner, secret relationship, backup option. Antonyms: exclusivity, transparency, respect. Savage Sentence: The Side Piece always thinks they're temporary—until they realize they were never the priority. UnExpert Advice: If they cheat with you, they'll cheat on you.

Silent Treatment /ˈsī-lənt ˈtrēt-mənt/ Withholding communication as a form of control or punishment. Synonyms: emotional shutdown, passive punishment, avoidance tactic. Antonyms: communication, resolution, emotional maturity. Savage Sentence: The Silent Treatment ended the conversation before it even had a chance to be resolved. UnExpert Advice: Silence isn't healing—it's avoidance.

Simping /ˈsimp-iŋ/ Excessive effort, attention, or praise given in hopes of earning affection or validation. Synonyms: overgiving, approval chasing, doormat energy. Antonyms: self-respect, balanced effort, confidence. Savage Sentence: The Simping didn't make you more attractive—it just made the imbalance obvious. UnExpert Advice: Effort should be matched, not begged for.

Situationship /ˌsi-chə-ˈwā-shən-ˌship/ A relationship with all the emotional labor and none of the commitment, clarity, or respect. Synonyms: unpaid girlfriend internship, confusion contract, commitment avoidance program. Antonyms: relationship, clarity, mutual effort. Savage Sentence: You're in a Situationship giving relationship energy to someone giving "let's see what happens" energy. UnExpert Advice: If you have to ask what you are, you already have your answer.

- **Core Dynamics (how it operates)**
  - **Situacation** /ˌsi-chə-ˈkā-shən/ Temporary escape, not a long-term investment.
  - **Situational Girlfriend** /ˌsi-chə-ˈwā-shə-nəl ˈgər(-ə)l-ˌfrend/ Girlfriend only when it benefits him.
  - **Situationshippery** /ˌsi-chə-ˈwā-shən-ˌship-ər-ē/ Prolonged confusion until it feels normal.
  - **Situationshipping** /ˌsi-chə-ˈwā-shən-ˌshi-piŋ/ Movement with no direction or outcome.
- **Identity / Personality Types**
  - **Situationship Scholar** /ˌsi-chə-ˈwā-shən-ˌship ˈskä-lər/ Expert in avoiding commitment while keeping access.
  - **Situationship Scholar (Female Edition)** Knows the pattern, still participates.

  - **Situationshipperette** /ˌsi-chə-ˈwā-shən-ˌship-ə-ˌret/ Says "it's chill" while emotionally unraveling.
  - **Situationshipcore** /ˌsi-chə-ˈwā-shən-ˌship kôr/ Confusion is his entire personality.
- **Psychological Traps (why you stay)**
  - **Situationship Syndrome** /ˌsi-chə-ˈwā-shən ˈsin-ˌdrōm/ Knows it's going nowhere but stays.
  - **Situationshipdelusioncore** /ˌsi-chə-ˈwā-shən də-ˈlü-zhən kôr/ Thinks confusion is normal.
  - **Situationshipnormalization** /ˌsi-chə-ˈwā-shən ˌnôr-mə-lə-ˈzā-shən/ Accepts dysfunction as standard.
  - **Situationshipspirituality** /ˌsi-chə-ˈwā-shən ˌspir-i-chə-ˈwa-lə-tē/ Calls it a "lesson" to justify staying.
- **Damage Effects (what it does to you)**
  - **Situationshipdecay** /ˌsi-chə-ˈwā-shən di-ˈkā/ Slowly erodes self-worth.
  - **Situationshipitis** /ˌsi-chə-ˈwā-shən-ˌī-təs/ Chronic acceptance of less.
  - **Situationshipwithdrawal** /ˌsi-chə-ˈwā-shən-with-ˈdrô-əl/ Feels addictive to leave.
  - **Situationshipslavery** /ˌsi-chə-ˈwā-shən-ˌslā-və-rē/ Stuck giving everything, receiving nothing.
  - **Situationshipstockholm** /ˌsi-chə-ˈwā-shən ˈstäk-ˌhōlm/ Defends the person hurting you.
- **Behavior Patterns**
  - **Situationshipmartyr** /ˌsi-chə-ˈwā-shən ˈmär-tər/ Suffers silently thinking it has value.
  - **Situationshiptherapist** /ˌsi-chə-ˈwā-shən ˈther-ə-pist/ Fixes him while neglecting herself.

Situationship Enabler /ˌsi-chü-ˈā-shən-ˌship en-ˈā-blər/ Someone who benefits from or prolongs undefined, non-committal dynamics. Synonyms: ambiguity extender, commitment avoider, gray-area dater. Antonyms: clarity, intentional dating, defined relationship. Savage Sentence: The Situationship Enabler kept things just undefined enough to keep all the benefits. UnExpert Advice: If it's unclear, it's usually intentional.

Situationship Translator ("Still Figuring It Out") /ˈsi-chə-ˌwā-shən tranz-ˈlā-tər/ Says they're figuring it out but actually avoiding commitment. Synonyms: non-committal dater, ambiguity addict, delay specialist. Antonyms: clarity, intention, decisiveness. Savage Sentence: The "Still Figuring It Out" line kept you stuck while they stayed exactly where they wanted. UnExpert Advice: If they don't know, they know.

Sledging /ˈsle-jing/ Making subtle digs, passive-aggressive comments, or undermining remarks disguised as jokes. Synonyms: low-key insults, passive aggression, disguised criticism. Antonyms: respect, direct communication, support. Savage Sentence: The Sledging came off as humor until you realized every joke had a target—and it was you. UnExpert Advice: If it hurts, it's not a joke.

Slow Fading /ˈslō ˈfā-diŋ/ Gradually disappearing instead of directly ending things. Synonyms: cowardly exit, emotional evaporation, passive rejection. Antonyms: direct communication, respectful ending, honesty. Savage Sentence: He pulled Slow Fading and expected you to quietly accept the disappearance instead of calling it what it was. UnExpert Advice: Silence is still an answer.

Sneaky Link /ˈsnē-kē liŋk/ A secret sexual or romantic connection kept hidden with no intention of going public. Synonyms: hidden hookup, undercover situationship, private benefits. Antonyms: transparency, public relationship, intentional connection. Savage Sentence: The Sneaky Link only existed at night, then disappeared the second daylight hit. UnExpert Advice: If it has to stay hidden, it's not building anything real.

Soft Ghosting / Hard Ghosting /gō-stiŋ/ Disappearing from communication—either gradually (soft) or abruptly (hard). Synonyms: vanishing act, digital disappearance, avoidance exit. Antonyms: closure, communication, respect. Savage Sentence: Whether it was soft or hard, Ghosting still said the same thing—no effort, no respect. UnExpert Advice: Don't chase people who disappear.

Soft Launch Trauma /sôft lônch ˈtrȯ-mə/ Being kept off social media while everything else is shared publicly. Synonyms: pocketing, hidden partner, half-claiming. Antonyms: public acknowledgment, pride, clarity. Savage Sentence: Soft Launch Trauma hits when you realize you're part of their life—but not part of their image. UnExpert Advice: If they won't show you, they don't fully claim you.

Soft Launching You Nowhere /ˈsôft ˈlôn-chiŋ yü ˈnō-ˌhwer/ Gives just enough attention to feel chosen but never actually claims you. Synonyms: almost-public relationship, invisible girlfriend energy, half-claiming. Antonyms: clear commitment, public acknowledgment, pride. Savage Sentence: You got Soft Launched Nowhere and stayed while he enjoyed all the benefits with none of the responsibility. UnExpert Advice: If he won't claim you, don't stay available to him.

Soulplaceholder /ˈsōl-ˌplās-ˌhōl-dər/ A temporary emotional filler while he waits for something else. Synonyms: emotional filler, temporary connection, interim partner. Antonyms: chosen partner, priority, long-term commitment. Savage Sentence: You were a Soulplaceholder giving real energy to someone who was just passing time. UnExpert Advice: If you feel temporary, leave permanently.

Spark Chaser /spärk ˈchā-sər/ Obsessed with chasing intense chemistry while ignoring compatibility and consistency. Synonyms: chemistry addict, intensity seeker, fireworks dater. Antonyms: compatibility, slow burn, stability. Savage Sentence: The Spark Chaser kept choosing chaos because calm never gave the same rush. UnExpert Advice: The spark fades—what's left is what matters.

Stalkerella /ˌstô-kə-ˈrel-ə/ Obsessively monitoring him instead of trusting or letting go. Synonyms: social media investigator, digital watcher, obsessive checker. Antonyms: trust, detachment, self-focus. Savage Sentence: You went full Stalkerella refreshing his page instead of focusing on your own life. UnExpert Advice: If you feel the need to monitor, something is already wrong.

Standards Hypocrite /ˈstan-dərdz ˈhī-pə-ˌkrit/ Demands high standards from others while offering little themselves. Synonyms: selective standards, double standard dater, entitlement mindset. Antonyms: consistency, reciprocity, self-awareness. Savage Sentence: The Standards Hypocrite expected everything while contributing almost nothing. UnExpert Advice: Standards only matter if you meet them too.

Stonewalling /ˈstōn-ˌwȯ-liŋ/ Shutting down emotionally and refusing to communicate during conflict. Synonyms: emotional shutdown, silent treatment, avoidance wall. Antonyms: communication, openness, conflict resolution. Savage Sentence: The Stonewalling ended the conversation before it ever had a chance to be resolved. UnExpert Advice: You can't fix what someone refuses to engage in.

Strategic Incompetence /strə-ˈtē-jik in-ˈkäm-pə-təns/ Pretends not to know how to show up so you stop expecting it. Synonyms: weaponized helplessness, effort avoidance, learned uselessness. Antonyms: capability, initiative, intentional effort. Savage Sentence: He used Strategic Incompetence and let you carry everything while acting like he couldn't figure it out. UnExpert Advice: If he can do it elsewhere, he can do it here.

Submarining /ˌsəb-mə-ˈrē-niŋ/ Disappearing completely, then resurfacing later like nothing happened. Synonyms: delayed ghosting, resurfacing ex, selective reappearance. Antonyms: consistency, accountability, closure. Savage Sentence: Submarining always shows up right when you've finally moved on. UnExpert Advice: If they disappeared once, they'll do it again.

Sugar Daddy / Sugar Baby / Sugar Mama /ˈshu̇-gər/ A transactional dynamic involving financial support in exchange for companionship or intimacy. Synonyms: transactional relationship, sponsored dating, exchange dynamic. Antonyms: mutual partnership, non-transactional love, independence. Savage Sentence: The arrangement worked until someone expected feelings in a situation built on transactions. UnExpert Advice: If it's built on exchange, it depends on what's being given.

Summer Fling /ˈsə-mər fliŋ/ A temporary, high-intensity connection with an expected ending. Synonyms: seasonal romance, short-term connection, temporary high. Antonyms: long-term relationship, sustained effort. Savage Sentence: The Summer Fling felt real until real life came back and it disappeared. UnExpert Advice: If it only works in perfect conditions, it's not built to last.

T

Taking Things Slow (Excuse) /ˈtā-kiŋ thiŋz slō/ Using "slow" as a delay tactic to avoid commitment while maintaining access. Synonyms: paced avoidance, commitment delay, soft stall. Antonyms: intentional pacing, clarity, direct communication. Savage Sentence: Taking Things Slow kept the benefits while postponing any real decision. UnExpert Advice: Slow is fine—indefinite is not.

Talking Stage /ˈtȯ-kiŋ stāj/ The early phase of texting and getting to know each other with no defined direction or commitment. Synonyms: pre-relationship limbo, texting phase, undefined connection. Antonyms: clear intention, defined relationship, progression. Savage Sentence: The Talking Stage dragged on so long it became the relationship instead of leading to one. UnExpert Advice: If it doesn't progress, it's not building anything.

Talking Stage Trap /ˈtȯ-kiŋ stāj trap/ Getting stuck in endless conversation with no real progression. Synonyms: text limbo, prolonged talking stage, stalled connection. Antonyms: movement, clarity, defined relationship. Savage Sentence: The Talking Stage Trap kept everything going without anything actually changing. UnExpert Advice: If it doesn't move forward, it's not building anything.

Temporary Partner /ˈtem-pə-ˌrer-ē ˈpärt-nər/ Plays the role perfectly in the beginning but fades when real effort or commitment is required. Synonyms: placeholder partner, short-term role filler, seasonal relationship. Antonyms: consistent partner, long-term investment, reliability. Savage Sentence: The Temporary Partner showed up fully at first—then disappeared when consistency mattered. UnExpert Advice: Consistency reveals intention.

Textationship /ˈtek-stə-ˌshən-ˌship/ A relationship that only exists in your phone and disappears in real life. Synonyms: digital delusion, keyboard romance, imaginary connection. Antonyms: real-life effort, actual dates, presence. Savage Sentence: You stayed in a Textationship building something in messages that never showed up in real life. UnExpert Advice: If it's not happening in real life, it's not happening.

- **Textinducedpsychosis** /tekst-in-ˈdüst sī-ˈkō-səs/ Builds a full relationship off inconsistent messages.
- **Textcrumbtrauma** /tekst-krəm ˈtrô-mə/ Emotional highs and lows triggered by texting patterns.
- **Textopath** /ˈtek-stə-ˌpäth/ Smooth over text, absent in real life.
- **Textorcist** /ˈtek-stôr-sist/ Communicates randomly, disappears mid-conversation.
- **Textspiralitis** /ˈtek-stə-ˌspī-rə-ˈlī-təs/ Overanalyzing messages into confusion.

Textpectations /tekst-ˈpek-ˌtā-shənz/ The anxiety and overanalysis tied to texting behavior, response times, and message tone. Synonyms: text anxiety, response obsession, digital overthinking. Antonyms: calm, clarity, emotional stability. Savage Sentence: Textpectations had you checking your phone like it controlled your entire mood. UnExpert Advice: If your peace depends on a reply, the connection already has too much power.

Texto /ˈtek-stō/ Someone who keeps texting despite receiving little or no response. Synonyms: over-texter, message chaser, one-sided communicator. Antonyms: reciprocity, self-respect, balanced communication. Savage Sentence: The Texto kept the conversation alive long after the other person had mentally left it. UnExpert Advice: If you're carrying the conversation, put it down.

Thirst Trap /ˈthərst trap/ Posting provocative or attention-seeking content to attract validation or reactions. Synonyms: attention bait, validation post, reaction fishing. Antonyms: authenticity, self-validation, grounded presence. Savage Sentence: The Thirst Trap pulled attention—but not the kind that leads to anything real. UnExpert Advice: Attention isn't connection.

Time Thief /tīm thēf/ Stays in your life knowing he doesn't want you long-term. Synonyms: time waster, emotional pickpocket, delay specialist. Antonyms: honesty, clarity, respect for your time. Savage Sentence: You let a Time Thief stay while he quietly knew you were never the end goal. UnExpert Advice: If he's unsure long-term, remove yourself immediately.

Time Traveler (Agefishing) /tīm ˈtrav-ə-lər/ Lies about age to access a different dating pool or demographic. Synonyms: age manipulator, demographic jumper, timeline liar. Antonyms: honesty, transparency, accuracy. Savage Sentence: The Time Traveler adjusted their age for matches, but reality showed up the second you met in person. UnExpert Advice: If they lie about the basics, trust nothing else.

Time Waster /tīm ˈwā-stər/ Engages your time and attention with no real intention of building anything. Synonyms: delay specialist, attention taker, non-committal dater. Antonyms: clarity, intention, respect for time. Savage Sentence: The Time Waster kept things going just enough to never have to end them. UnExpert Advice: If there's no direction, there's no destination.

Tinder Trash (App Trash) /ˈtin-dər trash/ Low-effort, disposable behavior on dating apps with no intention or respect. Synonyms: swipe culture chaos, low-effort dating, disposable matches. Antonyms: intentional dating, effort, respect. Savage Sentence: The Tinder Trash energy showed up in copy-paste messages and zero follow-through. UnExpert Advice: If it feels low effort, it is.

Too Much Too Soon /tü məch tü sün/ Rushing emotional intensity or connection before a real foundation exists. Synonyms: fast-track attachment, premature intensity, accelerated bonding. Antonyms: pacing, steady growth, intentional connection. Savage Sentence: Too Much Too Soon created a high that didn't last long enough to become real. UnExpert Advice: What builds fast often fades just as quickly.

Trauma Dumping /ˈtrȯ-mə ˈdəm-piŋ/ Oversharing heavy emotional baggage too early or inappropriately. Synonyms: emotional overshare, premature vulnerability, boundary overload. Antonyms: pacing, emotional awareness, appropriate sharing. Savage Sentence: Trauma Dumping turned a first date into a therapy session no one signed up for. UnExpert Advice: Depth needs timing—not immediacy.

Trauma-tainer /ˈtrô-mə-ˌtā-nər/ Turns his unresolved issues into your emotional responsibility. Synonyms: chaos creator, emotional burden distributor, unresolved mess. Antonyms: healed partner, self-awareness, emotional responsibility. Savage Sentence: You became a Trauma-tainer carrying issues that were never yours to fix. UnExpert Advice: Support is not the same as responsibility.

Travel Dipper /ˈtra-vəl ˈdi-pər/ Pops into your life while traveling, creates temporary connection, then disappears when they leave. Synonyms: vacation dater, temporary connection, location-based romance. Antonyms: consistency, long-term intention, real availability. Savage Sentence: The Travel Dipper made it feel meaningful until the return flight erased everything. UnExpert Advice: If it only works in transit, it won't last in reality.

Trickle Truth /ˈtri-kəl trüth/ Revealing the truth in small pieces over time instead of being fully honest upfront. Synonyms: slow-drip honesty, staggered confession, omission tactic. Antonyms: transparency, full disclosure, honesty.

Savage Sentence: The Trickle Truth kept changing the story every time a new detail "came up." UnExpert Advice: If the truth keeps evolving, it was never fully told.

Trophy Partner /ˈtrō-fē ˈpärt-nər/ Chosen for appearance, status, or external value rather than genuine connection. Synonyms: status symbol, image partner, ego accessory. Antonyms: authentic connection, mutual respect, depth. Savage Sentence: The Trophy Partner looked perfect publicly but felt empty privately. UnExpert Advice: Being admired isn't the same as being valued.

Typecasting /ˈtīp-ˌka-stiŋ/ Repeatedly choosing the same type of toxic partner while expecting a different outcome. Synonyms: pattern dating, same story cycle, repeated attraction loop. Antonyms: growth dating, intentional choice, pattern-breaking. Savage Sentence: The Typecasting showed when the same behavior appeared with a different face. UnExpert Advice: If the pattern feels familiar, it's not new.

Typing Indicator Manipulation /ˈtī-piŋ ˈin-də-ˌkā-tər mə-ˌni-pyə-ˈlā-shən/ Using the start-stop typing pattern to create anticipation or keep attention. Synonyms: digital teasing, message baiting, attention control. Antonyms: clear communication, directness, consistency. Savage Sentence: Typing Indicator Manipulation had you staring at three dots like something meaningful was coming. UnExpert Advice: Stop investing in what hasn't been said.

U

"U Up?" Guy /ˈyü əp gī/ Only reaches out late at night when bored, lonely, or horny—with zero intention of real connection. Synonyms: booty call specialist, midnight texter, low-effort opportunist. Antonyms: intentional dater, consistent communicator. Savage Sentence: The "U Up?" Guy kept your phone busy at 2 a.m. and your actual life completely empty. UnExpert Advice: If he only shows up after midnight, he's not offering anything worth waking up for.

Ultimatum Dodger /ˌəl-tə-ˈmā-təm ˈdä-jər/ Avoids or disappears when faced with boundaries or requests for clarity. Synonyms: boundary runner, pressure avoider, commitment escaper. Antonyms: accountability, growth, emotional maturity. Savage Sentence: The Ultimatum Dodger disappeared the moment things required a real answer. UnExpert Advice: If they run from standards, they were never planning to meet them.

Uncuffing Season /ˌən-ˈkə-fiŋ ˈsē-zən/ The breakup wave when people leave relationships to go back to casual dating and "see what's out there." Synonyms: freedom phase, seasonal dumping, field-playing season. Antonyms: commitment, settling down, long-term intention. Savage Sentence: Uncuffing Season hit and suddenly everyone who "wasn't ready" became very ready to be single. UnExpert Advice: If the relationship only worked in one season, it wasn't built to last through the next.

Undefined /ˌən-di-ˈfīnd/ Refusing to label or clarify the relationship to keep benefits without responsibility. Synonyms: situationship architect, label dodger, ambiguity king. Antonyms: clarity, intention, defined relationship. Savage Sentence: The Undefined kept everything just clear enough to stay and just vague enough to never commit. UnExpert Advice: If they won't define it, define your exit.

Unhealed /ˌən-ˈhēld/ Carrying unresolved baggage and using new people as coping mechanisms instead of doing the work. Synonyms: trauma carrier, emotional rebounder, unresolved dater. Antonyms: healed, self-aware, emotionally responsible. Savage Sentence: The Unhealed brought their past into everything and called it "just how I am." UnExpert Advice: You can support someone, but you can't heal them for them.

Upgrade Seeker /ˈəp-ˌgrād ˈsē-kər/ Treats partners as temporary until someone "better" comes along. Synonyms: ladder climber, serial upgrader, branch swiper. Antonyms: content partner, value-based dating, commitment. Savage Sentence: The Upgrade Seeker stayed just long enough to secure the next option. UnExpert Advice: If they're always looking for better, they'll never value what they have.

User /ˈyü-zər/ Takes time, energy, attention, or resources without intention of giving anything meaningful back. Synonyms: emotional extractor, benefit taker, one-way partner. Antonyms: reciprocity, mutual investment, real partner. Savage Sentence: The User kept taking until there was nothing left to give. UnExpert Advice: If they only show up to take, stop making yourself available.

V

Validation /ˌva-lə-ˈdā-shən/ Seeking external approval, attention, or reassurance to feel worthy or desirable. Synonyms: approval seeking, attention dependency, ego feeding. Antonyms: self-worth, internal validation, confidence. Savage Sentence: Validation had you chasing crumbs of attention like they were proof you mattered. UnExpert Advice: If you need someone else to confirm your value, you'll always be negotiating for it.

Validation Vulture /ˌva-lə-ˈdā-shən ˈvəl-chər/ Only shows up when he needs attention and disappears once he gets it. Synonyms: attention scavenger, emotional parasite, ego feeder. Antonyms: consistent presence, mutual support, genuine interest. Savage Sentence: He came back as a Validation Vulture, took what he needed, and disappeared again like clockwork. UnExpert Advice: You are not a refill station.

- **Validation Vampirex** /ˌva-lə-ˈdā-shən ˈvam-ˌpī(-ə)r eks/ Feeds on your energy, leaves, then returns when empty again.
- **Validationomics** /ˌva-lə-ˈdā-shə-ˌnä-miks/ Runs on taking attention without giving anything back.
- **Validationwithdrawal** /ˌva-lə-ˈdā-shən with-ˈdrô-əl/ Panic response when attention disappears.
- **Validationvixen** /ˌva-lə-ˈdā-shən ˈvik-sən/ Seeks constant external validation to feel secure.

Validation Whore /ˌva-lə-ˈdā-shən hȯr/ Constantly seeks attention, compliments, and admiration from multiple people to feel important. Synonyms: attention addict, ego collector, validation chaser. Antonyms: self-secure, internally validated. Savage Sentence: The Validation Whore kept a full audience just to feel chosen for five minutes at a time. UnExpert Advice: If they need everyone, they'll never choose one.

Vanilla /və-ˈni-lə/ Low-effort, basic, or uninspired behavior in dating or intimacy disguised as "chill." Synonyms: bare minimum dater, low-effort energy, flavorless connection. Antonyms: intentional effort, passion, depth. Savage Sentence: The Vanilla energy gave you nothing to complain about—

and nothing to stay for. UnExpert Advice: Stable is good. Boring with no effort is not.

Victim Mentality /ˈvik-təm men-ˈta-lə-tē/ Constantly positions themselves as the victim to avoid responsibility or accountability. Synonyms: blame shifter, accountability dodger, professional victim. Antonyms: ownership, self-awareness, responsibility. Savage Sentence: The Victim Mentality made sure every story had them as the innocent one—even when they caused the damage. UnExpert Advice: If everyone else is always the problem, it's not everyone else.

Vibe /vīb/ The emotional tone or energy of a connection, often used in place of clear communication or actual substance. Synonyms: energy, feeling, atmosphere. Antonyms: clarity, intention, substance. Savage Sentence: The Vibe felt amazing—until you realized it was the only thing holding it together. UnExpert Advice: Vibes can start something. They can't sustain it.

Vibe Merchant /vīb ˈmər-chənt/ Relies on charm, energy, and aesthetic to create attraction without substance or consistency. Synonyms: vibe dealer, aesthetic dater, illusion seller. Antonyms: substance, follow-through, consistency. Savage Sentence: The Vibe Merchant sold you a whole experience with nothing behind it to back it up. UnExpert Advice: Don't confuse how it feels with what it actually is.

Vibe Fishing /ˈvīb ˈfi-shiŋ/ Sending vague, low-effort messages to see who responds. Synonyms: lazy outreach, mass texting energy, bait-and-see behavior. Antonyms: intentional communication, direct interest, effort. Savage Sentence: He went Vibe Fishing and you answered like it was personal when it was clearly sent to five other people. UnExpert Advice: If it feels generic, it is.

Vibes Excuse /vībz ik-ˈskyüs/ Uses vague "vibe" language to avoid giving real reasons or accountability. Synonyms: cop-out explanation, vague rejection, emotional deflection. Antonyms: honesty, clarity, direct communication. Savage Sentence: The Vibes Excuse ended things without ever actually explaining anything. UnExpert Advice: If they can't say it clearly, they're choosing not to.

Volume Texter /ˈväl-yəm ˈtek-stər/ Floods you with messages when it suits them, then disappears when it doesn't. Synonyms: attention spammer, inconsistent communicator, digital overload. Antonyms: balanced communication, consistency, reciprocity. Savage Sentence: The Volume Texter gave you constant noise with zero reliability. UnExpert Advice: Consistency matters more than frequency.

Vulnerability Vampire /ˌvəl-nə-ˈrə-bəl-ˈvam-ˌpī(-ə)r/ Pulls deep emotional openness from you, then uses it for control, validation, or disappears after. Synonyms: emotional leech, trauma collector, fake safe space. Antonyms: safe connection, mutual vulnerability, trust. Savage Sentence: The Vulnerability Vampire took everything you shared and turned it into leverage. UnExpert Advice: If vulnerability starts feeling unsafe, it's not connection.

W

Walking Red Flag /ˈwȯ-kiŋ red flag/ A person whose behavior, patterns, or energy clearly signal toxicity or danger from the start. Synonyms: red flag parade, warning sign in human form, chaos magnet. Antonyms: green flag, safe partner, emotional stability. Savage Sentence: He wasn't a red flag—he was a full Walking Red Flag and you still tried to give him the benefit of the doubt. UnExpert Advice: If you have to convince yourself it's not that bad, it is.

Wallet Inspection /ˈwäl-ət in-ˈspek-shən/ Early probing into finances, status, or assets disguised as "compatibility" or curiosity. Synonyms: financial vetting, status screening, income check. Antonyms: genuine interest, value-based connection, organic curiosity. Savage Sentence: The Wallet Inspection started before the second drink and somehow turned into a full financial interview. UnExpert Advice: If they're assessing your worth in dollars, they're not looking for you—they're looking for what you provide.

Wallet Warrior /ˈwäl-ət ˈwȯr-ē-ər/ Uses money, gifts, or flashy spending to impress, attract, or control attention. Synonyms: money flasher, flex dater, transactional charmer. Antonyms: grounded partner, genuine connection, equal dynamic. Savage Sentence: The Wallet Warrior made a big show of paying—then acted like you owed him something for it. UnExpert Advice: Generosity without expectation feels good. This isn't that.

Weaponized Vulnerability /ˈwe-pən-ˌīzd ˌvəl-nə-ˈrə-bəl-ə-tē/ Using emotional sharing or trauma to gain sympathy, avoid accountability, or control the dynamic. Synonyms: pity play, trauma baiting, strategic openness. Antonyms: genuine vulnerability, healthy emotional exchange. Savage Sentence: The Weaponized Vulnerability flipped every conversation until you were apologizing for things you didn't do. UnExpert Advice: If vulnerability always redirects accountability, it's not real.

Weekend Warrior /ˈwēk-ˌend ˈwȯr-ē-ər/ Only shows up or puts in effort on weekends, then disappears or goes low-effort during the week. Synonyms: part-time partner, convenience dater, Friday-night special. Antonyms: consistent partner, full-week presence, reliable effort. Savage Sentence: The

Weekend Warrior gave you full romance for 48 hours and zero existence the other five days. UnExpert Advice: If you only get the highlight reel, you're not in the full relationship.

"We're Just Talking" /wēr jəst ˈtȯ-kiŋ/ A phrase used to maintain access to you while avoiding commitment or responsibility. Synonyms: situationship shield, label dodge, soft refusal. Antonyms: clarity, defined relationship, intention. Savage Sentence: "We're Just Talking" kept you loyal while they stayed completely free. UnExpert Advice: If it needs constant explaining, it's not evolving.

White Knight /wīt nīt/ Plays the savior role early on to gain admiration, control, or emotional leverage. Synonyms: rescuer performer, savior complex, hero act. Antonyms: equal partner, grounded support. Savage Sentence: The White Knight showed up strong at the start and expected permanent loyalty for temporary effort. UnExpert Advice: If they need to be the hero, they usually need something in return.

Wildflowering /ˈwīld-ˌflau̇-ər-iŋ/ Drifting through dating casually and directionlessly without clear intention or communication. Synonyms: free-floating dater, commitment avoider, casual drifter. Antonyms: intentional dating, clarity, rooted connection. Savage Sentence: The Wildflowering felt carefree at first—until you realized nothing was actually growing. UnExpert Advice: Going with the flow is fine—unless the flow is going nowhere.

Wishful Thinking Dater /ˈwish-fəl ˈthiŋ-kiŋ ˈdā-tər/ Projects hopes and potential onto someone while ignoring clear reality and patterns. Synonyms: fantasy dater, potential chaser, delusion romantic. Antonyms: discernment, reality-based dating, clarity. Savage Sentence: The Wishful Thinking Dater built a future in her head with someone who couldn't even show up in the present. UnExpert Advice: Patterns tell the truth—listen to them.

Work Spouse /wərk spous/ An emotionally intimate workplace connection that crosses boundaries and often replaces real relationship energy. Synonyms: office soulmate, emotional side piece, work partner. Antonyms: professional boundaries, appropriate connection. Savage Sentence: The Work Spouse got the attention, the jokes, and the emotional energy that should've been yours. UnExpert Advice: If someone else gets their best during the day, you're getting the leftovers.

Worthless Validation /ˈwərth-ləs ˌva-lə-ˈdā-shən/ Seeking attention or approval from people who don't meet your standards. Synonyms: misplaced validation, low-value approval, attention misalignment. Antonyms: self-worth, discernment, standards. Savage Sentence: You chased Worthless Validation and cared about the opinion of someone who didn't even qualify for your attention. UnExpert Advice: If they don't qualify, their validation doesn't count.

WYD Warlord /ˌdəb-əl-yü-ˌī-ˈdē ˈwȯr-ˌlȯrd/ Only communicates with "wyd" and expects full conversation in return. Synonyms: low-effort texter, conversation killer, bare minimum king. Antonyms: engaging communicator, effort, curiosity. Savage Sentence: The WYD Warlord sent three letters and expected a full personality back. UnExpert Advice: Low effort is the message.

XYZ

X-Ray Vision (Trash Version) /ˈeks-rā ˈvi-zhən/ Believing you can "see through" someone's red flags or fix them by understanding them deeply enough. Synonyms: over-empathizer goggles, potential projection, denial lens. Antonyms: discernment, reality-based judgment, acceptance. Savage Sentence: The X-Ray Vision had you searching for hidden potential while the obvious behavior kept proving itself. UnExpert Advice: Stop looking deeper for what isn't there—patterns are already visible.

Yap Trapping /yap ˈtrap-iŋ/ Overloading someone with nonstop talking to create the illusion of connection while avoiding real vulnerability or effort. Synonyms: verbal flooding, conversation hijack, false intimacy builder. Antonyms: balanced communication, intentional connection, emotional depth. Savage Sentence: The Yap Trapping kept you on the phone for hours while nothing meaningful ever actually moved forward. UnExpert Advice: Time spent talking isn't the same as progress—watch what actually develops.

Yellow Flag /ˈye-lō flag/ A small warning sign that feels off but is often dismissed until it escalates. Synonyms: soft red flag, early warning, subtle concern. Antonyms: green flag, clear compatibility, alignment. Savage Sentence: The Yellow Flag didn't seem like much—until it kept showing up in bigger ways. UnExpert Advice: Pay attention early or pay for it later.

"You're Not Like Other Girls" Trap /nät līk ˈə-thər gərlz trap/ A manipulative compliment that isolates you as "different" while subtly putting down other women. Synonyms: comparison bait, pick-me conditioning, selective flattery. Antonyms: genuine respect, equal appreciation, real compliment. Savage Sentence: The "You're Not Like Other Girls" Trap made you feel special while quietly lowering your standards. UnExpert Advice: Real compliments don't require putting anyone else down.

Zaddy /ˈza-dē/ An attractive, confident older man with style, presence, or financial stability. Synonyms: silver fox, daddy energy, polished provider. Antonyms: immature partner, unstable dater, low-effort energy. Savage Sentence: The Zaddy looked impressive on paper but offered nothing beyond surface-level appeal. UnExpert Advice: Attraction and status don't equal substance—pay attention to how he actually shows up.

Zero Effort King / Queen /ˈzir-ō ˈe-fərt/ Gives the bare minimum (or less) while expecting full access, attention, and loyalty. Synonyms: effort allergic, bare-minimum monarch, entitlement dater. Antonyms: reciprocity, intentional effort, mutual investment. Savage Sentence: The Zero Effort King expected full access while offering almost nothing in return. UnExpert Advice: Stop rewarding people for doing the least.

Zero Questioner /ˈzir-ō ˈkwes-chə-nər/ Never asks about your life, feelings, day, or opinions — conversations are one-way monologues about them. Synonyms: self-centered conversationalist, curiosity-free dater, me-monologue specialist Antonyms: engaged partner, curious communicator Savage Sentence: Dating a Zero Questioner feels like being an unpaid audience member at a one-man show that never ends. UnExpert Advice: Interest is shown through questions. If they never ask, they're not interested — they're just enjoying the sound of their own voice.

Zip-Coding /ˈzip-ˌkō-diŋ/ Restricting dating to an extremely small geographic radius out of convenience or low effort. Synonyms: proximity dating, lazy radius swiping, hyper-local limiting. Antonyms: open-minded dating, expanded options, intentional effort. Savage Sentence: The Zip-Coding kept your options small while your complaints about "no good options" kept getting louder. UnExpert Advice: If you limit your range, you limit your results.

Zombie Ex /ˈzäm-bē eks/ An ex who resurfaces at inconvenient times after disappearing, acting like nothing happened. Synonyms: undead texter, resurrection act, timing disruptor. Antonyms: closure, no contact, final ending. Savage Sentence: The Zombie Ex always came back right when you were finally moving on. UnExpert Advice: What ended once should stay ended.

Zombie-ing /ˈzäm-bē-iŋ/ When someone who ghosted you comes back like nothing happened. Synonyms: resurrection audacity, undead texter, selective revival. Antonyms: staying gone, closure, self-awareness. Savage Sentence: He tried Zombie-ing his way back in like you didn't already bury the situation. UnExpert Advice: If you had to heal from their absence, don't reopen the door.

Clinical Terms

Abandonment Issues /ə-ˈban-dən-mənt ˈi-shüz/ A deep fear of being left that drives clinginess, jealousy, or self-sabotage in relationships. Synonyms: fear of loss, attachment insecurity, emotional hypervigilance. Antonyms: security, trust, emotional stability. Savage Sentence: You moved like they were already leaving and ended up pushing them out before they ever had the chance. UnExpert Advice: Not everyone is going to leave. Stop treating them like they will.

Abuse Cycle (Cycle of Abuse) /ə-ˈbyüs ˈsī-kəl/ A repeating pattern of tension, conflict, reconciliation, and calm that keeps toxic relationships in motion. Synonyms: toxic loop, trauma cycle, repeated dysfunction. Antonyms: healthy conflict, stability, resolution. Savage Sentence: You keep waiting for the good part to last longer when it's literally built to reset. UnExpert Advice: If it keeps repeating, it's not a phase. It's the system.

Ambivalent Attachment (Anxious-Ambivalent) /am-ˈbi-və-lənt ə-ˈtach-mənt/ Craves closeness but fears it at the same time, creating emotional instability and push-pull behavior. Synonyms: push-pull dynamic, emotional inconsistency, unstable bonding. Antonyms: secure attachment, emotional clarity, stability. Savage Sentence: You want them close until they are, then suddenly it feels like too much. UnExpert Advice: If it feels chaotic, it probably is.

Anxious Attachment (Anxious-Preoccupied) /ˈaŋk-shəs ə-ˈtach-mənt/ A style marked by fear of abandonment, constant need for reassurance, and overanalyzing behavior. Synonyms: reassurance-seeking, emotional dependency, overthinking attachment. Antonyms: security, self-trust, emotional regulation. Savage Sentence: You turned one delayed reply into a full story about being replaced. UnExpert Advice: Not every silence is rejection.

Anxious-Avoidant Attachment (Fearful-Avoidant) /ˈaŋk-shəs ə-ˈvȯi-dənt ə-ˈtach-mənt/ Desires closeness but fears it deeply, resulting in intense push-pull cycles. Synonyms: chaotic bonding, emotional contradiction, instability loop. Antonyms: secure connection, consistency, emotional safety. Savage Sentence: They pull you in just enough to keep you, then push you away the second it feels real. UnExpert Advice: You can't stabilize someone who lives in contradiction.

Asexual (Ace / Aspec) /ā-ˈsek-shə-wəl/ A sexual orientation involving little to no sexual attraction, existing across a spectrum of emotional and romantic preferences. Synonyms: ace, low/no sexual attraction, aspec identity. Antonyms: allosexual, high sexual attraction. Savage Sentence: The issue wasn't the orientation, it was the lack of honesty about it from the start. UnExpert Advice: Clarity matters more than compatibility assumptions.

Attachment Anxiety /ə-ˈtach-mənt aŋ-ˈzī-ə-tē/ Persistent fear of being rejected, replaced, or not enough in a relationship. Synonyms: insecurity loop, fear response, emotional hyper-alertness. Antonyms: calm, trust, emotional grounding. Savage Sentence: You reacted to what you felt, not what was actually happening. UnExpert Advice: Not every feeling is a fact.

Attachment Injury /ə-ˈtach-mənt ˈin-jə-rē/ Deep emotional wounds from betrayal, abandonment, or neglect that distort future relationships. Synonyms: relational trauma, trust fracture. Antonyms: repair, safety, secure bonding. Savage Sentence: The Attachment Injury had you bracing for pain before anything even happened. UnExpert Advice: Heal the wound so it doesn't choose your next partner.

Avoidant Attachment /ə-ˈvȯi-dənt ə-ˈtach-mənt/ Finds closeness overwhelming and responds by withdrawing or creating emotional distance. Synonyms: emotional shutdown, intimacy resistance, distance-seeking. Antonyms: openness, vulnerability, connection. Savage Sentence: They didn't need space, they lived in it. UnExpert Advice: If they can't meet you emotionally, stop chasing them there.

BPD Relationship Cycle /ˌbē-pē-ˈdē ri-ˈlā-shən-ship ˈsī-kəl/ A pattern of intense attachment, emotional testing, devaluation, and separation seen in borderline dynamics. Synonyms: emotional rollercoaster, intensity loop, unstable bonding. Antonyms: stability, consistency, emotional safety. Savage Sentence: It starts like everything and ends like nothing with no in-between. UnExpert Advice: Intensity is not the same as stability.

Circumplex Model (Relationship Dynamics) /ˈsər-kəm-ˌpleks ˈmä-dəl/ A framework showing how too much closeness or too much distance creates dysfunction in relationships. Synonyms: imbalance model, relational extremes, dysfunction spectrum. Antonyms: balance, healthy boundaries, flexibility. Savage Sentence: You went from too close to completely disconnected and called it complicated. UnExpert Advice: Healthy relationships live in the middle.

Cluster B Personality Dynamics /ˈklə-stər bē ˌpər-sə-ˈna-lə-tē/ Patterns of dramatic, emotional, and erratic behavior often linked to narcissistic, borderline, antisocial, or histrionic traits. Synonyms: chaos dynamics, emotional volatility, manipulation patterns. Antonyms: stability, empathy, emotional regulation. Savage Sentence: One day you're everything, the next day you're nothing, and somehow you're expected to keep up. UnExpert Advice: Chaos is not passion.

Codependency /ˌkō-di-ˈpen-dən-sē/ An unhealthy dynamic where you over-function, over-give, or lose yourself trying to support someone else. Synonyms: overgiving, emotional overinvestment, enabling. Antonyms: independence, self-respect, balanced support. Savage Sentence: You gave everything trying to fix them and slowly lost yourself in the process. UnExpert Advice: Love doesn't require self-abandonment.

Cognitive Dissonance (Relationships) /ˈkäg-nə-tiv ˈdi-sə-nəns/ The mental conflict when what you believe about someone doesn't match how they actually treat you. Synonyms: mental conflict, self-justification, denial loop. Antonyms: clarity, alignment, acceptance. Savage Sentence: You felt it didn't add up and still kept trying to make it make sense. UnExpert Advice: When words and actions don't match, believe the actions.

Complex PTSD (in Relationships) /ˌkäm-pleks pē-tē-es-ˈdē/ Long-term trauma responses from repeated relational harm, leading to hypervigilance, trust issues, and emotional dysregulation. Synonyms: relational trauma, betrayal aftermath, nervous system imprint. Antonyms: regulation, healing, secure attachment. Savage Sentence: The Complex PTSD made even calm moments feel unsafe after everything you'd been through. UnExpert Advice: Healing your nervous system matters more than finding someone new.

DARVO /ˈdär-vō/ Deny, Attack, Reverse Victim and Offender—a manipulation tactic that flips accountability onto you. Synonyms: blame reversal, gaslighting tactic, accountability evasion. Antonyms: ownership, responsibility. Savage Sentence: The DARVO turned your boundary into the problem and your reaction into the crime. UnExpert Advice: When accountability disappears, so should you.

Demisexual /ˌde-mē-ˈsek-shə-wəl/ Experiences sexual attraction only after a strong emotional bond forms. Synonyms: emotional-first attraction, slow-burn sexuality, bond-dependent desire. Antonyms: instant physical attraction, hookup culture, low-bar chemistry. Savage Sentence: You invested like it was building something real while he treated it like a casual option. UnExpert Advice: Your wiring is valid. Protect it from low-effort people.

Dismissive-Avoidant Attachment /dis-ˈmi-siv ə-ˈvȯi-dənt ə-ˈtach-mənt/ Values extreme independence and emotional distance, viewing vulnerability as weakness and shutting down when relationships get too close. Synonyms: emotional island, hyper-independent attachment, intimacy phobic. Antonyms: secure attachment, emotional availability. Savage Sentence: They called it independence—the Dismissive-Avoidant Attachment disappeared the second feelings required presence. UnExpert Advice: You can't build closeness with someone who avoids it.

Earned Secure Attachment /ərnd sə-ˈkyu̇r ə-ˈtach-mənt/ Developing secure attachment through self-work, healing, and intentional change. Synonyms: healed attachment, conscious relating. Antonyms: unhealed patterns, reactive attachment. Savage Sentence: The Earned Secure Attachment stopped accepting what the old version of you used to tolerate. UnExpert Advice: This is built, not found—do the work and everything changes.

Emotional Neglect /i-ˈmō-shə-nəl ni-ˈglekt/ The consistent absence of emotional support, validation, or presence, leaving you feeling invisible. Synonyms: emotional starvation, absence of care, neglectful dynamic. Antonyms: attunement, support, emotional presence. Savage Sentence: The Emotional Neglect made silence feel louder than any argument. UnExpert Advice: Lack of harm isn't the same as presence.

Fawning /ˈfȯ-niŋ/ A trauma response of people-pleasing, over-accommodating, and suppressing your needs to avoid conflict or abandonment. Synonyms: people-pleasing, appeasement, survival compliance. Antonyms: boundaries, self-advocacy. Savage Sentence: The Fawning kept you agreeable while your needs quietly disappeared. UnExpert Advice: Peace that costs you yourself isn't peace.

Fearful-Avoidant Attachment (Disorganized) /ˈfir-fəl ə-ˈvȯi-dənt ə-ˈtach-mənt/ Desires connection but fears it, creating intense push-pull cycles and unstable bonding. Synonyms: chaotic attachment, approach-avoidance, disorganized pattern. Antonyms: secure attachment, consistency. Savage Sentence: The Fearful-Avoidant Attachment pulled you close, pushed you away, then panicked when you left. UnExpert Advice: You can't stabilize someone who fears the very thing they want.

Fraysexual /ˈfrā-sek-shə-wəl/ Attraction fades once emotional closeness develops, often disappearing when things get real. Synonyms: bond-killer sexuality, attachment fade, "liked you better as a stranger." Antonyms: demisexual, sustained attraction, emotional and physical compatibility. Savage Sentence: The closer it got, the faster the interest disappeared. UnExpert Advice: If attraction requires distance, don't chase it.

Idealization / Devaluation Cycle /ī-ˌdē-ə-lə-ˈzā-shən / dē-ˌval-yə-ˈwā-shən/ Rapid shifts between seeing someone as perfect and then worthless, often creating emotional instability and confusion. Synonyms: black-and-white relating, emotional flipping, pedestal to discard. Antonyms: stable perception, nuance, emotional consistency. Savage Sentence: The Idealization / Devaluation Cycle had you worshipped one week and dismissed the next without anything actually changing. UnExpert Advice: If their perception swings this fast, it's not love—it's instability.

Intermittent Reinforcement /ˌin-tər-ˈmit-ənt ˌrē-ən-ˈfȯrs-mənt/ Unpredictable rewards of attention or affection that create strong psychological attachment. Synonyms: hot-cold conditioning, inconsistency loop, addictive pattern. Antonyms: consistency, stability, reliability. Savage Sentence: The Intermittent Reinforcement kept you waiting for the next high that never lasted. UnExpert Advice: Consistency builds trust—randomness builds addiction.

Limerence /ˈli-mə-rən(t)s/ Intense, obsessive infatuation marked by intrusive thoughts, idealization, and emotional dependency on someone's response. Synonyms: obsessive crush, emotional addiction, fantasy attachment. Antonyms: grounded love, emotional regulation, secure connection. Savage Sentence: The Limerence had you building a whole relationship in your head with someone who barely showed up in real life. UnExpert Advice: If it feels all-consuming but not reciprocal, it's not connection—it's projection.

Projection /prə-ˈjek-shən/ Attributing their own behaviors, motives, or feelings to you. Synonyms: blame shifting, psychological mirroring, deflection. Antonyms: self-awareness, ownership. Savage Sentence: The Projection accused you of exactly what they were hiding. UnExpert Advice: Pay attention to repeated accusations—they reveal more than intended.

Reactive Abuse /rē-ˈak-tiv ə-ˈbyüs/ When someone provokes, pushes, or manipulates you over time until you finally react emotionally, then uses your reaction to paint you as the problem. Synonyms: provoked reaction, blame flip, manipulation trap. Antonyms: accountability, emotional safety, direct communication. Savage Sentence: The Reactive Abuse had you pushed to your limit, then labeled "crazy" the second you finally snapped. UnExpert Advice: If someone only points to your reaction and ignores what led to it, you're being set up—not seen.

Secure Attachment /sə-ˈkyu̇r ə-ˈtach-mənt/ Comfortable with intimacy and independence, communicates clearly, and handles conflict without extremes. Synonyms: emotionally balanced, safe base, healthy attachment. Antonyms: insecure attachment, fear-driven relating. Savage Sentence: The Secure Attachment didn't confuse you—they just showed up consistently. UnExpert Advice: This is the standard—not the exception.

Selfitis /self-ˈī-təs/ Excessive selfie posting with no variation or depth. Synonyms: selfie addiction, camera obsession, validation loop. Antonyms: balanced presence, real life, variety. Savage Sentence: The Selfitis profile had 47 angles of the same face and zero new information. UnExpert Advice: If they're obsessed with their image, expect the same in real life.

Splitting /ˈspli-tiŋ/ Viewing someone as all good or all bad with no middle ground. Synonyms: black-and-white thinking, emotional flipping, extreme perception. Antonyms: nuance, emotional balance, realistic perspective. Savage Sentence: You went from perfect to the problem overnight without changing anything. UnExpert Advice: Don't internalize someone else's extremes.

Trauma Bonding /ˈtrô-mə ˈbän-diŋ/ Becoming attached through cycles of emotional highs and lows, mistaking chaos for connection. Synonyms: chaos addiction, emotional rollercoaster, toxic attachment loop. Antonyms: stability, safety, healthy love. Savage Sentence: It felt intense because it kept breaking and pulling you back in. UnExpert Advice: Calm is not boring. Calm is safe.

Triangulation /trī-ˌaŋ-gyə-ˈlā-shən/ Bringing a third person into the dynamic to create jealousy, competition, or insecurity. Synonyms: comparison tactic, rivalry bait, supply management. Antonyms: direct communication, emotional security. Savage Sentence: The Triangulation showed up right on cue—another name dropped the moment you asked for clarity. UnExpert Advice: If a third person keeps appearing, the problem isn't them.

Historical & Old School Terms

Ancient / Classical Antiquity (Greek & Roman)

Adonis Complex /ə-ˈdä-nəs ˈkäm-ˌpleks/ Obsession with beauty, youth, and physical perfection as a measure of worth. Synonyms: vanity fixation, aesthetic obsession, beauty worship. Antonyms: self-acceptance, inner confidence, substance over appearance. Savage Sentence: He built his entire identity on Adonis Complex and still had nothing real to offer. UnExpert Advice: If all they bring is looks, that's all you get.

Adulterium /ə-ˌdəl-ˈtir-ē-əm/ Infidelity historically punished in women while often excused in men. Synonyms: infidelity, betrayal, extramarital affair. Antonyms: fidelity, loyalty, commitment. Savage Sentence: Funny how Adulterium was a crime for her and a "mistake" for him. UnExpert Advice: Double standards are not tradition, they're manipulation.

Agape /ä-ˈgä-pā/ Selfless, unconditional love given without expectation of return. Synonyms: unconditional love, altruistic love, sacrificial care. Antonyms: transactional love, conditional affection, self-serving attachment. Savage Sentence: You called it Agape while they called it convenient. UnExpert Advice: Selfless love should still be respected, not exploited.

Amor /ˈä-ˌmȯr/ Romantic, idealized love rooted in longing and admiration. Synonyms: romance, infatuation, idealized love. Antonyms: indifference, emotional detachment, realism. Savage Sentence: You were deep in Amor writing poetry in your head while they were barely replying. UnExpert Advice: Romanticizing someone doesn't make them worthy of it.

Aphrodisiac Influence /ˌa-frə-ˈdi-zē-ˌak ˈin-flə-wəns/ External stimulation that heightens desire or attraction. Synonyms: chemical attraction, induced desire, sensory trigger. Antonyms: natural connection, emotional grounding, genuine compatibility. Savage Sentence: It felt like connection but it was just

Aphrodisiac Influence and good lighting. UnExpert Advice: Chemistry isn't always compatibility.

Chthonic Attraction /ˈthä-nik ə-ˈtrak-shən/ A dark, consuming attraction tied to chaos and emotional intensity. Synonyms: toxic pull, destructive desire, obsessive attachment. Antonyms: healthy love, stability, emotional safety. Savage Sentence: You called it fate when it was really Chthonic Attraction dragging you into chaos. UnExpert Advice: If it feels consuming, it's not grounding.

Concubina /kän-ˈkyü-bə-nə/ A secondary partner without the rights or respect of a real commitment. Synonyms: kept woman, secondary partner, unofficial partner. Antonyms: equal partner, spouse, committed relationship. Savage Sentence: He gave you Concubina treatment and you still acted like you were the main character. UnExpert Advice: If you're not fully chosen, you're partially used.

Courtesan Culture /ˈkȯr-tə-zən ˈkəl-chər/ Relationships shaped by status, power, and exchange rather than genuine connection. Synonyms: transactional romance, status-based relationships, strategic intimacy. Antonyms: genuine connection, equal partnership, unconditional love. Savage Sentence: It looked like romance but it was Courtesan Culture with better branding. UnExpert Advice: If everything has a price, it's not love.

Cupiditas /kü-ˈpi-də-ˌtäs/ Intense, impulsive desire driven by urgency rather than reason. Synonyms: lust, craving, impulsive desire. Antonyms: restraint, clarity, emotional control. Savage Sentence: You moved on Cupiditas and ignored every logical red flag in the process. UnExpert Advice: Fast desire rarely leads to stable outcomes.

Divine Madness (Theia Mania) /ˈthī-ə ˈmā-nē-ə/ Love that feels irrational, overwhelming, and fated. Synonyms: obsessive love, fate-driven connection, irrational passion. Antonyms: grounded love, logic, emotional stability. Savage Sentence: You called it Divine Madness when it was really just emotional chaos with good timing. UnExpert Advice: Not everything intense is meant to last.

Electra Complex /i-ˈlek-trə ˈkäm-ˌpleks/ Subconscious paternal fixation influencing romantic patterns. Synonyms: paternal fixation, attachment distortion, unresolved imprinting. Antonyms: secure attachment, emotional independence, relational balance. Savage Sentence: You kept choosing the same man in different bodies and wondered why it never worked. UnExpert Advice: Patterns don't break until you see them.

Erastēs / Erōmenos (Paiderasteia) /e-ˈras-tēs • e-ˈrō-me-nōs/ A power-imbalanced relationship framed as mentorship but rooted in influence and control. Synonyms: exploitative mentorship, age-dynamic bonding, power imbalance. Antonyms: equal partnership, mutual agency, balanced connection. Savage Sentence: It was framed as guidance but operated like control from the start. UnExpert Advice: If power isn't equal, neither is the relationship.

Eros /ˈer-ˌōs/ Passionate, physical, and romantic desire rooted in attraction and intensity. Synonyms: passion, lust, romantic desire. Antonyms: indifference, restraint, emotional neutrality. Savage Sentence: It was all Eros and no substance, which is why it burned out fast. UnExpert Advice: Passion is powerful, but it's not enough on its own.

Fated Love (Moira-bound) /ˈmȯi-rə baůnd/ A connection believed to be destined and unavoidable, controlled by forces beyond choice. Synonyms: destined love, karmic bond, inevitable connection. Antonyms: free will, conscious choice, intentional love. Savage Sentence: You called it Fated Love and ignored every red flag like the universe personally approved him. UnExpert Advice: Destiny doesn't require you to suffer.

Forbidden Love /fər-ˈbi-dən ləv/ Love restricted by societal, moral, or external rules. Synonyms: taboo relationship, illicit romance, restricted desire. Antonyms: accepted union, approved relationship, social alignment. Savage Sentence: It felt intense because it was Forbidden Love, not because it was right. UnExpert Advice: Just because it's forbidden doesn't mean it's valuable.

Hedonistic Pursuit /ˌhē-də-ˈni-stik pər-ˈsüt/ Prioritizing pleasure over responsibility or long-term consequences. Synonyms: pleasure-seeking, indulgence, self-gratification. Antonyms: discipline, restraint, emotional accountability. Savage Sentence: He lived in Hedonistic Pursuit and expected you to deal with the consequences. UnExpert Advice: If they chase pleasure, you'll carry the fallout.

Heroic Devotion /hi-ˈrō-ik di-ˈvō-shən/ Extreme loyalty and sacrifice for a lover, often at personal cost. Synonyms: blind loyalty, sacrificial love, unwavering devotion. Antonyms: self-preservation, balance, mutual effort. Savage Sentence: You gave Heroic Devotion to someone who barely showed up. UnExpert Advice: Loyalty without reciprocity is self-betrayal.

Hetaira /he-ˈtī-rə/ A high-status companion valued for intellect, charm, and intimacy outside traditional roles. Synonyms: elite companion, cultivated mistress, social seductress. Antonyms: spouse, domestic partner, traditional wife. Savage Sentence: You were giving Hetaira energy while he was treating you like an option. UnExpert Advice: If you bring value, expect to be valued.

Idealized Beloved /ī-ˈdi-(ə-)ˌlīzd bə-ˈlə-vəd/ Loving someone as a fantasy rather than who they actually are. Synonyms: projection, romantic illusion, fantasy attachment. Antonyms: reality-based love, clarity, grounded connection. Savage Sentence: You fell for the Idealized Beloved and ignored the actual person standing in front of you. UnExpert Advice: Love what is, not what you imagined.

Immortal Longing /i-ˈmȯr-tᵊl ˈlȯŋ-iŋ/ A desire for a love that transcends time, loss, or reality. Synonyms: eternal love, undying desire, timeless attachment. Antonyms: fleeting connection, detachment, emotional closure. Savage Sentence: You held onto Immortal Longing while they moved on in real time. UnExpert Advice: Not all love is meant to last forever.

Kōmos (κῶμος) /ˈkō-mos/ A drunken, chaotic pursuit of pleasure and connection in public settings. Synonyms: drunken chaos, public courtship spectacle, intoxicated pursuit. Antonyms: restraint, privacy, composed behavior. Savage Sentence: He brought full Kōmos energy and called it flirting. UnExpert Advice: If it only exists drunk, it doesn't exist.

Libido /li-ˈbē-(ˌ)dō/ Raw sexual drive rooted in biological instinct. Synonyms: sexual urge, primal desire, physical craving. Antonyms: restraint, emotional control, asexuality. Savage Sentence: Don't confuse Libido with connection, they are not the same thing. UnExpert Advice: Attraction is easy. Compatibility is not.

Ludus /ˈlü-dəs/ Playful, flirtatious love centered on fun without commitment. Synonyms: casual dating, flirtation, non-serious romance. Antonyms: commitment, emotional investment, long-term partnership. Savage Sentence: It was all Ludus until you caught real feelings. UnExpert Advice: If it starts as a game, don't expect a relationship.

Mania (μανία) /ˈmā-nē-ə/ Obsessive, possessive love marked by emotional extremes. Synonyms: obsession, possessiveness, emotional volatility. Antonyms: stability, secure attachment, emotional regulation. Savage Sentence: You called it passion, it was Mania the entire time. UnExpert Advice: Intensity without stability is not love.

Mars/Venus Dynamic /märz ˈvē-nəs dī-ˈna-mik/ Attraction and tension between opposing masculine and feminine energies. Synonyms: opposites attract, polarity tension, gender dynamic conflict. Antonyms: alignment, harmony, emotional compatibility. Savage Sentence: You blamed Mars/Venus Dynamic when you were just incompatible. UnExpert Advice: Chemistry doesn't fix misalignment.

Meretrix / Scortum / Lupa /mə-ˈre-triks • ˈskȯr-təm • ˈlü-pə/ Roman terms reflecting different social views of transactional intimacy. Synonyms: transactional partner, paid companion, commodified intimacy. Antonyms: mutual partnership, non-transactional love, emotional connection. Savage Sentence: Different names, same dynamic, access without respect. UnExpert Advice: If it's transactional, don't call it love.

Moechus /ˈmē-kəs/ A person who engages in secret affairs outside commitment. Synonyms: cheater, adulterer, secret partner. Antonyms: loyal partner, faithful spouse, committed individual. Savage Sentence: He moved like a Moechus and still expected loyalty. UnExpert Advice: If they cheat with you, they'll cheat on you.

Moicheia / Moichos (μοιχεία / μοιχός) /moi-ˈkī-ə • ˈmoi-kos/ Adultery historically treated as a violation of ownership rather than partnership. Synonyms: infidelity, seduction, betrayal. Antonyms: fidelity, respect, relational integrity. Savage Sentence: Funny how Moicheia was about ownership, not betrayal. UnExpert Advice: Love is not possession.

Oedipal Desire /ē-ˈdi-pəl di-ˈzī(-ə)r/ Unconscious attraction patterns shaped by early parental dynamics. Synonyms: parental imprinting, subconscious attraction, attachment pattern. Antonyms: emotional autonomy, self-awareness, secure bonding. Savage Sentence: You keep dating the same dynamic in different bodies and calling it coincidence. UnExpert Advice: If the pattern feels familiar, it probably started way before them.

Ovidian Tactics /ō-ˈvi-dē-ən ˈtak-tiks/ Strategic seduction rooted in manipulation, performance, and calculated attraction. Synonyms: game-playing, manipulative flirting, seduction strategy. Antonyms: authenticity, honesty, genuine interest. Savage Sentence: He hit you with full Ovidian Tactics and you thought it was natural chemistry. UnExpert Advice: If it feels scripted, it probably is.

Paelex /ˈpī-ˌleks/ A rival mistress threatening the position of the primary partner. Synonyms: other woman, rival lover, secondary partner. Antonyms: primary partner, loyal spouse, exclusive relationship. Savage Sentence: You weren't confused, you were competing with a Paelex and pretending it was a relationship. UnExpert Advice: If there's competition, you've already lost the standard.

Paraklausithyron (παρακλαυσίθυρον) /ˌpa-rə-klau̇-sə-ˈthī-rän/ Public or dramatic pursuit after rejection, often emotional or intoxicated. Synonyms: public begging, emotional display, rejection pursuit. Antonyms: self-respect, detachment, emotional restraint. Savage Sentence: You showed up in full Paraklausithyron energy begging for access to someone who already closed the door. UnExpert Advice: If the door is closed, stop knocking.

Pallakē (παλλακή) /pa-lə-ˈkē/ A live-in mistress without full recognition or status. Synonyms: kept partner, side relationship, unofficial partner. Antonyms: spouse, equal partner, committed relationship. Savage Sentence: You accepted Pallakē treatment and still expected main character respect. UnExpert Advice: If the role isn't equal, the outcome won't be either.

Patron Lover /ˈpā-trən ˈlə-vər/ A relationship based on exchange of affection for status, money, or protection. Synonyms: transactional partner, benefactor relationship, sponsored romance. Antonyms: mutual love, equal partnership, independent connection. Savage Sentence: It looked like romance but it was Patron Lover dynamics with better lighting. UnExpert Advice: If support is the foundation, it's not love, it's leverage.

Philautia (φιλαυτία) /ˌfi-lau̇-ˈtē-ə/ Self-love ranging from healthy confidence to full-blown narcissism. Synonyms: narcissism, self-absorption, ego focus. Antonyms: empathy, humility, mutual care. Savage Sentence: There's a difference between Philautia and making everything about yourself. Learn it. UnExpert Advice: Self-love should not erase everyone else.

Philia /ˈfi-lē-ə/ Deep, loyal, friendship-based love built on trust and shared values. Synonyms: companionship, loyal love, emotional bond. Antonyms: superficial connection, lust, detachment. Savage Sentence: You skipped Philia and went straight to intensity, and that's why it didn't last. UnExpert Advice: Friendship is what makes love sustainable.

Pornē (πόρνη) /ˈpȯr-nē/ A lower-status transactional partner treated as a commodity. Synonyms: transactional partner, commodified intimacy, pay-for-play. Antonyms: mutual intimacy, respect-based connection, emotional bond. Savage Sentence: If the value is only physical, the treatment will be too. UnExpert Advice: If it's transactional, expect it to stay that way.

Possessive Passion /pə-ˈze-siv ˈpa-shən/ Love expressed through control, jealousy, and ownership. Synonyms: controlling love, jealousy-driven attachment, dominance. Antonyms: trust, freedom, secure attachment. Savage Sentence: You called it passion when it was just control in a nicer outfit. UnExpert Advice: If it feels restrictive, it's not love.

Pragma /ˈprag-mə/ Practical, enduring love built on compatibility and long-term effort. Synonyms: committed love, mature love, long-term partnership. Antonyms: impulsive love, fleeting attraction, instability. Savage Sentence: It's not fireworks, it's Pragma, and that's why it actually lasts. UnExpert Advice: Stability may feel boring at first, but it's what builds something real.

Pygmalion Effect /pig-ˈmā-lē-ən i-ˈfekt/ Shaping someone into an ideal through projection or expectation. Synonyms: projection, molding, expectation shaping. Antonyms: acceptance, authenticity, unconditional regard. Savage Sentence: You tried to Pygmalion him into potential and ignored who he actually was. UnExpert Advice: People are not projects.

Siren Call /ˈsī-rən kȯl/ A dangerous attraction that pulls you in despite the risk. Synonyms: seductive pull, fatal attraction, irresistible allure. Antonyms: safety, clarity, emotional stability. Savage Sentence: You heard the Siren Call and still swam straight toward it. UnExpert Advice: If it feels dangerous, it usually is.

Symposion (συμπόσιον) /sim-ˈpō-zē-ən/ A pleasure-driven social gathering centered on indulgence and excess. Synonyms: drinking party, indulgent gathering, pleasure-focused event. Antonyms: restraint, moderation, respectful conduct. Savage Sentence: He brought Symposion energy and expected you to take him seriously the next day. UnExpert Advice: If it starts in chaos, it ends in it.

Stuprum /ˈstü-prəm/ Illicit or socially condemned sexual misconduct outside accepted norms. Synonyms: sexual misconduct, violation, illicit encounter. Antonyms: consent, integrity, lawful union. Savage Sentence: Don't confuse Stuprum with rebellion, one has consequences the other just sounds exciting. UnExpert Advice: If it violates your values, it will cost you later.

Tragic Love /ˈtra-jik ləv/ Love that is destined to fail due to timing, circumstance, or inherent incompatibility. Synonyms: doomed romance, ill-fated love, star-crossed connection. Antonyms: enduring love, stable relationship, mutual success. Savage Sentence: You stayed in Tragic Love trying to fix something that was never built to work. UnExpert Advice: Not all love stories are meant to last. Some are meant to teach.

Venusian Love /və-ˈnü-zhən ləv/ Love driven by beauty, attraction, pleasure, and sensual experience. Synonyms: sensual love, aesthetic attraction, pleasure-based connection. Antonyms: pragmatic love, emotional depth, intellectual bond. Savage Sentence: You were in Venusian Love enjoying the vibe while ignoring the lack of substance. UnExpert Advice: Attraction can start it, but it can't sustain it.

Medieval / Old & Middle English

Amorous Courtesy /ˈa-mə-rəs ˈkər-tə-sē/ Polite, refined behavior used to express romantic interest while masking deeper intent. Synonyms: flirtatious politeness, charming conduct, romantic etiquette. Antonyms: bluntness, indifference, disrespect. Savage Sentence: He hid behind Amorous Courtesy so well you almost missed what he actually wanted. UnExpert Advice: Charm can be genuine or strategic. Pay attention to the follow-through.

Ballad Romance /ˈba-ləd rō-ˈmans/ A dramatic, often tragic love story built on emotion and storytelling rather than stability. Synonyms: tragic love story, poetic romance, emotional narrative. Antonyms: stable relationship, grounded love, realism. Savage Sentence: You lived a full Ballad Romance while ignoring how unsustainable it actually was. UnExpert Advice: If it feels like a story, it's probably not built for real life.

Bundling /ˈbən-dliŋ/ A restrained form of closeness designed to allow connection without crossing boundaries. Synonyms: controlled intimacy, supervised closeness, restrained courting. Antonyms: full intimacy, independence, unsupervised relationships. Savage Sentence: Bundling worked because both people respected the boundary, which is rare now. UnExpert Advice: Boundaries only work when both people honor them.

Canoodling /kə-ˈnü-dliŋ/ Affectionate physical behavior like cuddling or kissing, often kept private. Synonyms: cuddling, kissing, intimate affection. Antonyms: distance, formality, restraint. Savage Sentence: It started as Canoodling and somehow turned into emotional attachment real quick. UnExpert Advice: Physical closeness can accelerate feelings. Be aware of the shift.

Chivalric Devotion /ʃi-ˈval-rik di-ˈvō-shən/ Idealized, often performative loyalty and service to a romantic partner. Synonyms: performative loyalty, exaggerated romance, knightly devotion. Antonyms: balanced love, mutual effort, grounded connection. Savage Sentence: He gave Chivalric Devotion energy in the beginning and barely showed up after. UnExpert Advice: Effort that fades was never stable to begin with.

Clandestine Affair /klan-ˈde-stən ə-ˈfer/ A secret romantic or sexual relationship hidden from others. Synonyms: secret relationship, hidden romance, illicit affair. Antonyms: transparency, honesty, open relationship. Savage Sentence: If it has to stay hidden, it's already telling you everything you need to know. UnExpert Advice: Secrecy protects the situation, not you.

Courting / Courtship /ˈkȯr-tiŋ • ˈkȯrt-ˌship/ A formal, intentional pursuit of a partner with long-term commitment in mind. Synonyms: traditional dating, formal pursuit, intentional relationship. Antonyms: casual dating, situationship, non-commitment. Savage Sentence: Real Courtship requires effort, which is why so many avoid it now. UnExpert Advice: Intentional pursuit is rare for a reason. Value it when you see it.

Courtly Love /ˈkȯrt-lē ləv/ Idealized love marked by longing, devotion, and often emotional suffering. Synonyms: idealized romance, unrequited love, poetic devotion. Antonyms: mutual love, realistic relationship, emotional availability. Savage Sentence: You stayed in Courtly Love suffering for someone who never planned to choose you. UnExpert Advice: If it's one-sided, it's not love. It's projection.

Courtly Rivalry /ˈkȯrt-lē ˈrī-vəl-rē/ Competition between multiple suitors for one person's attention. Synonyms: romantic competition, love triangle, rival pursuit. Antonyms: exclusivity, commitment, mutual choice. Savage Sentence: You don't need to win Courtly Rivalry, you need to leave it. UnExpert Advice: If you're competing, you're not chosen.

Culver / Dove /ˈkəl-vər • dəv/ A term of endearment symbolizing gentleness and affection. Synonyms: sweetheart, beloved, darling. Antonyms: insult, detachment, indifference. Savage Sentence: He called you Dove while treating you like anything but. UnExpert Advice: Words mean nothing without matching behavior.

Faithless Swain /ˈfāth-ləs swān/ A lover who betrays or fails to uphold devotion. Synonyms: disloyal lover, betrayer, unreliable suitor. Antonyms: faithful partner, loyal lover, committed companion. Savage Sentence: He played Faithless Swain and still expected loyalty in return. UnExpert Advice: Disloyalty is a pattern, not a mistake.

Fealty in Love /ˈfē-əl-tē in ləv/ A sworn, unwavering loyalty to a romantic partner. Synonyms: unwavering loyalty, sworn devotion, romantic allegiance. Antonyms: betrayal, independence, emotional detachment. Savage Sentence: You gave Fealty in Love to someone who never even committed to you. UnExpert Advice: Loyalty should be mutual, not one-sided.

Fickle Heart /ˈfi-kəl härt/ A lover whose feelings change quickly and inconsistently. Synonyms: inconsistent lover, wavering affection, emotional instability. Antonyms: steady love, consistency, reliability. Savage Sentence: You tried to build something with a Fickle Heart and wondered why it never held. UnExpert Advice: Inconsistency is the answer.

Forbidden Courtship /fər-ˈbi-dən ˈkȯrt-ˌship/ A romantic pursuit restricted by social, moral, or external forces. Synonyms: taboo romance, restricted love, illicit pursuit. Antonyms: approved relationship, social acceptance, open union. Savage Sentence: It felt intense because it was Forbidden Courtship, not because it was right. UnExpert Advice: Intensity doesn't equal compatibility.

Fortune Hunter /ˈfȯr-chən ˈhən-tər/ Someone who pursues a relationship primarily for money, status, or gain. Synonyms: gold digger, opportunist, status seeker. Antonyms: genuine partner, self-sufficient lover, authentic connection. Savage Sentence: He wasn't interested in you, he was interested in what came with you. UnExpert Advice: If the benefit disappears, so will they.

Heart on One's Sleeve /härt on wənz slēv/ Openly expressing emotions and affection without restraint. Synonyms: emotional transparency, expressive affection, vulnerability. Antonyms: guardedness, emotional restraint, detachment. Savage Sentence: You wore your heart on your sleeve while they barely showed up with theirs. UnExpert Advice: Be open, but make sure it's being met.

Illicit Tryst /i-ˈli-sət trist/ A secret or forbidden meeting between lovers. Synonyms: secret rendezvous, hidden affair, forbidden meeting. Antonyms: open relationship, transparency, honesty. Savage Sentence: If it only exists as an Illicit Tryst, it's not a relationship, it's a situation. UnExpert Advice: Hidden connections rarely lead to real outcomes.

Inconstant Lover /in-ˈkän-stənt ˈlə-vər/ A partner who is emotionally inconsistent and unreliable. Synonyms: unreliable partner, inconsistent lover, emotional drifter. Antonyms: dependable partner, steady love, consistency. Savage Sentence: You tried to build something with an Inconstant Lover and called the instability "chemistry." UnExpert Advice: Inconsistency is not mystery, it's your answer.

Jealous Vigilance /ˈje-ləs ˈvi-jə-lən(t)s/ Constant monitoring driven by insecurity and fear of betrayal. Synonyms: possessiveness, suspicion, controlling behavior. Antonyms: trust, security, emotional freedom. Savage Sentence: You slipped into Jealous Vigilance and lost your peace trying to keep control. UnExpert Advice: If you have to monitor, you don't trust, and that matters.

Keepsake Devotion /ˈkēp-ˌsāk di-ˈvō-shən/ Maintaining emotional attachment through objects or memories. Synonyms: sentimental attachment, tokenized love, nostalgic bonding. Antonyms: emotional detachment, present focus, release. Savage Sentence: You held onto Keepsake Devotion while the relationship itself was long gone. UnExpert Advice: Let the memory stay a memory.

Knightly Pursuit /ˈnīt-lē pər-ˈsüt/ Relentless chasing framed as romantic or noble devotion. Synonyms: persistent pursuit, romantic chasing, performative devotion. Antonyms: mutual interest, respect, emotional balance. Savage Sentence: It felt like Knightly Pursuit until you realized it wasn't mutual. UnExpert Advice: Real interest doesn't require chasing.

Lady Fair /ˈlā-dē fer/ An idealized version of a woman placed on a pedestal. Synonyms: idealized woman, object of admiration, pedestal partner. Antonyms: equal partner, realistic perception, grounded connection. Savage Sentence: He treated you like Lady Fair until you showed real human complexity. UnExpert Advice: Being idealized is not the same as being known.

Lemman / Lef (Leof) /ˈlem-ən • lef • lāf/ A lover or beloved, sometimes in secret or unofficial contexts. Synonyms: lover, darling, secret partner. Antonyms: stranger, detached partner, formal spouse. Savage Sentence: You were his Lemman, just not the one he claimed publicly. UnExpert Advice: If it's hidden, it's limited.

Leof (Beloved) /lāf/ A deeply cherished and valued partner. Synonyms: beloved, dear one, cherished partner. Antonyms: indifference, neglect, emotional distance. Savage Sentence: You treated them like your Leof while they treated you like an option. UnExpert Advice: Value should be mutual.

Love-longing (Lovesickness) /ˈləv-ˌlȯŋ-iŋ/ Emotional distress caused by unfulfilled or unattainable love. Synonyms: yearning, romantic obsession, emotional ache. Antonyms: fulfillment, contentment, emotional stability. Savage Sentence: You stayed in Love-longing waiting for something that was never coming. UnExpert Advice: Longing is not a relationship.

Love Melancholy /ˈləv ˈme-lən-ˌkä-lē/ Lingering sadness tied to romantic dissatisfaction or loss. Synonyms: heartbreak, romantic sorrow, emotional heaviness. Antonyms: joy, fulfillment, emotional ease. Savage Sentence: You called it Love Melancholy when it was really just unmet reality. UnExpert Advice: Sit in it, but don't stay there.

Love Service /ˈləv ˈsər-vəs/ Acts performed to prove devotion or worth. Synonyms: performative effort, devotion acts, romantic proving. Antonyms: mutual effort, equal contribution, balanced love. Savage Sentence: You gave nonstop Love Service trying to earn something that should have been given freely. UnExpert Advice: Love is not something you prove, it's something you share.

Love Token /ˈləv ˈtō-kən/ A physical object symbolizing affection or connection. Synonyms: keepsake, sentimental object, romantic memento. Antonyms: detachment, release, emotional closure. Savage Sentence: The Love Token meant more to you than the relationship ever did to them. UnExpert Advice: Symbols don't replace substance.

Love Trial /ˈləv ˈtrī-əl/ Tests or challenges used to prove loyalty or devotion. Synonyms: loyalty test, romantic challenge, proof of love. Antonyms: ease, mutual trust, emotional security. Savage Sentence: If you're constantly in a Love Trial, you're not in a safe relationship. UnExpert Advice: Love should not feel like a test you're trying to pass.

Maiden /ˈmā-dən/ An unmarried woman idealized as pure, innocent, and unattainable. Synonyms: innocent woman, idealized partner, untouched figure. Antonyms: experienced woman, equal partner, realistic identity. Savage Sentence: He wanted a Maiden fantasy but couldn't handle a real woman. UnExpert Advice: If they need perfection, they're not ready for reality.

Masher /ˈma-shər/ A man who aggressively flirts or harasses without invitation or respect. Synonyms: catcaller, creep, aggressive flirt. Antonyms: respectful suitor, considerate admirer, restrained behavior. Savage Sentence: He thought he was charming, it was full Masher behavior. UnExpert Advice: Attention without respect is not a compliment.

Minstrel Love /ˈmin-strəl ləv/ Love expressed through performance, words, or art more than action. Synonyms: poetic love, performative romance, artistic devotion. Antonyms: practical love, consistent action, grounded connection. Savage Sentence: He gave Minstrel Love speeches and zero real effort. UnExpert Advice: If it sounds good but doesn't show up, it's not real.

Rake (Rakish Lover) /rāk/ A charming seducer who pursues many but commits to none. Synonyms: player, seducer, womanizer. Antonyms: loyal partner, committed lover, emotionally available partner. Savage Sentence: He played the Rake perfectly, right up until you expected consistency. UnExpert Advice: Charm without commitment is a pattern.

Romantic Idealization /rō-ˈman-tik ī-ˌdē-ə-lə-ˈzā-shən/ Elevating someone to a perfect fantasy while ignoring reality. Synonyms: projection, fantasy attachment, pedestal placement. Antonyms: realism, clarity, grounded love.

Savage Sentence: You romantic idealized him into someone he never actually was. UnExpert Advice: See them clearly, not hopefully.

Secret Love (Privy Love) /ˈsē-krət ləv/ A hidden romantic connection kept out of public view. Synonyms: hidden relationship, private affair, concealed love. Antonyms: open relationship, transparency, public commitment. Savage Sentence: If it's Secret Love to him, it's limited access for you. UnExpert Advice: Hidden love has hidden outcomes.

Sighing Love /ˈsī-iŋ ləv/ Love expressed through quiet longing instead of action. Synonyms: silent longing, unspoken love, emotional yearning. Antonyms: direct expression, action, clarity. Savage Sentence: You sat in Sighing Love waiting for something he was never going to do. UnExpert Advice: If it's not expressed, it's not progressing.

Spoony /ˈspü-nē/ Foolishly sentimental or overly emotional in love. Synonyms: lovestruck, overly emotional, infatuated. Antonyms: rational, composed, emotionally balanced. Savage Sentence: You went full Spoony and ignored every logical warning sign. UnExpert Advice: Feel it, but don't lose yourself in it.

Suitor /ˈsü-tər/ A man pursuing someone with intention of commitment. Synonyms: pursuer, admirer, courting partner. Antonyms: disinterested party, detached individual, non-committal dater. Savage Sentence: A real Suitor makes effort obvious, not confusing. UnExpert Advice: If you're guessing, he's not pursuing.

Swain /swān/ A young or naive romantic pursuer. Synonyms: young lover, admirer, romantic pursuer. Antonyms: experienced partner, detached individual, uninterested party. Savage Sentence: He had Swain energy, eager but not equipped. UnExpert Advice: Interest without maturity won't sustain anything.

Sweeting / Darling / My Honey /ˈswē-tiŋ • ˈdär-liŋ • ˈhə-nē/ Terms of endearment used to express affection, sometimes without substance. Synonyms: pet names, affectionate titles, romantic language. Antonyms: indifference, emotional distance, detachment. Savage Sentence: He called you everything but treated you like nothing. UnExpert Advice: Pet names don't equal real connection.

Token / Fairing /ˈtō-kən • ˈfer-iŋ/ A small symbolic gift representing affection or favor. Synonyms: love token, keepsake, symbolic gift. Antonyms: detachment, indifference, emotional absence. Savage Sentence: The Token meant more than the effort behind it. UnExpert Advice: Symbols don't replace consistency.

Unrequited Devotion /ˌən-ri-ˈkwī-təd di-ˈvō-shən/ Love given without return or acknowledgment. Synonyms: one-sided love, unreciprocated affection, emotional imbalance. Antonyms: mutual love, reciprocity, shared connection. Savage Sentence: You gave Unrequited Devotion and called it loyalty. UnExpert Advice: Love should be returned, not endured.

Virtuous Suffering /ˈvər-chü-əs ˈsə-fə-riŋ/ Enduring emotional pain as proof of love or loyalty. Synonyms: martyrdom in love, emotional endurance, sacrificial devotion. Antonyms: self-respect, emotional boundaries, balanced love. Savage Sentence: You thought it was Virtuous Suffering, it was just unnecessary pain. UnExpert Advice: Love is not supposed to hurt you consistently.

Wooing / To Woo /ˈwü-iŋ/ Actively pursuing someone through effort and intention. Synonyms: courting, pursuing, romantic effort. Antonyms: neglect, indifference, disinterest. Savage Sentence: If he's not Wooing you, he's not choosing you. UnExpert Advice: Effort is not optional.

Yearning Heart /ˈyər-niŋ härt/ A persistent emotional longing for someone, often without fulfillment. Synonyms: longing, desire, emotional ache. Antonyms: fulfillment, contentment, emotional closure. Savage Sentence: You stayed in Yearning Heart mode instead of facing reality. UnExpert Advice: Longing doesn't mean it's meant for you.

Renaissance / Shakespearean / Elizabethan

Battle of Wits /ˈba-təl əv wits/ Flirtation expressed through clever teasing, banter, and intellectual sparring. Synonyms: witty banter, intellectual flirtation, verbal sparring. Antonyms: dull conversation, emotional distance, lack of engagement. Savage Sentence: It started as a Battle of Wits and turned into you carrying the entire conversation. UnExpert Advice: Banter should be mutual, not one-sided entertainment.

Beau /bō/ A charming male admirer often valued for looks and charisma. Synonyms: suitor, admirer, boyfriend. Antonyms: disinterested man, indifferent partner, unattractive behavior. Savage Sentence: He looked like a Beau and behaved like a liability. UnExpert Advice: Attraction gets attention, behavior keeps it.

Buss /bəs/ A playful or affectionate kiss. Synonyms: kiss, peck, affectionate gesture. Antonyms: distance, rejection, avoidance. Savage Sentence: A Buss is cute until it's replacing actual effort. UnExpert Advice: Affection should match intention.

Carry a Torch /ˈka-rē ə tȯrch/ Holding onto feelings for someone, often one-sided or unreturned. Synonyms: longing, unrequited love, emotional attachment. Antonyms: moving on, detachment, emotional closure. Savage Sentence: You carried a torch while he barely carried a conversation. UnExpert Advice: Don't hold space for someone who isn't showing up in it.

Dainty Duck (Pet Names) /ˈdān-tē dək/ Playful or charming nicknames used to create affection. Synonyms: pet names, affectionate nicknames, romantic language. Antonyms: indifference, emotional coldness, detachment. Savage Sentence: He called you Dainty Duck and still treated you like an option. UnExpert Advice: Cute names don't equal real effort.

Death-Driven Devotion /deth ˈdri-vən di-ˈvō-shən/ Love framed as eternal, unbreakable, or lasting beyond all limits. Synonyms: eternal devotion, undying love, tragic loyalty. Antonyms: detachment, emotional closure, moving on. Savage Sentence: You gave Death-Driven Devotion to someone who couldn't even show up consistently. UnExpert Advice: Real love doesn't require suffering to prove it.

Deceptive Courtship /di-ˈsep-tiv ˈkȯrt-ˌship/ Romantic pursuit based on lies, manipulation, or false intentions. Synonyms: manipulation, false pursuit, misleading romance. Antonyms: honesty, transparency, genuine intention. Savage Sentence: It looked like effort until Deceptive Courtship revealed the motive. UnExpert Advice: If the foundation is false, the outcome will be too.

Eternal Love Oath /i-ˈtər-nəl ləv ōth/ A dramatic promise of forever, often made without real grounding. Synonyms: forever promise, romantic vow, undying pledge. Antonyms: realistic commitment, grounded love, measured intention. Savage Sentence: He gave you an Eternal Love Oath and couldn't even follow through for a week. UnExpert Advice: Don't believe forever from someone who can't handle consistency.

Fair Youth Obsession /fer yüth əb-ˈse-shən/ Fixation on beauty, youth, and physical perfection. Synonyms: beauty obsession, youth fixation, aesthetic attachment. Antonyms: maturity, depth, lasting connection. Savage Sentence: He was deep in Fair Youth Obsession and completely blind to substance. UnExpert Advice: If it's all surface, it won't last.

Faithless Lover /ˈfāth-ləs ˈlə-vər/ A partner who betrays or fails to remain loyal. Synonyms: cheater, betrayer, disloyal partner. Antonyms: faithful partner, loyal lover, committed individual. Savage Sentence: A Faithless Lover will always make you question yourself instead of their behavior. UnExpert Advice: Disloyalty is a decision, not confusion.

False Vows /fȯls vou̇z/ Promises of love or commitment made without intent to keep them. Synonyms: empty promises, insincere pledges, deceptive commitment. Antonyms: integrity, honesty, genuine devotion. Savage Sentence: He made False Vows like they were part of the script. UnExpert Advice: Words without action are just noise.

Fatal Attraction /ˈfā-tᵊl ə-ˈtrak-shən/ A powerful pull that leads to emotional or personal damage. Synonyms: destructive love, dangerous allure, toxic attraction. Antonyms: healthy love, stability, emotional safety. Savage Sentence: You knew it was a Fatal Attraction and still leaned in. UnExpert Advice: If it feels risky, believe that feeling.

Fated Union /ˈfā-təd ˈyün-yən/ A relationship believed to be destined or inevitable. Synonyms: destined love, soul tie, inevitable connection. Antonyms: conscious choice, free will, intentional relationship. Savage Sentence: You called it a Fated Union while ignoring every sign it wasn't working. UnExpert Advice: Destiny doesn't override reality.

Feign'd Affection /fānd ə-ˈfek-shən/ Pretending to feel love or attraction for personal gain. Synonyms: fake love, manipulation, insincere interest. Antonyms: authenticity, sincerity, genuine connection. Savage Sentence: It felt real until Feign'd Affection slipped and the truth showed. UnExpert Advice: If it feels inconsistent, question the intent.

Forbidden Desire /fər-ˈbi-dən di-ˈzī(-ə)r/ Attraction that goes against social or moral boundaries. Synonyms: taboo attraction, illicit desire, restricted longing. Antonyms: accepted love, appropriate relationship, social alignment. Savage Sentence: It felt intense because it was Forbidden Desire, not because it was right. UnExpert Advice: Intensity is not a justification.

Green-Eyed Jealousy /ˈgrēn-īd ˈje-lə-sē/ Envy and suspicion within a relationship that creates insecurity and conflict. Synonyms: jealousy, insecurity, possessiveness. Antonyms: trust, confidence, emotional security. Savage Sentence: You called it passion, it was Green-Eyed Jealousy ruining your peace. UnExpert Advice: If it creates anxiety, it's not strengthening the connection.

Honor-Bound Love /ˈä-nər baůnd ləv/ A relationship driven by duty, reputation, or obligation over genuine desire. Synonyms: duty-driven love, obligated relationship, social constraint. Antonyms: free love, personal choice, emotional authenticity. Savage Sentence: You stayed in Honor-Bound Love out of obligation, not desire. UnExpert Advice: Love should be chosen, not assigned.

Idealized Beauty /ī-ˈdi-(ə-)ˌlīzd ˈbyü-tē/ Viewing someone as flawless while ignoring reality. Synonyms: pedestalization, fantasy projection, perfection illusion. Antonyms: realism, acceptance, grounded perception. Savage Sentence: You saw Idealized Beauty while reality was quietly disagreeing. UnExpert Advice: Attraction fades, truth doesn't.

Inconstant Heart /in-ˈkän-stənt härt/ A lover whose emotions and loyalty change frequently. Synonyms: fickle lover, inconsistent partner, emotional drifter. Antonyms: steady love, loyalty, consistency. Savage Sentence: You tried to stabilize an Inconstant Heart and lost yourself in the process. UnExpert Advice: If it changes constantly, it's not dependable.

Jealous Rage /ˈje-ləs rāj/ Intense emotional reaction driven by insecurity and control. Synonyms: possessive anger, emotional volatility, reactive jealousy. Antonyms: calm, trust, emotional regulation. Savage Sentence: Jealous Rage doesn't come from love, it comes from insecurity. UnExpert Advice: Love feels safe, not explosive.

Love Betrayal /ləv bi-ˈtrā-əl/ Breaking trust through deception or disloyalty. Synonyms: betrayal, infidelity, deception. Antonyms: loyalty, honesty, fidelity. Savage Sentence: Once Love Betrayal happens, the dynamic is never the same. UnExpert Advice: Trust is not easily rebuilt, and that matters.

Lovesick Passion /ˈləv-ˌsik ˈpa-shən/ Overwhelming emotional intensity that borders on distress or obsession. Synonyms: obsession, infatuation, emotional overwhelm. Antonyms: emotional balance, clarity, stability. Savage Sentence: You were in Lovesick Passion and calling it connection. UnExpert Advice: If it consumes you, it's not grounded.

Mad Love (Love as Madness) /mad ləv/ Obsessive, chaotic attachment framed as romance. Synonyms: obsession, emotional instability, chaotic love. Antonyms: grounded love, emotional regulation, stability. Savage Sentence: You called it Mad Love when it was just emotional instability. UnExpert Advice: Chaos is not chemistry.

Masquerade Romance /ˈmas-kə-ˌrād rō-ˈmans/ A relationship built on illusion, disguise, or false identity. Synonyms: deceptive romance, illusion-based attraction, hidden identity. Antonyms: authenticity, transparency, truth. Savage Sentence: It felt real until the Masquerade Romance ended and the truth showed up. UnExpert Advice: If it starts with illusion, it ends with clarity.

Melancholy Love /ˈme-lən-ˌkä-lē ləv/ Love rooted in sadness, longing, and emotional heaviness. Synonyms: sorrowful love, romantic sadness, emotional depth. Antonyms: joy, fulfillment, lightness. Savage Sentence: You stayed in Melancholy Love thinking depth required pain. UnExpert Advice: Love is not supposed to feel heavy all the time.

Mistaken Identity Love /mi-ˈstā-kən ī-ˈden-tə-tē ləv/ A connection formed through misunderstanding who someone really is. Synonyms: confusion-based romance, illusion, misdirected love. Antonyms: clarity, truth, informed choice. Savage Sentence: You fell for who you thought he was, not who he actually is. UnExpert Advice: Pay attention to reality, not perception.

Paramour /ˈpa-rə-ˌmȯr/ A lover, often secret or outside a primary relationship. Synonyms: secret lover, affair partner, illicit romance. Antonyms: spouse, committed partner, exclusive relationship. Savage Sentence: You were the Paramour, not the priority. UnExpert Advice: If it's hidden, it's limited.

Passion Over Reason /ˈpa-shən ˈō-vər ˈrē-zən/ Choosing desire and emotion over logic and consequence. Synonyms: impulsive love, emotional decision-making, reckless desire. Antonyms: logic, restraint, thoughtful choice. Savage Sentence: Passion Over Reason feels exciting until you deal with the consequences. UnExpert Advice: Think past the feeling.

Petrarchan Love /pə-ˈträr-kən ləv/ One-sided devotion to an unattainable or idealized person. Synonyms: unrequited love, idealized obsession, poetic longing. Antonyms: mutual love, realistic connection, emotional reciprocity. Savage Sentence: You stayed in Petrarchan Love suffering for someone who was never going to choose you. UnExpert Advice: If it's not mutual, it's not sustainable.

Poetic Devotion /pō-ˈe-tik di-ˈvō-shən/ Expressing love through words and emotion more than action. Synonyms: performative love, expressive romance, dramatic affection. Antonyms: practical love, consistent effort, grounded connection. Savage Sentence: He gave Poetic Devotion speeches and zero follow-through. UnExpert Advice: Words should match behavior.

Possessive Love /pə-ˈze-siv ləv/ Love rooted in control, ownership, and restriction. Synonyms: controlling love, jealousy-driven attachment, dominance. Antonyms: trust, freedom, secure attachment. Savage Sentence: You called it Possessive Love, it was just control. UnExpert Advice: If it limits you, it's not love.

Reputation Stakes /ˌre-pyə-ˈtā-shən stāks/ Romantic decisions driven by image, status, or fear of judgment. Synonyms: social pressure, image management, public perception. Antonyms: authenticity, personal choice, emotional honesty. Savage Sentence: You chose Reputation Stakes over your actual happiness and called it "the right decision." UnExpert Advice: If you're choosing for the audience, you're losing for yourself.

Romantic Hyperbole /rō-ˈman-tik hī-ˈpər-bə-lē/ Exaggerated expressions of love or devotion that don't match reality. Synonyms: exaggeration, overstatement, dramatic expression. Antonyms: realism, honesty, grounded emotion. Savage Sentence: He gave full Romantic Hyperbole and barely showed up in real life. UnExpert Advice: If it sounds too big, check if it's backed by anything real.

Scandalous Affair /ˈskan-də-ləs ə-ˈfer/ A relationship that risks reputation, trust, or social standing. Synonyms: illicit affair, controversial relationship, public scandal. Antonyms: respectable union, approved relationship, transparency. Savage Sentence: It felt exciting because it was a Scandalous Affair, not because it was meaningful. UnExpert Advice: Chaos creates intensity, not stability.

Sonneteer's Love /ˌsä-nə-ˈtirz ləv/ Idealized affection expressed through poetic or performative language. Synonyms: poetic love, performative devotion, literary romance. Antonyms: practical love, grounded connection, consistent action. Savage Sentence: He gave Sonneteer's Love energy with words that never turned into action. UnExpert Advice: If it stays in language, it never becomes real.

Star-Crossed Lovers /stär kròst ˈlə-vərz/ Two people drawn together but ultimately separated by external forces. Synonyms: doomed romance, ill-fated love, tragic pair. Antonyms: successful relationship, mutual outcome, lasting union. Savage Sentence: You called it Star-Crossed Lovers when it was just incompatible timing and reality. UnExpert Advice: Not everything is fate, sometimes it just doesn't work.

Tragic Romance /ˈtra-jik rō-ˈmans/ A relationship that ends in loss, heartbreak, or emotional destruction. Synonyms: doomed love, heartbreaking relationship, emotional downfall. Antonyms: enduring love, stable relationship, mutual success. Savage Sentence: You stayed in a Tragic Romance hoping it would rewrite its own ending. UnExpert Advice: Patterns don't change just because you want them to.

Unrequited Love /ˌən-ri-ˈkwī-təd ləv/ Love or affection that is not returned. Synonyms: one-sided love, unreturned feelings, emotional imbalance. Antonyms: mutual love, reciprocity, shared connection. Savage Sentence: You gave Unrequited Love and still expected a mutual outcome. UnExpert Advice: If it's not returned, it's not a relationship.

Witty Courtship /ˈwi-tē ˈkȯrt-ˌship/ Romantic tension built through banter, teasing, and intellectual exchange. Synonyms: playful flirting, verbal sparring, intellectual attraction. Antonyms: dull interaction, emotional disconnect, lack of chemistry. Savage Sentence: It started as Witty Courtship until you realized it never moved beyond conversation. UnExpert Advice: Chemistry needs action to become something real.

18th-Century Libertine / Seduction Culture

The Art of the Affair /thē ärt əv thē ə-ˈfer/ A skillful orchestration and maintenance of secret or illicit romantic relationships. Synonyms: strategic infidelity, covert romance, calculated secrecy. Antonyms: transparency, fidelity, open commitment. Savage Sentence: He didn't slip up—he mastered The Art of the Affair while you thought you were the only one. UnExpert Advice: If it takes strategy to maintain, it's intentional.

Amorous Congress /ˈa-mə-rəs ˈkän-grəs/ Euphemistic language used to describe sexual activity while maintaining an illusion of refinement or decorum. Synonyms: sexual euphemism, coded intimacy, polite indecency. Antonyms: directness, honesty, emotional connection. Savage Sentence: Calling it Amorous Congress doesn't make it deeper—it just makes it sound better than it was. UnExpert Advice: Fancy language doesn't change the reality.

Bawd /bȯd/ A procuress or facilitator who arranges romantic or sexual encounters, often for personal gain. Synonyms: matchmaker, fixer, enabler. Antonyms: protector, boundary-setter, ethical guide. Savage Sentence: There's always a Bawd somewhere making sure the mess stays organized. UnExpert Advice: Pay attention to who benefits from your chaos.

Calculated Charm /ˈkal-kyə-ˌlā-təd chärm/ Deliberate use of charisma and likability to influence, seduce, or manipulate. Synonyms: strategic charm, manipulation, social engineering. Antonyms: authenticity, sincerity, genuine connection. Savage Sentence: That wasn't chemistry—it was Calculated Charm and you were the assignment. UnExpert Advice: If it feels too smooth, it's probably practiced.

Casanova vs. Don Juan /ˌka-sə-ˈnō-və • dän ˈwän/ Two archetypes of seduction—Casanova, the charming illusionist, and Don Juan, the ruthless collector. Synonyms: smooth talker, seducer, player. Antonyms: loyal partner, emotionally available partner, committed individual. Savage Sentence: Whether it's Casanova vs. Don Juan, the outcome is the same—you're not the one, you're just next. UnExpert Advice: Different style, same result.

Cold Seduction /kōld sə-ˈdək-shən/ A calculated romantic pursuit executed without genuine emotional investment. Synonyms: detached seduction, strategic pursuit, emotionless charm. Antonyms: emotional connection, sincerity, genuine interest. Savage Sentence: You felt something, but Cold Seduction means he didn't. UnExpert Advice: Technique is not connection.

Compromised Virtue /ˈkäm-prə-ˌmīzd ˈvər-chü/ Loss of innocence, reputation, or moral standing through romantic or sexual involvement. Synonyms: scandal, reputational damage, moral fall. Antonyms: integrity, reputation, social standing. Savage Sentence: Funny how Compromised Virtue only seemed to cost you, not him. UnExpert Advice: If the consequences aren't equal, neither is the situation.

Conquest Mentality /ˈkän-kwest men-ˈta-lə-tē/ Viewing romantic or sexual partners as achievements to win rather than people to connect with. Synonyms: game mindset, ego pursuit, competitive dating. Antonyms: emotional connection, mutual respect, partnership. Savage Sentence: You weren't a person in his world—you were a win in his Conquest Mentality. UnExpert Advice: If they treat dating like a game, don't play.

Control Through Desire /kən-ˈtrōl thru di-ˈzī(-ə)r/ Maintaining power by creating emotional dependency, longing, or imbalance. Synonyms: emotional manipulation, power play, strategic withholding. Antonyms: equality, transparency, emotional security. Savage Sentence: Control Through Desire kept you wanting more while he gave you less. UnExpert Advice: If you're always craving more, it's by design.

Courtesan /ˈkȯr-tə-zən/ A high-status companion offering charm and intimacy in exchange for support or status. Synonyms: elite companion, kept partner, transactional relationship. Antonyms: equal partner, non-transactional love, independent connection. Savage Sentence: She played Courtesan and still expected partner treatment. UnExpert Advice: If it's built on exchange, it depends on what you provide.

Cuckold /ˈkə-kəld/ A husband whose wife is unfaithful, often portrayed as oblivious or publicly humiliated. Synonyms: betrayed partner, deceived spouse, humiliated husband. Antonyms: faithful union, mutual loyalty, respected partner. Savage Sentence: He wasn't just cheated on—he became the Cuckold everyone else already knew about. UnExpert Advice: If you're the last to know, you're already being disrespected.

Cuckold-maker /ˈkə-kəld ˌmā-kər/ A seducer who deliberately pursues and sleeps with someone else's partner, often for ego or thrill. Synonyms: homewrecker, rival seducer, conquest-driven pursuer. Antonyms: respectful partner, boundary-respecting individual, ethical dater. Savage Sentence: The Cuckold-maker didn't want her—he wanted the ego boost of taking what wasn't his. UnExpert Advice: If someone enjoys crossing lines, they won't stop at yours.

Coxcomb /ˈkäks-ˌkōm/ A vain, self-obsessed individual focused on appearance, charm, and social performance over substance. Synonyms: narcissist, dandy, superficial charmer. Antonyms: grounded individual, authentic partner, emotionally aware person. Savage Sentence: The Coxcomb looked perfect until you realized there was nothing underneath it. UnExpert Advice: If all they offer is surface, that's all you'll ever get.

Disposal After Conquest /di-ˈspō-zəl ˈaf-tər ˈkän-kwest/ Abandoning a partner once the pursuit or seduction is complete. Synonyms: discard, emotional dumping, post-conquest abandonment. Antonyms: commitment, follow-through, sustained connection. Savage Sentence: Disposal After Conquest hit the second he got what he wanted and you finally saw who he was. UnExpert Advice: If they only value the chase, they won't value you after it.

Double Dealing /ˈdə-bəl ˈdē-liŋ/ Deceitful behavior involving dishonesty, betrayal, or hidden intentions in romantic relationships. Synonyms: deceit, manipulation, dishonesty. Antonyms: honesty, transparency, integrity. Savage Sentence: Double Dealing is why nothing ever added up—because he was never telling the full truth. UnExpert Advice: If something feels off, it probably is.

Duplicity in Love /du-ˈpli-sə-tē in ləv/ Maintaining multiple romantic interests, intentions, or personas simultaneously without honesty. Synonyms: two-timing, deception, parallel relationships. Antonyms: exclusivity, honesty, clear intention. Savage Sentence: Duplicity in Love means you weren't the only one—you were just the most convenient one. UnExpert Advice: If they can't be transparent, assume there's more you're not seeing.

Emotional Detachment /i-ˈmō-shə-nəl di-ˈta-chmənt/ Avoiding genuine emotional connection while still engaging in romantic or sexual interaction. Synonyms: emotional unavailability, distance, disengagement. Antonyms: vulnerability, connection, emotional presence. Savage Sentence: You kept trying to get closer while his Emotional Detachment made sure you never could. UnExpert Advice: If they won't connect, don't keep trying to pull them in.

Emotional Manipulation /i-ˈmō-shə-nəl mə-ˌni-pyə-ˈlā-shən/ The strategic use of affection, attention, or withdrawal to influence someone's feelings or behavior. Synonyms: control tactics, psychological influence, emotional control. Antonyms: honesty, emotional integrity, genuine care. Savage Sentence: You thought it was a rough patch, but it was Emotional Manipulation the entire time. UnExpert Advice: Inconsistency is often intentional.

False Seduction /fòls sə-ˈdək-shən/ Pursuing someone under the illusion of love or interest without genuine intention. Synonyms: deceptive pursuit, fake interest, manipulative attraction. Antonyms: sincere interest, genuine attraction, honest pursuit. Savage Sentence: You called it chemistry, but it was False Seduction doing exactly what it was designed to do. UnExpert Advice: If the outcome doesn't match the effort, it was never real.

Fan Flirting / Language of Fans /fan ˈflər-tiŋ/ A system of coded gestures using handheld fans to communicate romantic interest, rejection, or invitation in social settings. Synonyms: coded flirting, nonverbal signaling, indirect communication. Antonyms: direct communication, clarity, straightforward expression. Savage Sentence: He swore he could read signals, but Fan Flirting still left him guessing—and guessing wrong. UnExpert Advice: If it's confusing, it's not clear—and that's the problem.

Feign'd Devotion /fānd di-ˈvō-shən/ Performing affection or loyalty to gain trust, access, or advantage. Synonyms: fake loyalty, manipulative affection, performative love. Antonyms: sincerity, genuine care, authentic devotion. Savage Sentence: You called it loyalty, but Feign'd Devotion ended the second he got what he wanted. UnExpert Advice: If it disappears once you're invested, it was never real.

Fleeting Attachment /ˈflē-tiŋ ə-ˈta-chmənt/ A brief, noncommittal romantic involvement lacking depth or longevity. Synonyms: short-term fling, temporary connection, casual involvement. Antonyms: commitment, lasting bond, emotional investment. Savage Sentence: It felt intense in the moment, but Fleeting Attachment doesn't stick around for reality. UnExpert Advice: Short-lived doesn't mean meaningful.

Fop /fäp/ A man excessively concerned with appearance, fashion, and manners, often lacking depth or substance. Synonyms: dandy, narcissist, superficial performer. Antonyms: grounded individual, authentic partner, substance-driven person. Savage Sentence: The Fop looked flawless until you needed something real and got nothing. UnExpert Advice: Presentation isn't personality.

Gallant /ˈga-lənt/ A polished, attentive man whose charm and courtesy often mask strategic seduction or ulterior motives. Synonyms: charmer, smooth talker, calculated gentleman. Antonyms: genuine partner, honest suitor, sincere individual. Savage Sentence: He played the Gallant perfectly, which is exactly why it felt so convincing. UnExpert Advice: If it feels rehearsed, it probably is.

Hedonistic Living /ˌhē-də-ˈni-stik ˈli-viŋ/ A lifestyle centered on pleasure, indulgence, and excess without regard for consequence. Synonyms: indulgence, excess, pleasure-seeking. Antonyms: discipline, restraint, responsibility. Savage Sentence: He called it freedom, but Hedonistic Living always leaves someone else cleaning up the mess. UnExpert Advice: If someone avoids consequences, they'll leave you to handle them.

Illicit Intrigue /i-ˈli-sət in-ˈtrēg/ Romantic entanglements fueled by secrecy, risk, and hidden agendas. Synonyms: secret affair, hidden drama, risky romance. Antonyms: transparency, honesty, straightforward relationship. Savage Sentence: The thrill pulled you in, but Illicit Intrigue is what kept everything unstable. UnExpert Advice: If secrecy is the foundation, chaos is the outcome.

Kept Woman / Dame Entretenue / Mistress /kept ˈwu̇-mən/ A woman financially supported by a patron in exchange for companionship and intimacy, without formal partnership status. Synonyms: dependent partner, transactional relationship, sponsored companion. Antonyms: independent partner, equal relationship, mutual commitment. Savage Sentence: The lifestyle looked secure, but the Kept Woman role never comes with real power. UnExpert Advice: If everything depends on what he gives, so does your place.

Libertinage /ˈli-bər-tə-ˌnäzh/ A philosophy and lifestyle centered on sensual freedom, intellectual detachment, and strategic pleasure-seeking. Synonyms: hedonism, seduction strategy, emotional detachment. Antonyms: morality, commitment, emotional connection. Savage Sentence: He dressed it up as philosophy, but Libertinage was just an excuse to never commit. UnExpert Advice: If someone treats love like a concept, don't expect them to treat you like a person.

Libertine /ˈli-bər-ˌtēn/ A person who rejects moral or social constraints in favor of pleasure, indulgence, and personal freedom. Synonyms: hedonist, seducer, rule-breaker. Antonyms: disciplined individual, committed partner, morally grounded person. Savage Sentence: The Libertine loved the idea of freedom more than he ever loved you. UnExpert Advice: If someone believes in nothing, don't expect them to believe in you.

Lothario /lō-ˈthär-ē-ō/ A cold, unfeeling seducer who pursues and ruins lovers for sport without remorse. Synonyms: heartless seducer, ruthless player, emotional destroyer. Antonyms: empathetic partner, sincere lover, emotionally accountable individual. Savage Sentence: You thought it was chemistry until the Lothario pattern showed up and you realized you weren't the first. UnExpert Advice: If they enjoy the damage they cause, it's not accidental.

Love as Strategy /ləv az ˈstra-tə-jē/ Using romance as a calculated tool to gain power, access, influence, or advantage. Synonyms: strategic romance, manipulation, calculated connection. Antonyms: genuine love, emotional authenticity, sincere connection. Savage Sentence: You were feeling it, but to him Love as Strategy was just another move on the board. UnExpert Advice: If someone benefits more than they feel, it's not love.

Maîtresse-en-titre /mā-ˈtres än ˈtē-trə/ An officially recognized chief mistress with social influence and proximity to power, often rivaling or undermining the primary partner. Synonyms: primary mistress, power partner, influential lover. Antonyms: spouse, equal partner, legitimate relationship. Savage Sentence: She wasn't hidden because the Maîtresse-en-titre role already came with status and limits. UnExpert Advice: If the hierarchy is built in, so is the imbalance.

Man of Pleasure /man əv ˈple-zhər/ A man devoted to indulgence, sensuality, and personal gratification above all else. Synonyms: hedonist, pleasure-seeker, indulgent individual. Antonyms: disciplined partner, responsible individual, committed lover. Savage Sentence: You wanted consistency, but a Man of

Pleasure only shows up for what feels good in the moment. UnExpert Advice: If pleasure is the priority, you won't be.

Marriage as Transaction /ˈmer-ij az tran-ˈzak-shən/ Viewing romantic partnership primarily as an exchange of wealth, status, or social advantage. Synonyms: strategic marriage, economic partnership, social contract. Antonyms: love-based marriage, emotional connection, mutual bond. Savage Sentence: It looked stable on the outside, but Marriage as Transaction always comes with conditions. UnExpert Advice: If the foundation is exchange, the relationship will always depend on it.

Mistress Dynamic /ˈmis-trəs dī-ˈna-mik/ A romantic relationship outside of marriage or social norms, often defined by secrecy, imbalance, or compartmentalization. Synonyms: affair dynamic, side relationship, hidden partner. Antonyms: primary relationship, transparency, commitment. Savage Sentence: You felt chosen until the Mistress Dynamic reminded you exactly where you stood. UnExpert Advice: If you're hidden, you're not chosen.

Patronage Romance /ˈpā-trə-nij rō-ˈmans/ A relationship in which affection or intimacy is tied to financial support, status, or influence. Synonyms: sponsored relationship, transactional love, power-based connection. Antonyms: independent love, equal partnership, mutual connection. Savage Sentence: It felt secure until Patronage Romance made it clear everything had a price. UnExpert Advice: If love depends on what's being given, it can be taken away just as easily.

Pleasure Gardens / Assembly Rooms /ˈple-zhər ˈgär-dənz/ Social venues designed for entertainment, flirtation, and romantic encounters, often encouraging anonymity and indulgence. Synonyms: social playground, flirtation space, indulgent environment. Antonyms: private setting, intentional dating, structured courtship. Savage Sentence: It felt like freedom in Pleasure Gardens until you realized no one there was looking for anything real. UnExpert Advice: Environments built for chaos rarely produce clarity.

Pleasure-Seeking /ˈple-zhər ˈsē-kiŋ/ Prioritizing immediate gratification and desire over long-term consequence or responsibility. Synonyms: indulgence, impulsivity, gratification-driven behavior. Antonyms: restraint, foresight, responsibility. Savage Sentence: You were thinking long-term while his Pleasure-Seeking kept everything stuck in the moment. UnExpert Advice: If someone avoids consequences, they'll leave you with them.

Power Play Romance /ˈpaù-ər plā rō-ˈmans/ A relationship dynamic where control, dominance, or influence is used to shape attraction and outcomes.

Synonyms: dominance dynamic, control-based relationship, manipulation. Antonyms: equality, mutual respect, balanced partnership. Savage Sentence: You thought it was passion, but Power Play Romance was really about who stayed in control. UnExpert Advice: If it feels like a game of control, stop playing.

Reputation Ruin /ˌre-pyə-ˈtā-shən ˈrün/ Damage to one's social standing or honor as a result of romantic or sexual involvement. Synonyms: scandal, disgrace, social fallout. Antonyms: respectability, reputation, social standing. Savage Sentence: You paid the price while Reputation Ruin somehow skipped right over him. UnExpert Advice: If the consequences aren't equal, neither is the relationship.

Roué /ˈrü-ā/ A jaded, experienced libertine worn down by excess but still actively pursuing indulgence. Synonyms: aging player, seasoned seducer, cynical hedonist. Antonyms: reformed partner, disciplined individual, committed lover. Savage Sentence: He called it experience, but the Roué energy was just the same behavior on repeat. UnExpert Advice: Experience doesn't equal growth—sometimes it just means repetition.

Scandal Culture /ˈskan-dəl ˈkəl-chər/ Public fascination with affairs, betrayal, and romantic impropriety as entertainment. Synonyms: gossip culture, public drama, social spectacle. Antonyms: privacy, discretion, integrity. Savage Sentence: Your real pain turned into content once Scandal Culture got involved. UnExpert Advice: If it thrives on attention, it's not about connection.

Secret Correspondence /ˈsē-krət ˌkȯr-ə-ˈspän-dən(t)s/ Hidden communication between lovers intended to conceal romantic or illicit involvement. Synonyms: secret messaging, hidden contact, covert communication. Antonyms: transparency, openness, honesty. Savage Sentence: You called it harmless until Secret Correspondence made it something you couldn't say out loud. UnExpert Advice: What's done in secret rarely survives in the open.

Seduction as Sport /sə-ˈdək-shən az spȯrt/ Treating romantic conquest as a game, competition, or form of entertainment. Synonyms: conquest mindset, competitive dating, game-playing. Antonyms: emotional connection, sincerity, mutual respect. Savage Sentence: You were catching feelings while Seduction as Sport kept him focused on the win. UnExpert Advice: If they're playing to win, you're playing to lose.

Sensual Excess /ˈsen(t)-shə-wəl ik-ˈses/ Overindulgence in physical pleasure, desire, or romantic experience without restraint. Synonyms: indulgence, overconsumption, pleasure-seeking. Antonyms: moderation, restraint, balance. Savage Sentence: It felt intoxicating at first, but Sensual Excess never knows when to stop. UnExpert Advice: Too much of anything eventually turns into a problem.

Social Climbing Romance /ˈsō-shəl ˈklī-miŋ rō-ˈmans/ Pursuing romantic relationships for the purpose of gaining status, influence, or upward mobility. Synonyms: opportunistic dating, status-seeking, strategic relationship. Antonyms: genuine love, equal partnership, authentic connection. Savage Sentence: You thought it was connection, but Social Climbing Romance had you positioned, not chosen. UnExpert Advice: If you're part of their plan, you're not part of their heart.

Womanizer /ˈwu̇-mə-ˌnī-zər/ A man who habitually pursues multiple women without intention of commitment. Synonyms: player, seducer, serial dater. Antonyms: loyal partner, committed individual, faithful lover. Savage Sentence: You wanted something real, but the Womanizer pattern had already decided your role. UnExpert Advice: Patterns don't change just because you want them to.

Georgian / Regency / Victorian

Accomplished Woman /ə-ˈkäm-pli-sht ˈwu̇-mən/ A woman trained in social graces, arts, and manners to increase her desirability in marriage. Synonyms: refined lady, polished woman, socially trained partner. Antonyms: untrained, unconventional woman, socially indifferent. Savage Sentence: They called her an Accomplished Woman, but everything she mastered was designed for someone else's approval. UnExpert Advice: If your worth is based on performance, it's never truly yours.

Advantageous Marriage /ˌad-vən-ˈtā-jəs ˈmer-ij/ A union formed for financial security, status, or social advancement rather than emotional connection. Synonyms: strategic marriage, status union, economic partnership. Antonyms: love-based marriage, emotional connection, mutual bond. Savage Sentence: It checked every box, but the Advantageous Marriage still felt like a deal, not a connection. UnExpert Advice: If it's built on advantage, it will always feel like a trade.

Breach of Promise /brēch əv ˈprä-məs/ The act of breaking a formal engagement, sometimes resulting in legal or social consequences. Synonyms: broken engagement, betrayal, withdrawn commitment. Antonyms: follow-through, loyalty, upheld promise. Savage Sentence: He called it a change of heart, but the Breach of Promise showed exactly what his word was worth. UnExpert Advice: If someone can walk away from a promise easily, they never valued it.

Calling On / Paying Calls /ˈkȯ-liŋ än • ˈpā-iŋ kȯlz/ The formal practice of visiting a woman in her home, often under supervision, to express romantic interest. Synonyms: formal courting, structured visitation, supervised pursuit. Antonyms: casual dating, private interaction, informal connection. Savage Sentence: If it was real, Calling On meant showing up where it counted—not hiding behind convenience. UnExpert Advice: Effort used to be visible—if it's hidden now, question why.

Chaperoned Interaction /ˈsha-pə-ˌrōnd in-tər-ˈak-shən/ Supervised time between unmarried individuals to ensure propriety and prevent scandal. Synonyms: supervised meeting, controlled interaction, monitored courtship. Antonyms: privacy, independence, unsupervised connection. Savage Sentence: The Chaperoned Interaction existed because no one trusted what would happen without it. UnExpert Advice: If boundaries require a witness, they're already being tested.

Compromising Position /ˈkäm-prə-ˌmī-ziŋ pə-ˈzi-shən/ Being seen in a situation that suggests impropriety, potentially damaging reputation regardless of truth. Synonyms: scandal risk, reputational danger, suggestive situation. Antonyms: propriety, respectability, innocence. Savage Sentence: It didn't matter what actually happened—the Compromising Position told a story no one questioned. UnExpert Advice: Perception can carry consequences reality never intended.

Courtship Ritual /ˈkȯrt-ˌship ˈri-chə-wəl/ A structured, socially approved process of romantic pursuit governed by etiquette and expectation. Synonyms: formal dating, traditional courting, social protocol. Antonyms: casual dating, spontaneity, unstructured relationships. Savage Sentence: The Courtship Ritual looked perfect on the surface, even when nothing underneath it was real. UnExpert Advice: Following the rules doesn't guarantee genuine intention.

Dear John Letter /dir jän ˈle-tər/ A formal written message used to end a romantic relationship or engagement. Synonyms: breakup letter, rejection note, written dismissal. Antonyms: reconciliation, continued commitment, communication. Savage Sentence: The Dear John Letter said everything he didn't have the courage to say in person. UnExpert Advice: Closure delivered without courage still says everything.

Delayed Confession /di-ˈlāyd kən-ˈfe-shən/ Withholding romantic feelings until circumstances, timing, or social rules make them acceptable to express. Synonyms: suppressed feelings, postponed admission, restrained emotion. Antonyms: direct expression, openness, emotional honesty. Savage Sentence: By the time the Delayed Confession finally came out, it had already lost its chance to matter. UnExpert Advice: Timing matters—but so does speaking up.

Duty vs. Desire /ˈdü-tē vs di-ˈzī(-ə)r/ The internal conflict between personal feelings and societal or familial obligations. Synonyms: obligation conflict, emotional sacrifice, social pressure. Antonyms: alignment, freedom, personal choice. Savage Sentence: Choosing Duty vs. Desire looked right to everyone else—and wrong to you for the rest of it. UnExpert Advice: If you ignore your feelings long enough, they don't disappear—they linger.

Eligible Match /ˈe-lə-jə-bəl mach/ A socially approved partner deemed suitable based on wealth, status, or reputation. Synonyms: desirable partner, socially approved match, advantageous choice. Antonyms: unsuitable partner, social mismatch, disapproved relationship. Savage Sentence: Everyone approved the Eligible Match except the part of you that had to live with it. UnExpert Advice: Compatibility on paper doesn't guarantee connection in real life.

Emotional Constancy /i-ˈmō-shə-nəl ˈkän-stən-sē/ Steady, unwavering affection maintained over time despite challenges or distance. Synonyms: loyalty, consistency, enduring love. Antonyms: inconsistency, fickleness, emotional instability. Savage Sentence: You brought Emotional Constancy into something that only worked when it was one-sided. UnExpert Advice: Consistency is rare—recognize it when you see it.

Emotional Restraint /i-ˈmō-shə-nəl ri-ˈstrānt/ Controlling or limiting the outward expression of feelings to maintain composure and propriety. Synonyms: self-control, composure, emotional discipline. Antonyms: emotional expression, vulnerability, openness. Savage Sentence: Emotional Restraint kept everything contained—even the things that needed to be said. UnExpert Advice: Composure can protect you—but it can also isolate you.

Emotional Suppression /i-ˈmō-shə-nəl sə-ˈpre-shən/ Denying or burying personal feelings to conform to societal expectations or avoid conflict. Synonyms: repression, denial, emotional avoidance. Antonyms: expression, authenticity, emotional honesty. Savage Sentence: You called it control, but

Emotional Suppression is why it kept coming back stronger. UnExpert Advice: What you suppress doesn't disappear—it builds.

Enduring Attachment /en-ˈdu̇r-iŋ ə-ˈta-chmənt/ Long-term loyalty or emotional connection that persists despite obstacles, distance, or time. Synonyms: lasting bond, loyalty, persistent love. Antonyms: detachment, abandonment, fleeting connection. Savage Sentence: You stayed through everything, but Enduring Attachment only works when both people are still there. UnExpert Advice: Endurance only matters if it's mutual.

Forced Marriage /fȯrst ˈmer-ij/ A union compelled by social pressure, scandal, or obligation rather than genuine choice. Synonyms: coerced union, obligation marriage, pressured commitment. Antonyms: voluntary marriage, free choice, mutual decision. Savage Sentence: Everyone called it stability, but Forced Marriage was just pressure dressed up as a solution. UnExpert Advice: If it starts from pressure, it rarely leads to peace.

Formal Calling /ˈfȯr-məl ˈkȯ-liŋ/ Structured visits between potential partners conducted under strict social etiquette and supervision. Synonyms: formal visitation, structured courtship, regulated interaction. Antonyms: casual dating, informal meetings, spontaneity. Savage Sentence: It all looked proper, but Formal Calling doesn't guarantee anything underneath it is real. UnExpert Advice: Following rules doesn't guarantee real intention.

Inheritance-Driven Match /in-ˈher-ə-təns ˈdri-vən mach/ A marriage influenced or determined by property, wealth, or family lineage. Synonyms: strategic union, wealth-based marriage, legacy match. Antonyms: love-based union, emotional choice, independent partnership. Savage Sentence: The Inheritance-Driven Match made sense financially, just not emotionally. UnExpert Advice: If money is the reason, it will always be the condition.

Language of Flowers / Floriography /ˈflȯr-ē-ˌä-grə-fē/ A coded system of communication using flowers, accessories, or gestures to convey romantic interest, rejection, or hidden messages. Synonyms: symbolic communication, coded signals, indirect expression. Antonyms: direct communication, clarity, openness. Savage Sentence: You were searching for meaning in petals while Language of Flowers replaced real communication entirely. UnExpert Advice: If it requires interpretation, it invites misinterpretation.

Lingering Glance /ˈliŋ-gə-riŋ glans/ A prolonged look used to subtly express attraction, curiosity, or desire without words. Synonyms: suggestive look, silent signal, unspoken interest. Antonyms: indifference, avoidance, disinterest. Savage Sentence: You built a whole moment off that look, but the

Lingering Glance didn't mean he was staying. UnExpert Advice: Not every signal is a promise.

Making Love /ˈmā-kiŋ ləv/ The act of courting or expressing romantic affection, historically used for emotional pursuit rather than physical intimacy. Synonyms: courting, romantic expression, emotional pursuit. Antonyms: indifference, neglect, emotional distance. Savage Sentence: He knew how to sound convincing, but Making Love through words never turned into action. UnExpert Advice: Words can feel like love—until you look at the actions.

Marriage Market /ˈmer-ij ˈmär-kət/ The social system in which individuals seek partners based on status, wealth, and suitability. Synonyms: social matchmaking, status pairing, strategic dating. Antonyms: organic connection, love-based pairing, spontaneous relationship. Savage Sentence: It stopped feeling personal once the Marriage Market made it clear you were being compared, not chosen. UnExpert Advice: If it feels transactional, it probably is.

Marriage of Convenience /ˈmer-ij əv kən-ˈvēn-yəns/ A practical union formed for mutual benefit rather than emotional connection. Synonyms: strategic marriage, functional partnership, pragmatic union. Antonyms: romantic marriage, emotional bond, passionate connection. Savage Sentence: Everything functioned smoothly, but the Marriage of Convenience never had to feel anything. UnExpert Advice: Convenience can build a life—but not always a connection.

Meaningful Silence /ˈmē-niŋ-fəl ˈsī-ləns/ Unspoken communication that conveys emotion, tension, or understanding without words. Synonyms: silent connection, unspoken bond, emotional awareness. Antonyms: verbal expression, clarity, direct communication. Savage Sentence: You kept assigning depth to the quiet, but Meaningful Silence isn't always as meaningful as it feels. UnExpert Advice: Silence can be meaningful—or it can be avoidance.

Moral Superiority Complex /ˈmȯr-əl sü-ˌpir-ē-ˈȯr-ə-tē ˈkäm-ˌpleks/ Judging others' relationships through rigid standards of propriety, often masking insecurity or control. Synonyms: judgment, moral rigidity, social policing. Antonyms: empathy, understanding, open-mindedness. Savage Sentence: They stayed loud about your choices while Moral Superiority Complex kept theirs conveniently hidden. UnExpert Advice: Judgment says more about them than it does about you.

Mutual Understanding /ˈmyü-chə-wəl ˌən-dər-ˈstan-diŋ/ A shared emotional connection built through observation, subtlety, and unspoken agreement. Synonyms: silent connection, intuitive bond, shared awareness. Antonyms:

miscommunication, confusion, disconnect. Savage Sentence: It felt aligned in the moment, but Mutual Understanding without confirmation still leaves room for confusion. UnExpert Advice: Assumed understanding can still lead to misunderstanding.

Pinning / Going Steady /ˈpi-niŋ • ˈgō-iŋ ˈste-dē/ Symbolic acts or tokens used to indicate exclusivity or romantic commitment. Synonyms: commitment signal, exclusivity marker, relationship token. Antonyms: casual dating, non-commitment, ambiguity. Savage Sentence: You treated it like commitment, but Pinning was just a symbol without the follow-through. UnExpert Advice: Symbols don't replace consistency.

Polite Rejection /pə-ˈlīt ri-ˈjek-shən/ Declining romantic interest with courtesy, indirect language, or softened expression. Synonyms: gentle refusal, soft rejection, indirect no. Antonyms: acceptance, encouragement, direct interest. Savage Sentence: It sounded gentle, but Polite Rejection still closed the door all the same. UnExpert Advice: If it's not a yes, it's a no—no matter how politely it's said.

Proper Gentleman /ˈprä-pər ˈjen-təl-mən/ A man who embodies respectability, restraint, and adherence to social etiquette. Synonyms: honorable man, respectable suitor, well-mannered partner. Antonyms: rogue, libertine, disrespectful individual. Savage Sentence: He played the part well, but Proper Gentleman behavior doesn't guarantee real character. UnExpert Advice: Good manners don't guarantee good intentions.

Public Perception /ˈpə-blik pər-ˈsep-shən/ How a relationship is viewed, judged, or interpreted by society at large. Synonyms: reputation, social image, public opinion. Antonyms: privacy, authenticity, personal truth. Savage Sentence: Everyone believed the image, but Public Perception never tells the full story. UnExpert Advice: What people think isn't always what's real.

Repressed Passion /ri-ˈprest ˈpa-shən/ Intense romantic or emotional feelings hidden beneath controlled, socially acceptable behavior. Synonyms: suppressed desire, hidden intensity, restrained emotion. Antonyms: open expression, emotional release, vulnerability. Savage Sentence: You kept it together on the outside, but Repressed Passion was doing all the damage underneath. UnExpert Advice: What you bury doesn't disappear—it waits.

Reputation Management /ˌre-pyə-ˈtā-shən ˈma-nij-mənt/ Deliberate efforts to protect or shape one's social image in romantic or personal matters. Synonyms: image control, social strategy, perception management. Antonyms: authenticity, transparency, indifference to opinion. Savage Sentence: You thought it was about you, but Reputation Management made sure the image always came first. UnExpert Advice: If image comes first, truth comes last.

Reserved Affection /ri-ˈzərvd ə-ˈfek-shən/ Controlled or understated expression of romantic feeling, often to maintain propriety. Synonyms: restrained love, subtle affection, emotional control. Antonyms: open affection, emotional expression, demonstrative love. Savage Sentence: It never crossed the line into real security because Reserved Affection always stopped just short. UnExpert Advice: If it's always held back, it's never fully given.

Respectability Politics /ri-ˌspek-tə-ˈbi-lə-tē ˈpä-lə-tiks/ Regulating behavior to align with societal expectations in order to preserve reputation and status. Synonyms: social conformity, image control, behavioral restriction. Antonyms: authenticity, self-expression, independence. Savage Sentence: Happiness took a backseat the second Respectability Politics started running the show. UnExpert Advice: If you're performing for approval, you're not living for yourself.

Scandal Risk /ˈskan-dəl risk/ The potential damage to reputation caused by perceived or actual improper romantic behavior. Synonyms: reputational danger, social fallout, risk of disgrace. Antonyms: propriety, safety, social approval. Savage Sentence: It didn't have to be real for Scandal Risk to make it ruin everything anyway. UnExpert Advice: Perception can ruin what reality never did.

Secret Engagement /ˈsē-krət in-ˈgāj-mənt/ A hidden promise of marriage kept from public or familial knowledge. Synonyms: private commitment, concealed engagement, hidden promise. Antonyms: public engagement, open commitment, transparency. Savage Sentence: You had the promise, but Secret Engagement kept you invisible the entire time. UnExpert Advice: If it can't be acknowledged, it can't be secured.

Slow-Burn Romance /slō bərn rō-ˈmans/ A gradual development of romantic feelings over time, often built through familiarity and trust. Synonyms: gradual love, developing connection, steady bond. Antonyms: instant attraction, impulsive love, fleeting connection. Savage Sentence: It didn't rush, and that's exactly why the Slow-Burn Romance actually meant something. UnExpert Advice: What grows slowly often lasts longer.

Social Consequence /ˈsō-shəl ˈkän-sə-ˌkwens/ The impact on status, reputation, or future prospects resulting from romantic behavior. Synonyms: fallout, repercussion, societal impact. Antonyms: approval, acceptance, stability. Savage Sentence: One choice turned into a Social Consequence that followed you long after it was over. UnExpert Advice: Some risks don't just affect the moment—they follow you.

Social Climbing Courtship /ˈsō-shəl ˈklī-miŋ ˈkȯrt-ˌship/ Pursuing romantic relationships to elevate social class, status, or position. Synonyms: opportunistic dating, status-seeking, strategic courtship. Antonyms: genuine connection, equal partnership, authentic love. Savage Sentence: It felt personal until Social Climbing Courtship made it clear you were part of the strategy. UnExpert Advice: If you're part of their ladder, you're not part of their life.

Unrequited Admiration /ˌən-ri-ˈkwī-təd ˌad-mə-ˈrā-shən/ Silent or unexpressed affection that is not returned or acknowledged. Synonyms: one-sided admiration, hidden love, unreturned feelings. Antonyms: mutual admiration, shared affection, recognition. Savage Sentence: You kept showing up with Unrequited Admiration while he never even noticed. UnExpert Advice: If it's not acknowledged, it's not mutual.

Unspoken Attraction /ˌən-ˈspō-kən ə-ˈtrak-shən/ Romantic interest conveyed through subtle cues, behavior, or tension rather than direct expression. Synonyms: silent chemistry, subtle interest, nonverbal attraction. Antonyms: direct communication, clarity, explicit expression. Savage Sentence: It felt obvious, but Unspoken Attraction doesn't mean anything without actual action. UnExpert Advice: If it's never spoken, it can't be confirmed.

Veiled Disinterest /vāld dis-ˈin-trəst/ Subtle or indirect signals indicating lack of romantic interest while maintaining politeness. Synonyms: polite indifference, soft rejection, indirect dismissal. Antonyms: clear interest, direct attraction, open engagement. Savage Sentence: They kept it polite, but Veiled Disinterest made sure you never actually got anything real. UnExpert Advice: If the energy isn't there, don't try to translate it into something else.

Virtue Signaling (Historical) /ˈvər-chü ˈsig-nə-liŋ/ Performing moral behavior or propriety to maintain social status and public approval. Synonyms: moral performance, social posturing, reputation control. Antonyms: authenticity, genuine character, private integrity. Savage Sentence: It looked righteous on the surface, but Virtue Signaling made sure the image mattered more than the truth. UnExpert Advice: If it's done for an audience, it's not about values—it's about image.

Window Signaling / Fan Flirtation / Parasol Codes /ˈwin-dō ˈsig-nə-liŋ/ Non-verbal gestures and signals using objects or positioning to communicate romantic interest, curiosity, or dismissal discreetly. Synonyms: coded flirting, subtle signaling, indirect communication. Antonyms: direct communication, clarity, explicit expression. Savage Sentence: You kept reading into it, but Window Signaling was never clear enough to mean anything solid. UnExpert Advice: If it's unclear, it's unreliable.

Yearning Beneath Restraint /ˈyər-niŋ bi-ˈnēth ri-ˈstrānt/ Deep romantic desire hidden beneath controlled behavior, distance, or social decorum. Synonyms: suppressed longing, hidden desire, restrained emotion. Antonyms: open expression, emotional release, vulnerability. Savage Sentence: You held it all in, and Yearning Beneath Restraint made sure nothing ever actually happened. UnExpert Advice: What stays unexpressed rarely gets fulfilled.

Early 20th Century / Old Hollywood Romance

Welcome to Old Hollywood — where everything looks glamorous and everything is falling apart behind the scenes.

Blind Date /ˈblīnd dāt/ A social outing with someone previously unknown, often arranged by a third party. Synonyms: setup date, arranged meeting, unknown match. Antonyms: familiar partner, known connection, established relationship. Savage Sentence: It could go either way, and the Blind Date made sure you had zero control over which. UnExpert Advice: Low expectations make for better outcomes.

Broken Idealism /ˈbrō-kən ī-ˈdi-(ə-)ˌlī-zəm/ Continuing to believe in romantic ideals despite repeated disappointment or disillusionment. Synonyms: romantic denial, hopeful persistence, emotional disillusionment. Antonyms: realism, acceptance, emotional clarity. Savage Sentence: You kept holding on, but Broken Idealism was doing all the heavy lifting against reality. UnExpert Advice: Hope is powerful—but it shouldn't ignore reality.

Carry a Torch /ˈka-rē ə tȯrch/ To remain emotionally attached to someone, often unrequited or from the past. Synonyms: lingering attachment, unresolved feelings, unrequited love. Antonyms: closure, moving on, emotional release. Savage Sentence: You kept Carrying a Torch long after they stopped even thinking about you. UnExpert Advice: If it's not returned, it's not meant to stay.

Casting Couch /ˈkas-tiŋ kau̇ch/ The exploitation of power in which opportunities are exchanged for sexual favors, often under coercion. Synonyms: exploitation, coercion, abuse of power. Antonyms: merit-based success, ethical opportunity, consent. Savage Sentence: It looked like opportunity, but the Casting Couch made the real cost impossible to ignore. UnExpert Advice: If power is involved, consent gets complicated.

Curated Romance /ˈkyůr-ā-təd rō-ˈmans/ Presenting a relationship as perfect or ideal while concealing its flaws or reality. Synonyms: performative relationship, image control, filtered love. Antonyms: authenticity, transparency, real connection. Savage Sentence: Everyone believed it, but Curated Romance only showed what was safe to see. UnExpert Advice: If it's curated, it's not complete.

Dangerous Charm /ˈdān-jə-rəs chärm/ An alluring personality that masks risk, instability, or harmful intent. Synonyms: seductive danger, risky attraction, toxic charisma. Antonyms: safety, sincerity, emotional stability. Savage Sentence: You felt pulled in, and Dangerous Charm made it hard to care about the warning signs. UnExpert Advice: Attraction doesn't cancel out danger.

Dramatic Breakup /drə-ˈma-tik ˈbrāk-ˌəp/ An emotionally intense or public separation marked by conflict, spectacle, or heightened emotion. Synonyms: explosive breakup, emotional fallout, public split. Antonyms: calm separation, mutual closure, peaceful ending. Savage Sentence: It escalated fast, and the Dramatic Breakup made sure everyone felt it. UnExpert Advice: The louder it ends, the less stable it was.

Drugstore Cowboy /ˈdrəg-ˌstȯr ˈkaů-ˌbȯi/ A man who loiters in public spaces seeking to flirt with or pick up women, often lacking substance or sincerity. Synonyms: street flirt, opportunist, pickup artist. Antonyms: intentional dater, respectful pursuer, genuine partner. Savage Sentence: It felt personal until the Drugstore Cowboy proved he approached everyone the same way. UnExpert Advice: If they're always available, they're rarely intentional.

Emotional Detachment (Modern) /i-ˈmō-shə-nəl di-ˈta-chmənt/ Withholding vulnerability or emotional connection while still participating in romantic involvement. Synonyms: emotional unavailability, distance, guardedness. Antonyms: vulnerability, connection, emotional presence. Savage Sentence: You kept trying to connect, but Emotional Detachment kept every door closed. UnExpert Advice: If they won't connect, stop trying to force it.

Emotional Isolation /i-ˈmō-shə-nəl ˌī-sə-ˈlā-shən/ Feeling alone or disconnected despite being in a romantic relationship. Synonyms: loneliness, disconnection, emotional distance. Antonyms: closeness, intimacy, emotional support. Savage Sentence: You stayed in it, but Emotional Isolation made it feel like you were doing it alone. UnExpert Advice: If you feel alone in a relationship, something's missing.

Emotional Substitution /i-ˈmō-shə-nəl ˌsəb-stə-ˈtü-shən/ Using a new partner to replace unresolved feelings from a previous relationship. Synonyms: rebound, emotional replacement, avoidance. Antonyms: healing, closure, emotional processing. Savage Sentence: It felt real to you, but Emotional Substitution made it temporary from the start. UnExpert Advice: If they haven't healed, you're filling a gap—not building something new.

Emotional Turbulence /i-ˈmō-shə-nəl ˈtər-byə-lən(t)s/ Volatile, unstable romantic dynamics marked by highs, lows, and unpredictability. Synonyms: chaos, instability, emotional swings. Antonyms: stability, balance, consistency. Savage Sentence: The highs kept you hooked, but Emotional Turbulence made sure the lows always followed. UnExpert Advice: If it's always up and down, it's not grounded.

Fast Love /fast ləv/ Rapid, intense romantic involvement that escalates quickly without a stable foundation. Synonyms: whirlwind romance, instant connection, impulsive love. Antonyms: slow-burn romance, gradual connection, stability. Savage Sentence: It felt undeniable in the moment, but Fast Love skipped everything that actually makes something last. UnExpert Advice: Speed can feel like chemistry—but it often skips the important parts.

Femme Fatale /fem fə-ˈtal/ A captivating, seductive woman whose allure leads others into emotional or personal downfall. Synonyms: seductress, dangerous woman, alluring manipulator. Antonyms: safe partner, grounded individual, emotionally stable person. Savage Sentence: You thought you were in control until the Femme Fatale dynamic made it clear you never were. UnExpert Advice: Not all attraction is safe—some of it is designed to destabilize.

Flapper /ˈfla-pər/ A bold, liberated young woman embracing independence, pleasure, and social rebellion against traditional norms. Synonyms: free spirit, party girl, rebellious woman. Antonyms: traditional woman, restrained individual, conservative partner. Savage Sentence: They called her too much, but the Flapper energy was just freedom they couldn't control. UnExpert Advice: Freedom will always be criticized by those who don't have it.

Flat Tire (Pill / Pickle / Drag) /flat tī(-ə)r/ A dull, disappointing, or uninspiring romantic partner or date. Synonyms: bore, dud, low-energy partner. Antonyms: exciting partner, engaging date, dynamic personality. Savage Sentence: You kept trying to revive it, but Flat Tire energy doesn't suddenly come to life. UnExpert Advice: If it's draining, it's not worth forcing.

Forbidden Affair (Modernized) /fər-ˈbi-dən ə-ˈfer/ A relationship that defies social, moral, or relational boundaries in a more modern context. Synonyms: taboo romance, illicit relationship, hidden affair. Antonyms: accepted relationship, transparency, ethical connection. Savage Sentence: The excitement pulled you in, but the Forbidden Affair made sure the consequences stayed. UnExpert Advice: If the thrill comes from the risk, the fallout comes with it.

Gigolo /ˈji-gə-ˌlō/ A man who provides companionship or intimacy in exchange for financial benefit or gifts. Synonyms: paid companion, transactional partner, sponsored dater. Antonyms: independent partner, mutual relationship, non-transactional love. Savage Sentence: It felt like attention, but the Gigolo dynamic made it clear it came with a price. UnExpert Advice: If it's tied to what you provide, it's not unconditional.

Glamour Illusion /ˈgla-mər i-ˈlü-zhən/ The projection of a perfect, enviable relationship while concealing dysfunction or instability. Synonyms: image control, performative perfection, curated reality. Antonyms: authenticity, transparency, real connection. Savage Sentence: Everyone envied it, but the Glamour Illusion kept the truth completely out of sight. UnExpert Advice: Perfection is usually edited.

Gold Digger /ˈgōld ˌdi-gər/ Someone who pursues romantic relationships primarily for financial gain or status. Synonyms: opportunist, status-seeker, transactional dater. Antonyms: genuine partner, independent individual, authentic connection. Savage Sentence: It looked like love from the outside, but the Gold Digger motive was always driving it. UnExpert Advice: If money is the motive, it will always be the measure.

Hopeful Cynicism /ˈhōp-fəl ˈsi-nə-ˌsi-zəm/ Simultaneously desiring love while expecting disappointment or failure. Synonyms: guarded hope, romantic skepticism, emotional conflict. Antonyms: optimism, trust, emotional openness. Savage Sentence: You kept showing up, but Hopeful Cynicism made sure you never fully believed in it. UnExpert Advice: If you expect failure, you'll find it.

Impulsive Affair /im-ˈpəl-siv ə-ˈfer/ A spontaneous romantic involvement driven by emotion rather than intention or thought. Synonyms: reckless romance, spur-of-the-moment connection, emotional decision. Antonyms: intentional relationship, thoughtful choice, stability. Savage Sentence: It felt right for a second, but the Impulsive Affair couldn't hold up anywhere else. UnExpert Advice: Impulse fades—consequences don't.

It Girl / "It" Factor /it gərl/ A woman possessing magnetic charm, charisma, and effortless allure that draws attention and admiration. Synonyms: charismatic figure, social magnet, captivating personality. Antonyms: overlooked individual, low presence, lack of appeal. Savage Sentence: Everyone wanted access, but the It Girl reality was that no one actually saw her. UnExpert Advice: Attention isn't the same as connection.

Lonely Together /ˈlōn-lē tə-ˈge-thər/ Being in a relationship while feeling emotionally disconnected or alone. Synonyms: emotional isolation, disconnected partnership, hollow relationship. Antonyms: intimacy, connection, emotional closeness. Savage Sentence: You stayed in it, but Lonely Together made it clear presence isn't the same as connection. UnExpert Advice: Company doesn't guarantee connection.

Love Addiction (Early Concept) /ləv ə-ˈdik-shən/ Dependence on romantic intensity, validation, or emotional highs as a source of identity or fulfillment. Synonyms: emotional dependency, validation-seeking, obsession. Antonyms: independence, emotional balance, self-sufficiency. Savage Sentence: It felt like love, but Love Addiction kept pulling you back for the feeling, not the person. UnExpert Advice: If you need it to feel whole, it's not healthy.

Love as Performance /ləv az pər-ˈfȯr-məns/ Acting out romance for appearance, validation, or public approval rather than genuine connection. Synonyms: performative love, staged relationship, image-driven romance. Antonyms: authenticity, private connection, genuine intimacy. Savage Sentence: You thought it was real, but Love as Performance only existed when someone was watching. UnExpert Advice: If it needs an audience, it's not real.

Missed Connection /mist kə-ˈnek-shən/ A romantic opportunity that never fully develops due to timing, circumstance, or hesitation. Synonyms: lost chance, timing issue, unrealized connection. Antonyms: fulfilled relationship, mutual timing, successful connection. Savage Sentence: It felt like it could've been something, but Missed Connection is where timing wins over potential. UnExpert Advice: Potential means nothing without timing.

Modern Love /ˈmä-dərn ləv/ Romance shaped by shifting roles, independence, and evolving social expectations. Synonyms: contemporary dating, evolving relationships, independent partnership. Antonyms: traditional courtship, rigid roles, structured relationships. Savage Sentence: You had options, but Modern Love made clarity harder to find. UnExpert Advice: More options don't always mean better outcomes.

Necking (Necking Party) /ˈne-kiŋ/ Passionate kissing and physical affection short of intercourse, often considered scandalous in its time. Synonyms: heavy makeout, physical affection, intimate contact. Antonyms: restraint, distance, formality. Savage Sentence: You said it was casual, but Necking still crossed a line that feelings don't ignore. UnExpert Advice: Physical closeness still carries emotional weight.

On-Again, Off-Again Love /än ə-ˈgen, ȯf ə-ˈgen ləv/ A cyclical relationship marked by repeated breakups and reunions. Synonyms: unstable relationship, recurring romance, inconsistent bond. Antonyms: stable relationship, consistency, commitment. Savage Sentence: You kept giving it another chance, but On-Again, Off-Again Love never actually changes the outcome. UnExpert Advice: If it keeps ending, that's your answer.

Performative Passion /pər-ˈfȯr-mə-tiv ˈpa-shən/ Exaggerated displays of affection or emotion intended to impress or influence others. Synonyms: dramatic affection, staged intensity, emotional display. Antonyms: genuine emotion, quiet connection, authenticity. Savage Sentence: It felt overwhelming, but Performative Passion was more about impact than truth. UnExpert Advice: If it feels like a show, it probably is.

Petting (Petting Party) /ˈpe-tiŋ/ Physical intimacy involving touching, caressing, and affectionate behavior short of intercourse, often in social group settings. Synonyms: heavy foreplay, intimate touching, group affection. Antonyms: restraint, distance, formality. Savage Sentence: You thought it stayed light, but Petting blurred lines faster than you expected. UnExpert Advice: Physical intimacy doesn't stay casual for everyone.

Public Romance /ˈpə-blik rō-ˈmans/ A relationship openly displayed and subject to attention, scrutiny, or commentary. Synonyms: visible relationship, exposed love, public display. Antonyms: private relationship, discretion, intimacy. Savage Sentence: Everyone had an opinion, but Public Romance never showed what was actually happening. UnExpert Advice: Visibility doesn't equal depth.

Push-Pull Dynamic /ˈpu̇sh-ˈpu̇l dī-ˈna-mik/ A pattern of alternating closeness and distance that creates emotional instability. Synonyms: hot-and-cold behavior, inconsistency, emotional fluctuation. Antonyms: stability, consistency, secure attachment. Savage Sentence: You kept reacting, but the Push-Pull Dynamic was controlling the entire pace. UnExpert Advice: If it's inconsistent, it's intentional.

Rebound Romance /ˈrē-ˌbau̇nd rō-ˈmans/ A relationship entered quickly after a breakup to cope with unresolved emotions. Synonyms: emotional replacement, quick recovery attempt, distraction. Antonyms: healing, closure, emotional processing. Savage Sentence: It felt real in the moment, but Rebound Romance was never meant to last. UnExpert Advice: If they haven't healed, you're not building—you're covering.

Reputation Fallout /ˌre-pyə-ˈtā-shən ˈfȯl-ˌau̇t/ Negative impact on one's image or standing following romantic exposure or scandal. Synonyms: backlash, social damage, reputational harm. Antonyms: approval, stability, positive perception. Savage Sentence: The relationship ended, but Reputation Fallout stayed long after it was over. UnExpert Advice: Some choices follow you longer than the moment.

Romantic Disillusionment /rō-ˈman-tik ˌdi-sə-ˈlü-zhən-mənt/ The loss of belief in idealized love after disappointment or repeated failure. Synonyms: emotional burnout, lost faith, cynicism. Antonyms: hope, optimism, belief in love. Savage Sentence: You didn't plan on it, but Romantic Disillusionment built slowly with every letdown. UnExpert Advice: Disappointment teaches—but don't let it define everything.

Romantic Escapism /rō-ˈman-tik i-ˈskā-ˌpi-zəm/ Using romance as a way to avoid reality, problems, or personal growth. Synonyms: avoidance, fantasy living, emotional escape. Antonyms: accountability, realism, personal growth. Savage Sentence: It felt like love, but Romantic Escapism was just a break from everything you didn't want to face. UnExpert Advice: Love shouldn't be an escape—it should add to your reality.

Scandalous Affair /ˈskan-də-ləs ə-ˈfer/ A highly visible or socially risky romantic relationship that invites judgment or controversy. Synonyms: public scandal, illicit romance, controversial relationship. Antonyms: private relationship, accepted union, discretion. Savage Sentence: It felt exciting at first, but a Scandalous Affair doesn't stay hidden for long. UnExpert Advice: If it thrives on secrecy, it won't survive exposure.

Secret Romance /ˈsē-krət rō-ˈmans/ A romantic relationship deliberately kept hidden from public or social awareness. Synonyms: hidden relationship, private affair, concealed love. Antonyms: public relationship, transparency, openness. Savage Sentence: It felt intimate at first, but Secret Romance made sure you stayed invisible the entire time. UnExpert Advice: If it has to stay hidden, ask who benefits from that.

Self-Destructive Love /self di-ˈstrək-tiv ləv/ Engaging in relationships that cause emotional, mental, or personal harm. Synonyms: toxic love, harmful attachment, destructive relationship. Antonyms: healthy love, self-respect, emotional safety. Savage Sentence: You saw the damage clearly, but Self-Destructive Love kept pulling you back anyway. UnExpert Advice: If it's breaking you, it's not building anything.

Serial Romance /ˈsir-ē-əl rō-ˈmans/ Repeated cycles of intense but short-lived romantic relationships. Synonyms: serial dating, repeated flings, pattern relationships. Antonyms: long-term commitment, stability, consistency. Savage Sentence: It felt different this time, but Serial Romance always ends the same way. UnExpert Advice: If the pattern repeats, it's not coincidence.

Sheba /ˈshē-bə/ A woman with strong sex appeal, charisma, and seductive presence, often aware of her influence. Synonyms: siren, seductress, magnetic woman. Antonyms: understated individual, low-profile presence, reserved partner. Savage Sentence: She didn't chase anything, and the Sheba energy made sure everything came to her instead. UnExpert Advice: Power is fine—how it's used is what matters.

Sheik /shēk/ A charismatic, brooding man whose allure and mystique create intense romantic attraction. Synonyms: heartthrob, seducer, charismatic man. Antonyms: unremarkable partner, emotionally unavailable individual, dull presence. Savage Sentence: You felt everything instantly, but the Sheik effect disappeared just as fast. UnExpert Advice: Charisma can pull you in—but it won't keep you grounded.

Sleep Around /slēp ə-ˈrau̇nd/ Engaging in casual sexual relationships with multiple partners without commitment. Synonyms: promiscuity, casual sex, non-commitment. Antonyms: exclusivity, commitment, monogamy. Savage Sentence: They called it freedom, but Sleep Around behavior left you feeling anything but fulfilled. UnExpert Advice: If there's no consistency, don't expect stability.

Spooning /ˈspü-niŋ/ Close physical cuddling or affectionate contact, often leading to deeper intimacy. Synonyms: cuddling, physical closeness, affectionate contact. Antonyms: distance, detachment, formality. Savage Sentence: It started off simple, but Spooning blurred the line between comfort and attachment fast. UnExpert Advice: Physical closeness rarely stays casual for everyone involved.

Struggle Buggy /ˈstrə-gəl ˈbə-gē/ A car used as a private space for romantic or physical encounters. Synonyms: makeout spot, private escape, hidden space.

Antonyms: public setting, structured environment, supervision. Savage Sentence: You thought it was just a drive, but the Struggle Buggy made the situation a lot more than that. UnExpert Advice: If the setting changes, so do the expectations.

Studio System Affairs /ˈstü-dē-ō ˈsi-stəm ə-ˈferz/ Hidden or managed romantic relationships within the entertainment industry, often controlled or concealed for image purposes. Synonyms: managed romance, secret industry relationship, controlled narrative. Antonyms: authentic relationship, transparency, personal freedom. Savage Sentence: It looked perfect publicly, but Studio System Affairs kept the truth completely controlled. UnExpert Advice: If it's being managed, it's not fully yours.

Sugar Daddy /ˈshu̇-gər ˈda-dē/ An older, wealthy individual who provides financial support or gifts in exchange for companionship or intimacy. Synonyms: benefactor, patron, transactional partner. Antonyms: equal partner, independent relationship, mutual support. Savage Sentence: It felt secure, but the Sugar Daddy dynamic always depended on what was being provided. UnExpert Advice: If it depends on what's given, it can be taken away.

Timing Tragedy /ˈtī-miŋ ˈtra-jə-dē/ A relationship that fails due to circumstances or timing rather than incompatibility. Synonyms: missed timing, situational failure, lost opportunity. Antonyms: aligned timing, successful relationship, mutual readiness. Savage Sentence: You both felt it, but Timing Tragedy made sure it never actually worked out. UnExpert Advice: Right person, wrong time is still wrong.

Two-Time / Two-Timer /ˈtü-ˌtīm/ Engaging in deception or infidelity by maintaining multiple romantic partners simultaneously. Synonyms: cheater, double-dealer, dishonest partner. Antonyms: faithful partner, honest individual, committed lover. Savage Sentence: You believed the story, but the Two-Timer reality meant you were never the only one. UnExpert Advice: If they can lie once, they can lie twice.

Whirlwind Romance /ˈwərl-ˌwind rō-ˈmans/ A fast-moving, passionate relationship that develops quickly and intensely. Synonyms: rapid romance, intense connection, impulsive love. Antonyms: slow-burn romance, gradual development, stability. Savage Sentence: It felt like everything at once, but Whirlwind Romance rarely gives anything time to last. UnExpert Advice: Fast beginnings don't guarantee lasting endings.

Acronyms & Text Culture

AF / ASF (As Fuck) /ˌā-ˈef • ˌā-ˈes-ˈef/ Used to intensify attraction or behavior, often exaggerating feelings or perceptions in early dating stages. Synonyms: emotional amplification, hype language, intensity inflation. Antonyms: grounded perception, emotional regulation, realism. Savage Sentence: The AF had you calling him "perfect ASF" after two dates like your judgment took a vacation. UnExpert Advice: If everything feels extreme that fast, it's probably not depth—it's dopamine.

AYCE (All You Can Eat) /ˌā-ˈwī-ˈsē-ˈē/ Treating dating like unlimited access—consuming attention, validation, sex, or options without intention or limits. Synonyms: unlimited access mindset, validation binge, roster gluttony. Antonyms: intentional dating, boundaries, selective investment. Savage Sentence: The AYCE energy had him sampling everyone while committing to absolutely no one. UnExpert Advice: If someone treats dating like a buffet, don't volunteer to be on the menu.

BDE (Big Dick Energy) /big dik ˈe-nər-jē/ Effortless confidence, calm presence, and secure energy that doesn't need validation or attention. Synonyms: quiet confidence, grounded energy, secure presence. Antonyms: try-hard energy, insecurity, overcompensation. Savage Sentence: The BDE walked in, said nothing, and still had more presence than everyone else trying too hard. UnExpert Advice: If someone has to prove it, they don't have it.

BDSM /ˌbē-dē-ˌes-ˈem/ Consensual power dynamics involving dominance, submission, and control within clearly defined boundaries. Synonyms: power play dynamic, consensual control, kink structure. Antonyms: coercion, manipulation, non-consensual dynamics. Savage Sentence: The BDSM only works when both people actually respect the rules—otherwise it's just control disguised as kink. UnExpert Advice: Without consent and communication, it's not a dynamic—it's a problem.

DL (Down Low) /ˈdī-ˈel/ Secretly engaging in same-sex relationships or behavior while presenting as heterosexual publicly. Synonyms: hidden sexuality, double life, secret identity. Antonyms: openness, authenticity, transparency. Savage Sentence: The DL kept two completely separate lives and expected both to never collide. UnExpert Advice: If someone is hiding core parts of themselves, you're not getting the full picture.

DTR (Define The Relationship) /ˌdē-tē-ˈär/ The conversation meant to clarify intentions, labels, and expectations. Synonyms: clarity talk, label conversation, relationship checkpoint. Antonyms: avoidance, ambiguity, situationship limbo. Savage Sentence: The DTR kept getting delayed because clarity would've ended the benefits. UnExpert Advice: If someone avoids defining it, they're benefiting from not doing so.

DTF (Down To Fuck) /ˌdē-tē-ˈef/ Openly seeking casual sex without emotional involvement or commitment. Synonyms: hookup ready, casual intent, no-strings energy. Antonyms: relationship-minded, intentional dating. Savage Sentence: The DTF energy was clear—just not honest about what came after. UnExpert Advice: Believe the intention when it's shown early.

ENM (Ethical Non-Monogamy) /ˌē-ˌen-ˈem/ Open relationship structures based on consent, communication, and agreed boundaries. Synonyms: open relationship, poly dynamics, consensual non-exclusivity. Antonyms: cheating, secrecy, dishonesty. Savage Sentence: The ENM only works when it's actually ethical—otherwise it's just cheating with better branding. UnExpert Advice: Transparency is the only thing that makes it ethical.

FB (F*ck Buddy) /ˌef-ˈbē/ A purely physical arrangement with little to no emotional connection, often less "friendly" than FWB. Synonyms: casual hookup partner, physical-only connection, no-strings sex. Antonyms: emotional relationship, mutual connection, commitment. Savage Sentence: The FB kept things simple—just not respectful or meaningful. UnExpert Advice: If it's only physical, don't expect emotional depth to magically appear.

FOMO Dating /ˈfō-mō ˈdā-tiŋ/ Constantly keeping options open out of fear something better is around the corner. Synonyms: option addiction, grass-is-greener mindset, roster mentality. Antonyms: presence, commitment, intentional choice. Savage Sentence: The FOMO Dating had you chasing possibilities while missing what was right in front of you. UnExpert Advice: If you're always looking for better, you'll never recognize good.

FWB (Friends with Benefits) /ef-də-bəl-yü-bē/ A supposedly casual sexual arrangement between "friends" that almost always becomes emotionally messy, unbalanced, or one-sided. Synonyms: situationship with orgasms, benefits without labels, delayed heartbreak Antonyms: clear boundaries, mutual emotional detachment, genuine friendship Savage Sentence: They started as FWB and somehow she was catching feelings while he was still treating her like a scheduled subscription. UnExpert Advice: "No strings" almost never stays that way. If you can't handle the emotional fallout, don't sign up for the benefits.

GFE (Girlfriend Experience) /ˌjē-ef-ˈē/ A transactional or semi-transactional dynamic where someone provides emotional and physical "girlfriend" energy without actual commitment. Synonyms: rented intimacy, paid companionship, simulated relationship. Antonyms: genuine partnership, mutual emotional investment. Savage Sentence: The GFE gave him girlfriend access while he made sure you never got the title. UnExpert Advice: If you're doing relationship work without relationship security, you're being used.

HABs (Husbands and Boyfriends) /habz/ Male partners of high-profile women, often referenced in media or social circles. Synonyms: male counterpart, partner label, tabloid term. Antonyms: single status, independent identity. Savage Sentence: The HABs were present—but rarely the main story. UnExpert Advice: Labels don't define value—behavior does.

ILY / ILU (I Love You) /ˌī-el-ˈwī/ Expressing love—often prematurely or casually in modern dating, sometimes used to fast-track intimacy. Synonyms: emotional escalation, early attachment signal, love inflation. Antonyms: paced connection, earned intimacy, emotional restraint. Savage Sentence: The ILY showed up before the consistency did—and disappeared just as fast. UnExpert Advice: Love said too early is often about feeling, not commitment.

IOI (Indicators of Interest) /ˌī-ō-ˈī/ A pickup-artist term for reading and interpreting signals of attraction, often used to "game" interactions rather than build real connection. Synonyms: attraction cues, scripted flirting, calculated reading. Antonyms: natural chemistry, genuine interaction. Savage Sentence: The IOI had him analyzing your every move instead of just acting like a normal human. UnExpert Advice: If someone is studying you instead of connecting with you, you're being played.

IRL (In Real Life) /ˌī-ˌär-ˈel/ The reality of a person or connection outside of apps, texts, or curated online presence. Synonyms: offline reality, real-world interaction, actual behavior. Antonyms: online persona, curated identity, digital illusion. Savage Sentence: The IRL didn't match the energy they sold online. UnExpert Advice: Always trust what shows up in real life.

LBH (Loser Back Home) /ˈel-bē-ˈāch/ Someone who seeks validation or dating success abroad because they struggle to attract partners in their own environment. Synonyms: passport dater, validation traveler, relocation player. Antonyms: confident dater, self-sufficient attraction. Savage Sentence: The

LBH had to leave the country to feel chosen. UnExpert Advice: Changing locations doesn't fix patterns.

LDR (Long-Distance Relationship) /ˌel-ˌdē-ˈär/ A relationship maintained across physical distance, requiring high communication and trust. Synonyms: distance dating, remote relationship, long-distance love. Antonyms: proximity dating, local relationship. Savage Sentence: The LDR worked—until distance became an excuse. UnExpert Advice: Effort matters more when distance exists.

MIA (Missing In Action) /ˌem-ī-ˈā/ Someone who suddenly disappears from communication or plans with no explanation. Synonyms: sudden vanish, soft ghost, unexplained absence. Antonyms: consistent communicator, reliable presence. Savage Sentence: The MIA turned daily texts into complete silence like the connection never existed. UnExpert Advice: Disappearing is communication—just not the kind you should tolerate.

NRE (New Relationship Energy) /ˌen-är-ˈē/ The intense excitement and chemical high at the start of a new connection that can distort judgment. Synonyms: honeymoon phase, dopamine rush, early infatuation. Antonyms: grounded attachment, long-term compatibility. Savage Sentence: The NRE convinced you it was special when it was just new. UnExpert Advice: Don't make permanent decisions based on temporary chemistry.

NSA (No Strings Attached) /ˌen-ˌes-ˈā/ A casual arrangement with no emotional expectations or commitment. Synonyms: casual sex, detached involvement, no-commitment setup. Antonyms: emotional investment, relationship intent. Savage Sentence: The NSA stayed simple—until one person started wanting more. UnExpert Advice: Be honest about what you can actually handle.

ONS (One Night Stand) /ˌwən nīt stand/ A single sexual encounter with no expectation of continuation. Synonyms: one-time hookup, casual encounter, single night connection. Antonyms: ongoing relationship, emotional bond. Savage Sentence: The ONS was exactly what it was—nothing more, nothing less. UnExpert Advice: Don't rewrite it into something it wasn't.

OOC (Out of Character) /ˌō-ō-ˈsē/ A sudden shift in behavior that doesn't match how someone previously showed up—often an early sign of a mask slipping. Synonyms: personality shift, early mask slip, behavior glitch. Antonyms: consistency, authenticity, stable behavior. Savage Sentence: The OOC moment turned "perfect guy" into "who the hell is this" overnight. UnExpert Advice: When someone shows you a version that doesn't match, believe the shift—not the story.

OTP (One True Pairing) /ˌō-tē-ˈpē/ The belief or projection that two people are perfectly meant to be together, often based on fantasy rather than reality. Synonyms: idealized couple, fantasy match, perfection projection. Antonyms: realistic connection, grounded compatibility. Savage Sentence: The OTP existed more in your head than in the actual relationship. UnExpert Advice: Perfect on paper doesn't mean real in practice.

PDA (Public Displays of Affection) /ˌpē-dē-ˈā/ Physical affection shown openly in public settings. Synonyms: public affection, visible intimacy, performative romance. Antonyms: privacy, restraint, subtlety. Savage Sentence: The PDA felt more like a performance than a connection. UnExpert Advice: If it's for an audience, question the intention.

PMO (Put Me On) /ˌpē-em-ˈō/ Asking to be introduced, included, or connected—often revealing opportunistic intentions in dating or social circles. Synonyms: access seeking, social climbing, connection leveraging. Antonyms: genuine interest, organic connection, independent approach. Savage Sentence: The PMO came real quick once he realized who you knew. UnExpert Advice: If someone is more interested in your network than you, you're a stepping stone, not a connection.

PP (Pay Pig / Pay Piggy) /ˌpē-ˈpē/ Someone who derives gratification from giving money or gifts, often in transactional or power-based dynamics. Synonyms: financial submissive, wallet simp, transactional giver. Antonyms: equal partnership, mutual exchange. Savage Sentence: The PP kept paying for attention and calling it connection. UnExpert Advice: If money is the main driver, it's a transaction—not a relationship.

PPM (Pay Per Meet) /ˌpē-ˌpē-ˈem/ A transactional arrangement where payment is exchanged for time or companionship per meeting. Synonyms: transactional dating, compensated companionship, pay structure. Antonyms: emotional connection, mutual relationship. Savage Sentence: The PPM kept everything clear—just not meaningful. UnExpert Advice: If it's transactional, it will always feel conditional.

RN (Right Now) /ˌär-ˈen/ Signals temporary interest or availability with no intention of long-term investment. Synonyms: short-term interest, temporary attention, moment-based desire. Antonyms: long-term intention, commitment, consistency. Savage Sentence: The RN energy wanted you in the moment but had no plan for you beyond it. UnExpert Advice: "Right now" rarely turns into "forever."

SDE (Small Dick Energy) /smȯl dik ˈe-nər-jē/ Insecure, loud, overcompensating behavior masking fragility and ego issues. Synonyms: overcompensation, fragile ego, try-hard energy. Antonyms: BDE, confidence, grounded presence. Savage Sentence: The SDE was loud enough to prove exactly what it was trying to hide. UnExpert Advice: Real confidence doesn't need volume.

SMV (Sexual Market Value) /ˌes-ˌem-ˈvē/ A reductive ranking system assigning worth based on looks, status, and desirability. Synonyms: value ranking, attraction scale, market mindset. Antonyms: human connection, intrinsic worth. Savage Sentence: The SMV reduced real people into numbers that said more about the system than the person. UnExpert Advice: Anyone who reduces people to value will treat them like it.

THOT (That Ho Over There) /thät/ A derogatory label used to shame someone (usually women) for perceived promiscuity or attention-seeking behavior. Synonyms: slut-shaming term, projection label, insecurity insult. Antonyms: sexual autonomy, respect, non-judgment. Savage Sentence: The THOT insult said more about his insecurity than anything about her behavior. UnExpert Advice: Anyone using this word is telling you exactly who they are.

VBD (Very Bad Date) /ˌvē-bē-ˈdē/ A disastrous or uncomfortable dating experience often shared as a cautionary tale. Synonyms: nightmare date, dating fail, awkward encounter. Antonyms: great date, positive experience. Savage Sentence: The VBD was unforgettable for all the wrong reasons. UnExpert Advice: Bad dates are data—use them.

WAGS (Wives and Girlfriends) /wagz/ Partners of high-profile men, especially in sports or celebrity culture. Synonyms: partner circle, social label, media term. Antonyms: independent identity, single status. Savage Sentence: The WAGS were known—but not always valued beyond the label. UnExpert Advice: Don't confuse association with identity.

Archetypes & Roles

THE CORE MALE ARCHETYPES

ATTENTION ADDICT

Needs constant validation from multiple sources and uses romantic attention as fuel, not connection.

What It Sounds Like

- "I just like talking to people."
- "I'm not ready for anything serious right now."
- "I didn't think it was a big deal."
- "You're overthinking it."
- "I like attention, I won't lie."

What It Looks Like

- Always active on social media, especially with opposite sex
- Flirty with everyone, loyal to no one
- Keeps conversations going with multiple people at once
- Thrives on reactions, compliments, and being desired
- Pulls back once real emotional depth is required

The Psychological Play. Validation is their currency. They're not looking for love. they're looking to feel wanted, admired, and chosen… by as many people as possible.

Why It Works (On You)

- You mistake attention for interest
- You feel chosen when they focus on you
- You believe you can "win" their full attention
- The inconsistency keeps you hooked

Long-Term Effects

- Constant comparison to others
- Anxiety and insecurity
- Feeling replaceable
- Emotional exhaustion

How to Recognize It Early

- Their attention feels intense… but not exclusive
- You notice other people always in the background
- They love the chase but avoid depth
- You feel like you're competing without signing up for a competition

The Trap: You think if you give just a little more… they'll finally choose you.

The Reality Check: They already chose. Just not exclusively.

Your Dating UnExpert Truth: "If they need an audience, they're not ready for a relationship."

Your Dating UnExpert Move

- Stop rewarding inconsistent attention
- Pull your energy back
- Watch what they do when you're not feeding them validation

AVOIDANT

Emotionally unavailable by design. Craves connection but withdraws the moment it becomes real.

What It Sounds Like

- "I just need space."
- "I don't like labels."
- "I've been hurt before."
- "I'm just really busy right now."
- "I don't want to rush anything."

What It Looks Like

- Strong connection early, then sudden distance

- Pulls away after emotional or physical closeness
- Avoids defining the relationship
- Keeps conversations surface-level when things get real
- Disappears when expectations increase

The Psychological Play: Intimacy feels like a threat. They want connection, but only at a distance where they still feel in control.

Why It Works (On You)

- You confuse emotional unavailability with depth
- You want to "earn" their vulnerability
- You interpret distance as something you need to fix
- The push-pull dynamic creates addiction

Long-Term Effects

- Chronic confusion
- Overanalyzing everything
- Emotional burnout
- Lowered self-worth
- Feeling "too much" for asking for normal needs

How to Recognize It Early

- Hot at the beginning, cold when it matters
- Avoids emotional conversations
- You feel closer than they act
- Effort drops the moment things stabilize

The Trap: You keep trying to prove you're "safe enough" to love.

The Reality Check: They're not avoiding you. They're avoiding intimacy.

Your Dating UnExpert Truth: "You're not asking for too much. You're asking the wrong person."

Your Dating UnExpert Move:

- Stop chasing clarity from someone avoiding it
- Match their effort (you won't like what you see)
- Choose consistency over potential

BREADCRUMBER

Gives just enough attention to keep you interested… but never enough to move things forward.

What It Sounds Like

- "Hey stranger"
- "I've just been busy"
- "I miss you" (with zero follow-up)
- "We should hang soon"
- "I've been thinking about you"

What It Looks Like

- Random check-ins with no real plans
- Flirty messages that go nowhere
- Disappears, then reappears like nothing happened
- Keeps you emotionally engaged without commitment
- Always "almost" doing something

The Psychological Play: They want access without responsibility. You stay on the hook… without them ever having to show up fully.

Why It Works (On You)

- You hold onto the potential
- You fill in the gaps with hope
- You believe the next message will be different
- Intermittent reinforcement keeps you addicted

Long-Term Effects

- Emotional dependency on inconsistency
- Confusion and self-doubt
- Wasted time and energy
- Difficulty trusting real effort later

How to Recognize It Early

- Conversations never turn into plans
- Effort comes in random bursts
- You're always waiting for the next message

- You feel more invested than they act

The Trap: You think the next breadcrumb will turn into a full meal.

The Reality Check: If they wanted to see you, they would.

Your Dating UnExpert Truth: "You're not building something. You're being kept."

Your Dating UnExpert Move

- Stop responding to low-effort messages
- Require plans, not vibes
- Exit anything that lives in "almost"

THE COMEBACK GUY

Disappears when it's convenient... then resurfaces like nothing happened, expecting access to you again.

What It Sounds Like

- "Hey... I know it's been a while."
- "I've been thinking about you."
- "Life just got crazy."
- "I didn't mean to disappear like that."
- "Can we start over?"

What It Looks Like

- Ghosts or fades... then randomly reappears
- Slides back in casually, no real accountability
- Picks up where things left off without earning it
- Shows up when lonely, bored, or rejected elsewhere
- Leaves again once the emotional supply is refilled

The Psychological Play: You are familiar. Easy. Available. They return because they know you once cared... and hope you still do.

Why It Works (On You)

- You crave closure
- You remember the good parts, not the ending
- You want to believe they've changed
- The history creates emotional leverage

Long-Term Effects

- Emotional whiplash
- Reopened wounds
- Loss of self-respect
- Difficulty moving on
- Getting stuck in cycles that never evolve

How to Recognize It Early

- They reappear with words, not changed behavior
- No real acknowledgment of what they did
- Same energy, same patterns
- You feel hopeful... but uneasy

The Trap: You think this time will be different.

The Reality Check: If they respected you, they wouldn't have disappeared in the first place.

Your Dating UnExpert Truth: "Access to you is not a free trial they can keep restarting."

Your Dating UnExpert Move

- Don't reward re-entry without accountability
- Judge them by patterns, not apologies
- Close doors that only open when it's convenient for them

COMMITMENT-PHOBE

Wants all the benefits of a relationship... without ever agreeing to one.

What It Sounds Like

- "I just don't want labels."
- "Let's not rush things."
- "I like what we have right now."
- "Why do we need to define it?"
- "I'm just going with the flow."

What It Looks Like

- Acts like a partner but avoids the title
- Keeps things undefined for as long as possible

- Resists conversations about the future
- Gives just enough to keep you around
- Pulls back when commitment is brought up

The Psychological Play: Commitment feels like loss of freedom. They want connection... without responsibility, expectation, or accountability.

Why It Works (On You)

- You don't want to pressure them
- You believe time will change their mind
- You accept less to keep them
- You confuse consistency with commitment

Long-Term Effects

- Wasted time in undefined relationships
- Emotional insecurity
- Feeling "not quite chosen"
- Difficulty asking for your needs

How to Recognize It Early

- Avoids defining anything clearly
- Deflects serious conversations
- Keeps you in a gray area
- You feel like you're in a relationship... but can't say it

The Trap: You wait for them to "be ready."

The Reality Check: They are ready. Just not for you.

Your Dating UnExpert Truth: "If they want the benefits without the title, they don't want you — they want access."

Your Dating UnExpert Move

- Define what you want early
- Don't negotiate your standards
- Walk away from anything undefined for too long

EGO FEEDER

Uses your attention, admiration, and emotional energy to boost their self-worth… without reciprocating real connection.

What It Sounds Like

- "You're amazing."
- "I don't deserve you."
- "You're too good for me."
- "I just have a lot going on right now."
- "You make me feel so good."

What It Looks Like

- Loves compliments, gives little back
- Keeps you emotionally invested without progressing
- Opens up just enough to keep you engaged
- Comes to you for validation, not partnership
- Disappears once their ego is refilled

The Psychological Play: You are their confidence source. They don't want you — they want how you make them feel about themselves.

Why It Works (On You)

- You feel needed
- You enjoy being appreciated
- You believe your love can "build them up"
- You mistake emotional reliance for connection

Long-Term Effects

- Emotional depletion
- One-sided attachment
- Feeling used but unable to explain why
- Loss of boundaries
- Confusion between love and validation

How to Recognize It Early

- Conversations revolve around them
- You give more than you receive

- They show up when they need something
- You feel drained instead of fulfilled

The Trap: You think if you love them enough, they'll become the partner you want.

The Reality Check: They're not growing. They're feeding.

Your Dating UnExpert Truth: "You're not their partner. You're their confidence supply."

Your Dating UnExpert Move

- Stop over-giving emotionally
- Notice what they *don't* give back
- Choose mutual investment, not one-sided energy

EMOTIONALLY UNAVAILABLE MAN

Capable of connection in moments... but fundamentally unable or unwilling to sustain emotional intimacy.

What It Sounds Like

- "I'm just not in the right place right now."
- "I don't know what I want."
- "I care about you, I just can't give you what you deserve."
- "I've been through a lot."
- "I don't want to hurt you."

What It Looks Like

- Shows depth in short bursts, then disappears emotionally
- Avoids vulnerability when it actually matters
- Keeps conversations safe or surface-level
- Pulls back when expectations increase
- Gives mixed signals that never fully resolve

The Psychological Play: They want connection... but not the responsibility that comes with it. So they give you just enough to keep you close, but never enough to build anything real.

Why It Works (On You)

- You see glimpses of who they *could* be

- You want to be the one they open up to
- You interpret emotional distance as depth
- You believe patience will unlock them

Long-Term Effects

- Emotional confusion
- Constant overthinking
- Feeling "too much" for having needs
- Lowered standards over time
- Attachment to potential instead of reality

How to Recognize It Early

- Words show care, actions lack consistency
- Vulnerability is rare or controlled
- You feel emotionally alone... even with them
- Effort doesn't deepen over time

The Trap: You fall in love with their potential, not their pattern.

The Reality Check: If they can't show up consistently, they're not available — no matter what they say.

Your Dating UnExpert Truth: "Almost available is still unavailable."

Your Dating UnExpert Move

- Stop romanticizing inconsistency
- Pay attention to patterns, not moments
- Choose someone who shows up without being unlocked

FUTURE FAKER

Creates a fantasy of a future together to secure your emotional investment... with no intention of following through.

What It Sounds Like

- "We're going to travel together."
- "I can see us living together one day."
- "You'd be such a great partner long-term."
- "I've never felt like this before."
- "I want something real with you."

What It Looks Like

- Talks about the future early and often
- Makes plans that never materialize
- Speaks in "we" language without building anything real
- Creates emotional security... without actual effort
- Disappears or pulls back once you're invested

The Psychological Play: They fast-forward intimacy to lock you in emotionally. You fall for the *vision*, not the reality.

Why It Works (On You)

- You feel chosen and secure quickly
- You trust the consistency of their words
- You start building a future in your head
- You invest emotionally before seeing real proof

Long-Term Effects

- Feeling misled and betrayed
- Difficulty trusting future partners
- Emotional attachment to something that never existed
- Confusion between words and real intention

How to Recognize It Early

- Big promises with little follow-through
- Talks about the future before building the present
- Plans stay hypothetical
- You feel emotionally committed faster than the relationship justifies

The Trap: You believe the version of the relationship they described... instead of the one they're actually building.

The Reality Check: If it's not happening in the present, it's not happening in the future.

Your Dating UnExpert Truth: "Consistency builds a future. Not words."

Your Dating UnExpert Move

- Ignore future talk — watch present behavior
- Require follow-through, not fantasy
- Slow down emotional investment

GASLIGHTER

Manipulates your perception of reality to avoid accountability and maintain control.

What It Sounds Like

- "That's not what I said."
- "You're imagining things."
- "You're way too emotional."
- "You always twist things."
- "You're remembering it wrong."
- "You're crazy, just like your mother."

What It Looks Like

- Denies things that clearly happened
- Rewrites conversations or events
- Minimizes your feelings and reactions
- Turns situations around to make you the problem
- Creates confusion until you question yourself

The Psychological Play: Control through confusion. If you don't trust your own perception, you become easier to manage.

Why It Works (On You)

- You want to be fair and understanding
- You question yourself before questioning them
- You try to "fix" the miscommunication
- You slowly lose confidence in your own memory and instincts

Long-Term Effects

- Loss of self-trust
- Anxiety and mental exhaustion
- Emotional instability
- Dependence on their version of reality
- Identity erosion

How to Recognize It Early

- You leave conversations feeling confused
- You start doubting things you were sure about
- You apologize when you didn't do anything wrong
- You feel like you're always the problem

The Trap: You try harder to explain yourself... instead of questioning them.

The Reality Check: Confusion is not miscommunication.: It's manipulation.

Your Dating UnExpert Truth: "You're not crazy. You're being controlled."

Your Dating UnExpert Move

- Trust your initial perception
- Stop over-explaining your feelings
- Document patterns if needed
- Leave anything that makes you question your reality

GHOST

Disappears without explanation, closure, or accountability... leaving you to make sense of something they chose not to explain.

What It Sounds Like

- "I thought everything was fine..." *(you, to yourself)*
- "Did I do something?"
- "Maybe something happened?"
- "I'll just give it a few days..."
- *...silence*

What It Looks Like

- Stops responding out of nowhere
- Disappears mid-conversation or after intimacy
- No goodbye, no explanation, no closure
- Watches your stories but doesn't engage
- Reappears later like nothing happened (optional upgrade: Comeback Guy)

The Psychological Play: Avoidance of discomfort. Instead of communicating honestly, they exit silently and leave you holding the emotional weight.

Why It Works (On You)

- You search for answers that don't exist
- You replay everything trying to find "the moment"
- You blame yourself for the disappearance
- Lack of closure keeps you emotionally stuck

Long-Term Effects

- Overthinking and self-blame
- Fear of sudden abandonment
- Difficulty trusting new connections
- Emotional lingering without resolution

How to Recognize It Early

- Inconsistent communication patterns
- Avoids difficult conversations
- Disappears during minor conflict
- Effort drops without explanation

The Trap: You wait for closure from someone who chose not to give it.

The Reality Check: Closure is something you give yourself.

Your Dating UnExpert Truth: "Silence is an answer. Just not the one you wanted."

Your Dating UnExpert Move

- Stop chasing an explanation
- Don't romanticize their return
- Decide that disappearing is disqualifying

HOT-AND-COLD GUY

Alternates between intense interest and emotional distance... creating confusion, dependency, and emotional instability.

What It Sounds Like

- "I miss you so much."
- "You're all I want."

  ...then...

  "I've just been busy."

- "I need space."
- "You're overthinking this."

What It Looks Like

- Intense attention followed by sudden withdrawal
- Affection that feels real… but isn't consistent
- Disappears, then comes back strong
- Keeps you emotionally off-balance
- Effort comes in waves, not stability

The Psychological Play. Intermittent reinforcement. The inconsistency creates a dopamine loop — making you crave the "high" when they're good.

Why It Works (On You)

- You chase the version of them you liked
- You think the "hot" version is the real one
- The inconsistency creates emotional addiction
- You confuse intensity with connection

Long-Term Effects

- Anxiety and emotional instability
- Obsessive thinking
- Loss of emotional grounding
- Addiction to unpredictability
- Difficulty accepting calm, stable love later

How to Recognize It Early

- Their energy changes without explanation
- You feel secure one day, anxious the next
- Effort is inconsistent
- You're constantly trying to "get back" to how it was

The Trap: You think if you act right, they'll stay consistent.

The Reality Check: Consistency isn't something you earn. It's something they either are… or aren't.

Your Dating UnExpert Truth: "If you feel anxious more than secure, that's your answer."

Your Dating UnExpert Move

- Stop rewarding inconsistent behavior
- Step back instead of leaning in
- Choose stability over emotional highs

LOVEBOMBER

Overwhelms you with intense affection, attention, and promises early on… to fast-track emotional attachment.

What It Sounds Like

- "I've never felt this way before."
- "You're different from anyone I've met."
- "I can see a future with you."
- "I've been waiting for someone like you."
- "You're perfect."

What It Looks Like

- Excessive compliments and attention early
- Constant texting, calling, and validation
- Fast emotional intimacy
- Big promises early on
- Pushes the relationship forward quickly

The Psychological Play: They create intensity to build attachment quickly. The faster you bond, the harder it is for you to pull away later.

Why It Works (On You)

- You feel deeply seen and chosen
- It feels like a rare, instant connection
- You drop your guard quickly
- You trust the intensity as real

Long-Term Effects

- Emotional crash when behavior changes
- Confusion and betrayal
- Attachment to a version of them that disappears
- Difficulty trusting future connections

How to Recognize It Early

- Feels "too much" too fast
- Talks about the future immediately
- Over-the-top attention early on
- Emotional intensity without foundation

The Trap: You think you've found something rare.

The Reality Check: Real connection builds. It doesn't explode.

Your Dating UnExpert Truth: "If it feels like a fantasy this early… it probably is."

Your Dating UnExpert Move

- Slow everything down
- Watch for consistency over time
- Don't match their intensity — observe it

NARCISSIST

Prioritizes their own needs, image, and control above all else… while maintaining just enough charm to keep you engaged.

What It Sounds Like

- "You're lucky to have me."
- "No one else would put up with you."
- "You're too sensitive."
- "I never said that."
- "You're the problem in all your relationships."

What It Looks Like

- Charming and magnetic at first
- Needs admiration and control
- Lacks real empathy
- Turns conflict into your fault
- Punishes you with withdrawal, silence, or attitude
- Keeps you off-balance emotionally

The Psychological Play: Control through validation and devaluation. They build you up just enough… so they can slowly tear you down and keep you dependent.

Why It Works (On You)

- You want to prove your worth
- You hold onto who they were in the beginning
- You believe if you love them right, it will go back
- You confuse emotional intensity with connection

Long-Term Effects

- Loss of self-worth
- Emotional dependency
- Confusion and self-doubt
- Walking on eggshells
- Identity erosion

How to Recognize It Early

- Everything revolves around them
- Apologies feel rare or fake
- You feel drained, not supported
- Conflict never resolves — it shifts
- You question yourself more than them

The Trap: You keep trying to get back to the version of them you met first.

The Reality Check: That version was the hook. This version is the pattern.

Your Dating UnExpert Truth: "You're not hard to love. You're just loving someone who can't."

Your Dating UnExpert Move

- Stop explaining yourself endlessly
- Set boundaries and watch the reaction
- Leave anything that makes you feel smaller over time

PLAYER

Actively engages with multiple romantic or sexual options while presenting just enough interest to keep you invested.

What It Sounds Like

- "I'm just seeing what's out there."
- "I don't like labels."
- "I'm not tied down to anyone."
- "You're the only one I really like though."
- "I'm just going with the flow."

What It Looks Like

- Talks to multiple people at once
- Keeps things casual and undefined
- Flirty, charming, and socially active
- Avoids exclusivity conversations
- Gives attention... but spreads it thin

The Psychological Play: Options equal power. The more people they have, the less they have to invest in any one person.

Why It Works (On You)

- You want to be "the one they choose"
- Competition creates urgency
- You mistake attention for commitment
- You believe you can stand out

Long-Term Effects

- Comparison and insecurity
- Emotional instability
- Feeling replaceable
- Wasted time in undefined dynamics

How to Recognize It Early

- Vague about intentions
- Always "busy" but active socially
- Avoids exclusivity

- You feel like one of many

The Trap: You think if you stand out enough, they'll stop playing.

The Reality Check: Players don't stop playing because of one person.: They stop when they decide to.

Your Dating UnExpert Truth: "If they act single, believe them."

Your Dating UnExpert Move

- Don't compete — remove yourself
- Ask direct questions early
- Walk away from vague answers

SITUATIONSHIP KING

Keeps you emotionally involved in a relationship that never gets defined… while still receiving all the benefits.

What It Sounds Like

- "I don't want to label this."
- "I like what we have."
- "Let's just go with the flow."
- "Why complicate it?"
- "I'm not ready for anything serious."

What It Looks Like

- Acts like a partner without committing
- Regular contact, emotional connection, sometimes physical intimacy
- Avoids defining the relationship
- Keeps things in a comfortable gray area
- Progress never actually happens

The Psychological Play: Maximum benefit, minimum responsibility. They get connection, attention, and access… without commitment.

Why It Works (On You)

- It feels like a relationship
- You don't want to "ruin it" by pushing
- You believe time will naturally progress things

- You accept less to keep them

Long-Term Effects

- Wasted time
- Emotional attachment without security
- Confusion and frustration
- Difficulty moving on
- Feeling "almost chosen"

How to Recognize It Early

- No clear label after a reasonable amount of time
- Avoids future planning
- Deflects serious conversations
- You feel like you're in something… but can't define it

The Trap: You think patience will turn it into a relationship.

The Reality Check: If it hasn't progressed, it's not going to.

Your Dating UnExpert Truth: "You're not building something. You're maintaining access."

Your Dating UnExpert Move

- Set a timeline for clarity
- Ask directly where it's going
- Walk away from anything undefined

SLOW FADER

Gradually reduces effort and communication instead of ending things directly… hoping you'll eventually get the hint.

What It Sounds Like

- "Sorry, I've just been really busy."
- "I've had a lot going on."
- "I didn't see your message."
- "Work has been crazy."
- "Let's catch up soon."

What It Looks Like

- Responses get slower and shorter

- Plans become less frequent, then nonexistent
- Effort declines steadily over time
- Energy shifts without explanation
- No clear ending — just less and less

The Psychological Play: Avoiding confrontation. They don't want to have the uncomfortable conversation… so they slowly disappear instead.

Why It Works (On You)

- You keep adjusting to their decreasing effort
- You don't want to overreact
- You believe it's temporary
- You hold onto how it used to be

Long-Term Effects

- Prolonged confusion
- Emotional draining over time
- Difficulty letting go
- Loss of clarity and closure

How to Recognize It Early

- Noticeable drop in effort
- More excuses than action
- You're initiating everything
- Conversations feel forced or minimal

The Trap: You keep giving them time to "come back."

The Reality Check: They're not busy. They're disengaging.

Your Dating UnExpert Truth: "Slow fade is still a no."

Your Dating UnExpert Move

- Stop matching low effort with patience
- Address it directly once
- If nothing changes — exit cleanly

MODERN DATING MALE ARCHETYPES

THE BARE MINIMUM KING

Does the absolute least required to keep you around... and expects to be praised for it.

What It Sounds Like

- "I text you every day, don't I?"
- "I told you I like you."
- "What more do you want?"
- "I'm not like those other guys."
- "I'm trying."

What It Looks Like

- Inconsistent effort passed off as consistency
- Last-minute plans or low-effort dates
- Minimal communication but expects access
- Does one small thing... and acts like it's a grand gesture
- Stops trying once you show interest

The Psychological Play: Effort reduction. Once they know you're invested, they lower the standard and see how little they can give without losing you.

Why It Works (On You)

- You don't want to seem "high maintenance"
- You appreciate small effort... even when it's not enough
- You compare them to worse experiences
- You convince yourself "at least he's trying"

Long-Term Effects

- Lowered standards
- Feeling underappreciated
- Emotional dissatisfaction
- Resentment over time
- Accepting less than you deserve

How to Recognize It Early

- Effort drops once you reciprocate
- You're doing more to maintain the connection
- Dates and communication feel lazy or repetitive
- You feel like you're asking for basic things

The Trap: You start overvaluing small effort because you've seen worse.

The Reality Check: Bare minimum is not potential. It's the preview of what you'll keep getting.

Your Dating UnExpert Truth: "If you have to explain effort, it's not enough."

Your Dating UnExpert Move

- Raise your standards quietly
- Stop rewarding low effort
- Let him meet the bar — or miss it

THE CRYPTO BRO

Obsessed with money, status, and "the next big thing"... often using ambition as a personality and a distraction from emotional depth.

What It Sounds Like

- "I'm about to make a huge move."
- "You just don't understand the market."
- "I don't work a 9–5."
- "I'm building something big right now."
- "I'll have time later once this takes off."

What It Looks Like

- Constantly talking about investments, trades, or "opportunities"
- Prioritizes money and status over connection
- Unpredictable schedule, always "busy"
- Uses future success to justify present absence
- Emotionally unavailable but intellectually overactive

The Psychological Play: Identity through success. They tie their worth to achievement, so emotional availability feels secondary or unnecessary.

Why It Works (On You)

- Ambition is attractive
- You believe in their "future"
- You see potential lifestyle, not current behavior
- You excuse absence as "grind mode"

Long-Term Effects

- Feeling like you come second to everything
- Emotional neglect
- Waiting for a future version of them
- Loneliness inside the relationship

How to Recognize It Early

- Conversations revolve around money or success
- Rarely emotionally present
- Always building, rarely connecting
- You feel like an accessory to their life

The Trap: You fall in love with who they say they're going to become.

The Reality Check: If they don't have time for you now, they won't magically have time later.

Your Dating UnExpert Truth: "You're not dating potential profits. You're dating current behavior."

Your Dating UnExpert Move

- Pay attention to how they show up *now*
- Don't compete with their priorities
- Choose someone who makes space for you

THE "GO WITH THE FLOW" GUY

Avoids direction, decisions, and commitment by hiding behind a laid-back, nonchalant persona.

What It Sounds Like

- "I'm just going with the flow."
- "Let's see what happens."
- "I don't like putting pressure on things."
- "Why define it?"
- "I'm just vibing."

What It Looks Like

- No clear intentions or direction
- Avoids making plans or decisions
- Lets you carry the structure of the relationship
- Drifts instead of progressing
- Comfortable in ambiguity

The Psychological Play: Avoidance through passivity. If nothing is defined, nothing is required of them.

Why It Works (On You)

- It feels easy and low-pressure at first
- You don't want to "ruin the vibe"
- You think things will naturally evolve
- You step in to create structure

Long-Term Effects

- Lack of progression
- Emotional uncertainty
- One-sided effort
- Wasted time in undefined dynamics

How to Recognize It Early

- Avoids direct answers about intentions
- Doesn't initiate or plan consistently
- Keeps everything vague
- You feel like you're steering the connection

The Trap: You think patience will turn "flow" into direction.

The Reality Check: No direction is a direction.

Your Dating UnExpert Truth: "Go with the flow usually means go nowhere slowly."

Your Dating UnExpert Move

- Ask clear questions early
- Require clarity, not vibes
- Walk away from anything that drifts too long

THE GYM PERSONALITY

Builds their identity around fitness, discipline, and aesthetics... but often lacks emotional depth, availability, or relational effort.

What It Sounds Like

- "I've got legs today."
- "I'm on a strict routine."
- "I don't skip the gym."
- "I'm really focused on myself right now."
- "I just don't have time for distractions."

What It Looks Like

- Life revolves around workouts, diet, and physique
- Highly disciplined physically... inconsistent emotionally
- Prioritizes routine over connection
- Conversations stay surface-level or performance-based
- Uses "self-improvement" to avoid emotional intimacy

The Psychological Play: Control and identity. They've mastered their body... but often avoid the vulnerability required to connect emotionally.

Why It Works (On You)

- Discipline is attractive
- They seem "put together"
- You associate physical effort with emotional maturity
- You respect their focus

Long-Term Effects

- Feeling secondary to their routine
- Lack of emotional depth
- Surface-level connection
- Loneliness despite consistency in seeing them

How to Recognize It Early

- Conversations revolve around gym, diet, or routine
- Rarely opens up emotionally
- Schedules life around themselves, not the relationship

- You feel like you're fitting into *their* life, not building one together

The Trap: You think structure equals stability.

The Reality Check: Being disciplined in the gym doesn't mean they're capable of emotional discipline.

Your Dating UnExpert Truth: "Abs are not a personality."

Your Dating UnExpert Move

- Look for emotional consistency, not just physical discipline
- Don't confuse routine with readiness
- Choose depth, not just aesthetics

THE "I DON'T DO LABELS" GUY

Rejects defining the relationship to maintain freedom, avoid accountability, and keep access without commitment.

What It Sounds Like

- "I don't like labels."
- "Why do we need to define this?"
- "I like what we have right now."
- "Let's not complicate it."
- "I'm just being real with you."

What It Looks Like

- Acts like a partner but refuses the title
- Avoids exclusivity conversations
- Keeps things intentionally vague
- Benefits from relationship-level access
- Pulls back when clarity is requested

The Psychological Play: If it's undefined, it's unaccountable. They remove structure so they're never responsible for meeting expectations.

Why It Works (On You)

- You don't want to seem pushy
- You believe labels aren't "that important"

- You think time will naturally define things
- You accept less to keep them

Long-Term Effects

- Emotional confusion
- Lack of security
- Wasted time
- Feeling unchosen
- Difficulty asking for your needs

How to Recognize It Early

- Avoids direct answers about what you are
- Deflects relationship conversations
- Keeps everything in gray areas
- You feel committed… but can't say it

The Trap: You convince yourself the label doesn't matter.

The Reality Check: The label isn't the problem. Their refusal is.

Your Dating UnExpert Truth: "If they don't define it, they don't value it."

Your Dating UnExpert Move

- Be clear about what you want
- Don't downplay your needs
- Walk away from intentional ambiguity

THE INSTAGRAM WATCHER

Consistently watches your stories and keeps tabs on you… without ever engaging, progressing, or showing real intention.

What It Sounds Like: *Nothing.* (That's the point.)

What It Looks Like

- Watches every story… instantly
- Never replies, reacts, or initiates
- Pops up in your views but not your messages
- Stays silently present in your life
- Occasionally likes something… just enough to stay relevant

The Psychological Play: Passive presence. They stay on your radar without risking rejection, effort, or actual involvement.

Why It Works (On You)

- You interpret watching as interest
- You feel "noticed" without interaction
- You wonder why they're watching but not acting
- Curiosity keeps them in your mental space

Long-Term Effects

- Mental distraction
- False sense of connection
- Wasted emotional energy on someone inactive
- Delayed closure

How to Recognize It Early

- High visibility, zero effort
- No real communication
- You notice them… but nothing ever happens
- You feel like you're being observed, not pursued

The Trap: You think watching means they care.

The Reality Check: If they wanted to talk to you… they would.

Your Dating UnExpert Truth: "Watching is not pursuing."

Your Dating UnExpert Move

- Stop assigning meaning to silent behavior
- Don't engage first just because they're watching
- Remove access if it's distracting you

THE JEALOUS NON-BOYFRIEND

Acts possessive, protective, and emotionally reactive… without ever actually committing to you.

What It Sounds Like

- "Who's that guy?"
- "I don't like you posting stuff like that."
- "You're talking to other guys now?"

- "I just care about you, that's all."
- "I don't want to lose you."

What It Looks Like

- Gets jealous but avoids commitment
- Monitors your behavior without claiming you
- Reacts to your independence as a threat
- Wants exclusivity... without offering it
- Pulls emotional control without relationship responsibility

The Psychological Play: Control without commitment. They don't want to lose access to you... but they also don't want to fully choose you.

Why It Works (On You)

- Jealousy can feel like interest or care
- You feel wanted or "claimed"
- You believe it means they secretly care deeply
- You hope it will lead to commitment

Long-Term Effects

- Confusion about where you stand
- Restricted behavior without security
- Emotional dependency
- Loss of freedom without gaining a relationship

How to Recognize It Early

- Jealous reactions without defining the relationship
- Questions your behavior but avoids accountability
- Wants access but resists commitment
- You feel controlled... but not chosen

The Trap: You mistake jealousy for investment.

The Reality Check: If they wanted you, they'd claim you. Not control you.

Your Dating UnExpert Truth: "You don't get boyfriend privileges on a situationship contract."

Your Dating UnExpert Move

- Call out the contradiction directly
- Don't adjust your behavior without commitment
- Require clarity or remove access

THE LATE-NIGHT TEXTER

Only shows up when it's convenient, lonely, or late… offering attention in moments that require the least effort.

What It Sounds Like

- "You up?"
- "Hey stranger 😏"
- "What are you doing tonight?"
- "Come over."
- "I've been thinking about you…"

What It Looks Like

- Messages primarily late at night
- Rarely engages during the day
- Conversations are short, flirty, or physical
- No real plans outside of convenience
- Disappears once the moment passes

The Psychological Play: Convenience over connection. You become an option for entertainment, validation, or physical access… not a priority.

Why It Works (On You)

- Late-night vulnerability lowers your guard
- You feel chosen in the moment
- You hope it will turn into something more
- Attention, even inconsistent, feels good

Long-Term Effects

- Feeling used or secondary
- Emotional dissatisfaction
- Confusion about their intentions
- Lowered standards over time

How to Recognize It Early

- Messages only come at night
- No effort to see you during the day
- No real progression
- You feel like a convenience, not a plan

The Trap: You think late-night attention will turn into daytime effort.

The Reality Check: If they wanted to see you in the daylight, they would.

Your Dating UnExpert Truth: "Midnight interest is not real intention."

Your Dating UnExpert Move

- Stop responding to late-night-only messages
- Require effort in real hours
- Don't accept convenience as connection

THE ORBITING EX

A former partner who never fully leaves... staying in your life through subtle presence, check-ins, and digital lurking.

What It Sounds Like

- "Hey... just checking in."
- "I saw something that reminded me of you."
- "I hope you're doing well."
- "No one gets me like you do."
- "I miss what we had."

What It Looks Like

- Watches your stories consistently
- Reaches out just as you're moving on
- Keeps communication open but vague
- Doesn't commit to rebuilding anything
- Reappears during your moments of growth or happiness

The Psychological Play: Emotional tethering. They don't want to be with you... but they don't want you fully free either.

Why It Works (On You)

- History creates emotional attachment
- Familiarity feels safe
- You remember the good more than the ending
- You wonder "what if"

Long-Term Effects

- Delayed healing
- Emotional confusion

- Difficulty moving forward
- Reopening old wounds

How to Recognize It Early

- Reaches out at emotionally vulnerable times
- Keeps things nostalgic but not actionable
- No real effort to rebuild
- You feel pulled backward instead of forward

The Trap: You think the history means something still needs to be explored.

The Reality Check: If it was meant to work, it would have.

Your Dating UnExpert Truth: "Familiar doesn't mean right."

Your Dating UnExpert Move

- Stop entertaining unfinished cycles
- Limit or remove access
- Choose forward movement over emotional nostalgia

THE PEN PAL

Maintains constant communication through texting or calls… but avoids ever meeting, progressing, or turning it into real life.

What It Sounds Like

- "Good morning ☀"
- "How was your day?"
- "I feel like I can talk to you about anything."
- "We should definitely hang out soon."
- "I've just been busy lately."

What It Looks Like

- Texts all day, every day
- Deep conversations… with no real plans
- Always "about to" meet, never actually does
- Builds emotional connection without physical presence
- Keeps you engaged through words alone

The Psychological Play: Low-risk connection. They get emotional intimacy without vulnerability, effort, or real-life accountability.

Why It Works (On You)

- You feel connected through constant communication
- It mimics a real relationship
- You build emotional attachment quickly
- You believe meeting is just around the corner

Long-Term Effects

- Emotional attachment to someone not showing up
- Wasted time
- Frustration and confusion
- Difficulty trusting future connections

How to Recognize It Early

- Plans are always vague or postponed
- Communication is high, action is low
- You've been talking longer than makes sense without meeting
- You feel close… but haven't built anything real

The Trap: You think the connection is real because the conversation is.

The Reality Check: If they wanted to meet you, they would have.

Your Dating UnExpert Truth: "Texting is not a relationship."

Your Dating UnExpert Move

- Set a timeline for meeting
- Stop investing in words without action
- Cut off anything that lives only on your phone

PLACEHOLDER

Keeps you around to fill time, attention, or emotional space… while waiting for something "better" or different.

What It Sounds Like

- "I really like you, I'm just not ready right now."
- "I don't want to lose you."
- "You mean a lot to me."

- "I just need time to figure things out."
- "I'm not sure what I want yet."

What It Looks Like

- Keeps you close but not committed
- Gives emotional access without progression
- Doesn't let you go… but doesn't choose you
- Shows up when it benefits them
- Keeps you in rotation, not priority

The Psychological Play: Security without commitment. You provide comfort, attention, and consistency… while they remain open to other options.

Why It Works (On You)

- You believe patience will pay off
- You feel emotionally connected
- You don't want to lose what you've built
- You hope to become "the one"

Long-Term Effects

- Feeling stuck
- Loss of time
- Lowered self-worth
- Emotional dependency
- Difficulty walking away

How to Recognize It Early

- No clear progression over time
- Mixed signals about intentions
- Keeps you close but undefined
- You feel like you're waiting

The Trap: You think staying proves your value.

The Reality Check: You're not being chosen. You're being kept.

Your Dating UnExpert Truth: "Someone who wants you doesn't risk losing you."

Your Dating UnExpert Move

- Stop waiting for clarity that isn't coming
- Choose yourself before they don't
- Walk away from anything that feels like a holding pattern

THE PODCAST PHILOSOPHER

Speaks fluently in therapy language, self-awareness, and emotional insight… but doesn't actually apply any of it in real life.

What It Sounds Like

- "I've done a lot of inner work."
- "I'm very self-aware."
- "I understand attachment styles."
- "I'm on a healing journey."
- "I just need to protect my energy."

What It Looks Like

- Can articulate emotions… but doesn't regulate them
- Talks about growth more than demonstrating it
- Uses therapy language to justify poor behavior
- Appears emotionally intelligent… but lacks consistency
- Avoids accountability under the guise of "boundaries"

The Psychological Play: Intellectualized self-awareness. They understand the language of growth… but use it as a shield instead of a tool.

Why It Works (On You)

- Emotional intelligence is attractive
- You feel understood and seen
- You believe they've "done the work"
- You trust their awareness as proof of readiness

Long-Term Effects

- Confusion between words and actions
- Frustration when behavior doesn't match insight
- Emotional exhaustion
- Difficulty trusting future "self-aware" partners

How to Recognize It Early

- Talks about growth constantly... but patterns don't change
- Uses therapy terms in place of real accountability
- You feel confused because they *sound* healthy
- Their actions don't align with their insight

The Trap: You believe awareness equals change.

The Reality Check: Knowing better and doing better are not the same thing.

Your Dating UnExpert Truth: "Self-awareness without action is just performance."

Your Dating UnExpert Move

- Watch behavior, not vocabulary
- Don't be impressed by language alone
- Require consistency, not concepts

THE REFORMED FUCKBOY

Claims he's changed, healed, and grown... but still operates with the same patterns, just packaged more respectfully.

What It Sounds Like

- "I'm not like I used to be."
- "I've done a lot of work on myself."
- "I used to be toxic, but I've changed."
- "I just move differently now."
- "I'm trying to do things right this time."

What It Looks Like

- More self-aware... but still inconsistent
- Uses "growth" language while repeating old behaviors
- Moves slightly slower, but ends in the same place
- Aware of his patterns... but doesn't break them
- Presents as evolved, but still avoids real commitment

The Psychological Play: Rebranding. They upgrade the language, not the behavior... making it harder to call out.

Why It Works (On You)

- You believe in growth and second chances
- Self-awareness feels like progress
- You think "at least he knows now"
- You want to believe this version is real

Long-Term Effects

- Repeating the same emotional cycle
- Disappointment disguised as hope
- Confusion between effort and actual change
- Emotional burnout

How to Recognize It Early

- Talks about growth more than demonstrating it
- Patterns feel familiar despite new language
- Progress is inconsistent or short-lived
- You feel like you've been here before

The Trap: You believe awareness means transformation.

The Reality Check: If the behavior hasn't changed, neither has he.

Your Dating UnExpert Truth: "New words don't mean new patterns."

Your Dating UnExpert Move

- Watch for sustained change over time
- Don't reward early "growth talk"
- Believe consistent behavior, not rebrands

THE RESURFACER

Disappears for months at a time... then reappears like clockwork, expecting to pick things back up without explanation.

What It Sounds Like

- "Hey you... it's been a minute."
- "I saw something that reminded me of you."
- "Random, but I thought of you today."
- "How have you been?"
- "I've been meaning to reach out."

What It Looks Like

- Pops back up every few months
- No real accountability for disappearing
- Casual re-entry, like nothing happened
- Tests if you're still available
- Leaves again once the interaction fades

The Psychological Play: Access testing. They check if the door is still open... without ever intending to walk through it properly.

Why It Works (On You)

- Nostalgia hits hard
- You're curious why they came back
- You hope this time has changed them
- The timing always feels oddly intentional

Long-Term Effects

- Interrupted healing
- Emotional resets
- Difficulty moving forward
- Lingering attachment

How to Recognize It Early

- Pattern of disappearing and reappearing
- No growth or change between cycles
- Reaches out during emotionally vulnerable times
- Feels familiar... but not different

The Trap: You think the return means something.

The Reality Check: It means you're still accessible.

Your Dating UnExpert Truth: "You're not a bookmark in someone else's story."

Your Dating UnExpert Move

- Stop responding to repeat cycles
- Break the pattern once and for all
- Close doors that only reopen out of convenience

TRAUMA DUMPER

Overshares deeply personal trauma early on to fast-track emotional intimacy… without the foundation to support it.

What It Sounds Like

- "I've never told anyone this before…"
- "My ex really messed me up."
- "I've been through a lot."
- "You're the only person I can talk to about this."
- "I just feel safe with you."

What It Looks Like

- Deep, heavy conversations very early
- Shares emotional wounds before real trust is built
- Leans on you for emotional processing quickly
- Creates instant emotional closeness
- Doesn't balance vulnerability with stability

The Psychological Play: Forced intimacy. By accelerating emotional depth, they create a bond that feels real… without actually building it.

Why It Works (On You)

- You feel trusted and chosen
- You want to support and understand them
- It creates instant emotional connection
- You confuse vulnerability with readiness

Long-Term Effects

- Emotional exhaustion
- Feeling responsible for their healing
- Imbalanced dynamic
- Burnout and confusion

How to Recognize It Early

- Heavy emotional topics too soon
- You feel like their therapist, not their partner
- The connection feels intense but unstable
- There's no gradual build — just immediate depth

The Trap: You think depth equals compatibility.

The Reality Check: Sharing trauma isn't the same as being emotionally available.

Your Dating UnExpert Truth: "Vulnerability without stability is just emotional dumping."

Your Dating UnExpert Move

- Slow the pace of emotional intimacy
- Don't take on the role of healer
- Look for balance, not intensity

THE VACATION BOYFRIEND

Creates a perfect, romantic, all-in connection... but only within a temporary environment where real life doesn't apply.

What It Sounds Like

- "I wish this could last forever."
- "This feels so right."
- "I've never felt this way before."
- "Why don't we just stay here?"
- "I'm going to miss you so much."

What It Looks Like

- Intense connection during trips, events, or short-term settings
- Fully present and attentive... in the moment
- Feels like a real relationship quickly
- No real plan once normal life resumes
- Fades or disappears once reality returns

The Psychological Play: Fantasy environment. Without real-life responsibilities, they can show up fully... temporarily.

Why It Works (On You)

- The setting amplifies emotions
- It feels effortless and magical
- You experience them at their best
- You want to carry that feeling into real life

Long-Term Effects

- Emotional crash after the high
- Attachment to a moment, not a person
- Confusion about what was real
- Difficulty letting go of the experience

How to Recognize It Early

- Intensity tied to a specific environment
- No real-life integration or planning
- Avoids discussing what happens after
- Feels perfect... but contained

The Trap: You try to turn a moment into a relationship.

The Reality Check: It wasn't the relationship. It was the environment.

Your Dating UnExpert Truth: "Not everything that feels real is meant to continue."

Your Dating UnExpert Move

- Enjoy the experience without attaching to it
- Don't build a future off a temporary high
- Judge connection in real life, not just escape mode

THE "WYD" GUY

Initiates low-effort, repetitive communication with no intention of building conversation, plans, or connection.

What It Sounds Like

- "wyd"
- "what you doing"
- "u up"
- "hey"
- "what's good"

What It Looks Like

- Minimal effort texts with no substance
- Repeats the same messages daily
- Doesn't build conversation or direction

- Rarely turns messages into plans
- Keeps interaction at the lowest possible level

The Psychological Play: Effort minimization. They keep the line open... without investing anything meaningful.

Why It Works (On You)

- It keeps them on your radar
- You respond out of habit or curiosity
- You hope it will turn into something more
- Small attention still feels like attention

Long-Term Effects

- Wasted time and energy
- Mental distraction
- Lack of real connection
- Frustration from going nowhere

How to Recognize It Early

- Conversations never evolve
- Messages are repetitive and low effort
- No plans are made
- You're carrying the interaction

The Trap: You keep responding, hoping the conversation will improve.

The Reality Check: Low effort in the beginning doesn't turn into high effort later.

Your Dating UnExpert Truth: "If 'wyd' is the best they've got, that's all they're bringing."

Your Dating UnExpert Move

- Stop engaging with low-effort texts
- Don't carry the conversation
- Require intention, not filler

PSYCHOLOGICAL / BEHAVIORAL MALE TYPES

THE APPROVAL SEEKER

Shapes their behavior, opinions, and identity around what will be liked, accepted, or approved... rather than what's authentic.

What It Sounds Like

- "I just want everyone to be happy."
- "I don't like conflict."
- "Whatever you want is fine."
- "I'm easy."
- "I just go along with things."

What It Looks Like

- Avoids conflict at all costs
- Changes opinions depending on who they're with
- Struggles to make decisions
- Prioritizes being liked over being real
- Lacks clear boundaries or direction

The Psychological Play: Acceptance over authenticity. They avoid rejection by becoming whatever they think people want.

Why It Works (On You)

- They're easy to be around
- They don't challenge you
- It feels smooth and conflict-free
- You feel comfortable initially

Long-Term Effects

- Lack of real connection
- Frustration from indecisiveness
- Emotional shallowness
- Feeling like you don't truly know them
- Instability in who they are

How to Recognize It Early

- Avoids giving real opinions
- Always agrees or defers

- Struggles with decisions
- You feel like you're leading everything

The Trap: You think easy means compatible.

The Reality Check: If they don't know who they are, they can't show up fully for you.

Your Dating UnExpert Truth: "Agreeable isn't the same as authentic."

Your Dating UnExpert Move

- Pay attention to consistency in identity
- Don't over-lead the dynamic
- Choose someone with a clear sense of self

THE BOUNDARY PUSHER

Gradually tests, ignores, or overrides your boundaries to see how much they can get away with over time.

What It Sounds Like

- "You're being a little dramatic."
- "It's not that big of a deal."
- "Relax."
- "You're overreacting."
- "Why are you so strict about that?"

What It Looks Like

- Dismisses your limits as unreasonable
- Repeats behavior you've already addressed
- Pushes small boundaries first... then bigger ones
- Frames your standards as the problem
- Slowly conditions you to accept more than you should

The Psychological Play: Desensitization. If they can get you to tolerate small violations, they can escalate over time.

Why It Works (On You)

- You don't want to seem difficult
- You second-guess your standards
- You compromise to keep the peace
- You assume it's not "worth a fight"

Long-Term Effects

- Eroded boundaries
- Loss of self-respect
- Confusion about what's acceptable
- Increased tolerance for poor behavior
- Emotional exhaustion

How to Recognize It Early

- Repeatedly ignores your stated boundaries
- Makes you feel unreasonable for having them
- Tests limits instead of respecting them
- You feel pressured to loosen your standards

The Trap: You think flexibility will improve the relationship.

The Reality Check: Respect isn't negotiated. It's revealed.

Your Dating UnExpert Truth: "If they push your boundaries, they don't respect them."

Your Dating UnExpert Move

- Hold your boundaries without over-explaining
- Watch how they respond, not what they say
- Walk away from repeated disrespect

THE CONTROL FREAK

Needs to control situations, outcomes, and often you... to maintain emotional security and power.

What It Sounds Like

- "Why didn't you tell me that?"
- "I just like to know what's going on."
- "I'm not controlling, I just care."
- "That's not how I would do it."
- "I just want things done right."

What It Looks Like

- Questions your choices, timing, or decisions
- Needs constant updates or information
- Gets uncomfortable when they're not in control

- Subtly (or not subtly) tries to direct your behavior
- Frames control as "care" or "concern"

The Psychological Play: Control = safety. If they can control the environment, they don't have to deal with uncertainty or vulnerability.

Why It Works (On You)

- It can feel like protection at first
- You interpret it as involvement or care
- You adjust to avoid conflict
- You slowly normalize their expectations

Long-Term Effects

- Loss of independence
- Walking on eggshells
- Reduced confidence in your own decisions
- Emotional restriction
- Power imbalance

How to Recognize It Early

- Over-involvement in your choices
- Subtle pressure to do things their way
- Discomfort when you act independently
- You start second-guessing yourself

The Trap: You think they're just "very invested."

The Reality Check: Control isn't care. It's fear disguised as authority.

Your Dating UnExpert Truth: "If you have to shrink to keep the peace, it's not peace."

Your Dating UnExpert Move

- Hold your independence firmly
- Don't over-explain your choices
- Watch how they react to boundaries

THE EMOTIONAL LEECH

Feeds off your emotional energy, support, and attention… without giving the same in return.

What It Sounds Like

- "I just need to vent."
- "You're the only one who understands me."
- "I don't know what I'd do without you."
- "Can I call you? I'm having a rough time."
- "You always know what to say."

What It Looks Like

- Constantly unloads emotional problems onto you
- Relies on you for support, but doesn't reciprocate
- Comes to you when they need something
- Rarely asks about or supports your emotional needs
- Leaves you feeling drained after interactions

The Psychological Play: Emotional dependency. They attach to your ability to support them… without developing their own stability.

Why It Works (On You)

- You're empathetic and supportive
- You feel needed and important
- You want to help
- You mistake emotional reliance for connection

Long-Term Effects

- Emotional burnout
- One-sided relationship
- Feeling drained and overwhelmed
- Loss of personal emotional energy
- Resentment

How to Recognize It Early

- Conversations revolve around their problems
- Little to no support for you
- You feel exhausted after talking to them
- They show up when they need you, not consistently

The Trap: You think helping them creates connection.

The Reality Check: You're not in a relationship. You're in an emotional support role.

Your Dating UnExpert Truth: "Support should be mutual, not one-sided."

Your Dating UnExpert Move

- Set limits on emotional availability
- Notice what you're not receiving
- Choose reciprocity, not depletion

THE MARTYR

Positions himself as the one who sacrifices the most… using it to gain sympathy, control, or moral superiority.

What It Sounds Like

- "I do everything for everyone."
- "No one ever shows up for me."
- "I guess I'll just handle it like I always do."
- "I'm used to being the one who gives more."
- "It's fine, I don't expect anything anymore."

What It Looks Like

- Over-gives… then resents it
- Keeps score silently
- Uses sacrifice to create obligation
- Plays the "I do more" narrative
- Makes you feel guilty for not matching their effort

The Psychological Play: Control through guilt. By positioning themselves as the one who gives the most, they create an unspoken expectation that you owe them.

Why It Works (On You)

- You don't want to seem ungrateful
- You feel pressure to "balance it out"
- You empathize with their struggle
- You try harder to meet their expectations

Long-Term Effects

- Guilt-driven relationship dynamic
- Emotional pressure
- Resentment on both sides
- Feeling like you're never doing enough
- Loss of emotional ease

How to Recognize It Early

- Frequent comments about how much they give
- Subtle guilt when you don't reciprocate equally
- Keeps track of effort
- Gives with expectation, not generosity

The Trap: You feel responsible for their sacrifices.

The Reality Check: Healthy giving doesn't come with a receipt.

Your Dating UnExpert Truth: "If it feels like a debt, it's not love."

Your Dating UnExpert Move

- Don't overcompensate for guilt
- Call out unspoken expectations
- Look for balanced, voluntary effort

THE PROJECTIONIST

Projects their own behaviors, insecurities, or intentions onto you... accusing you of what they're actually doing or feeling.

What It Sounds Like

- "You're being shady."
- "You're probably talking to other people."
- "You don't care about me."
- "You're the one acting weird."
- "I feel like you're hiding something."

What It Looks Like

- Accuses you without evidence
- Reflects their own behavior onto you
- Creates conflict based on assumption
- Makes you defend yourself constantly
- Shifts focus away from their actions

The Psychological Play: Deflection. By placing the focus on you, they avoid scrutiny of themselves.

Why It Works (On You)

- You want to clear your name
- You get pulled into defending yourself
- You try to prove your intentions
- You shift focus away from their behavior

Long-Term Effects

- Constant defensiveness
- Emotional confusion
- Distrust
- Loss of self-confidence
- Draining, circular conflict

How to Recognize It Early

- Accusations don't match your behavior
- You're always explaining yourself
- Conflict feels misplaced
- You feel blamed for things that aren't yours

The Trap: You try to prove you're not what they're accusing you of.

The Reality Check: What they accuse you of often says more about them.

Your Dating UnExpert Truth: "Projection is confession in disguise."

Your Dating UnExpert Move

- Don't over-defend yourself
- Redirect focus to facts and patterns
- Step back from circular arguments

THE TESTER

Pushes limits early on to see what you'll tolerate... often disguised as jokes, sarcasm, or "just seeing how you react."

What It Sounds Like

- "I'm just joking."
- "Relax, I didn't mean it like that."
- "You're too sensitive."

- "I just wanted to see what you'd say."
- "You can't take a joke?"

What It Looks Like

- Makes borderline inappropriate comments early
- Uses humor to mask disrespect
- Pushes emotional or physical limits quickly
- Watches your reaction closely
- Adjusts behavior based on what you tolerate

The Psychological Play: Boundary mapping. They're gathering data on what you'll accept… so they know how far they can go later.

Why It Works (On You)

- You don't want to seem uptight
- You laugh things off to keep it light
- You give benefit of the doubt
- You assume it's harmless

Long-Term Effects

- Normalization of disrespect
- Gradual boundary erosion
- Confusion about intent
- Loss of confidence in your reactions

How to Recognize It Early

- "Jokes" that don't feel good
- Comments that cross a line, then get minimized
- You feel uncomfortable… but brush it off
- They pay attention to how much you tolerate

The Trap: You minimize it to avoid making it a big deal.

The Reality Check: If it doesn't feel good, it's not harmless.

Your Dating UnExpert Truth: "Testing you is them showing you who they are."

Your Dating UnExpert Move

- Address it immediately
- Don't laugh off discomfort
- Watch if behavior changes or continues

THE VALIDATION ADDICT

Relies on external attention, praise, and reassurance to feel worthy… often at the expense of real connection.

What It Sounds Like

- "Do you think I'm doing well?"
- "Be honest, do you like me?"
- "I just need reassurance sometimes."
- "I like knowing where I stand."
- "Tell me how you feel about me."

What It Looks Like

- Constantly seeks compliments or reassurance
- Needs frequent emotional affirmation
- Feels insecure without external feedback
- Can become distant or reactive when not validated
- Uses multiple people or platforms to fill the need

The Psychological Play: External worth. They don't feel secure internally, so they depend on others to confirm their value.

Why It Works (On You)

- You enjoy making them feel good
- It creates a sense of closeness
- You feel needed
- You believe reassurance equals emotional depth

Long-Term Effects

- Emotional exhaustion
- One-sided effort
- Feeling responsible for their self-worth
- Loss of emotional balance
- Burnout from constant reassurance

How to Recognize It Early

- Frequent need for validation
- Mood shifts based on your attention

- You feel like you're "maintaining" them emotionally
- They seek attention beyond just you

The Trap: You think your love can fill what they're missing internally.

The Reality Check: No amount of reassurance fixes internal insecurity.

Your Dating UnExpert Truth" "You're not their confidence system."

Your Dating UnExpert Move

- Stop over-giving reassurance
- Notice how much you're pouring in
- Choose emotional balance, not dependency

THE VICTIM MINDSET GUY

Sees himself as the one who's always been wronged, misunderstood, or treated unfairly... avoiding accountability by staying the victim.

What It Sounds Like

- "My ex was crazy."
- "People always do me wrong."
- "No one ever gives me a fair shot."
- "I just have bad luck with relationships."
- "I'm always the one who gets hurt."

What It Looks Like

- Blames past partners for everything
- Rarely takes responsibility
- Repeats the same patterns with new people
- Seeks sympathy over solutions
- Uses past pain to justify current behavior

The Psychological Play: Avoidance of accountability. If they're always the victim, they never have to change.

Why It Works (On You)

- You want to be the one who treats them better
- You empathize with their past
- You believe their story
- You think you can change their experience

Long-Term Effects

- One-sided emotional labor
- Repeated cycles
- Frustration and burnout
- Feeling responsible for fixing things
- Lack of growth in the relationship

How to Recognize It Early

- Every ex is the problem
- No personal accountability
- Same story, different people
- You feel like their emotional support system

The Trap: You think you'll be the exception.

The Reality Check: If everyone else was the problem... you'll be next.

Your Dating UnExpert Truth: "Someone who avoids accountability can't build a healthy relationship."

Your Dating UnExpert Move

- Listen for patterns, not just stories
- Don't take on the role of fixer
- Watch for ownership of behavior

FEMALE ARCHETYPES

ANXIOUS ANALYZER

Overthinks every word, action, and delay... trying to decode meaning, predict outcomes, and gain emotional security.

What It Sounds Like

- "What did he mean by that?"
- "Why did he take three hours to respond?"
- "His tone felt off."
- "Do you think he's losing interest?"
- "I shouldn't have said that, should I?"

What It Looks Like

- Re-reads texts multiple times
- Analyzes tone, timing, and wording
- Seeks reassurance from friends
- Over-adjusts behavior based on perceived signals
- Struggles to feel secure without constant clarity

The Psychological Play: Control through analysis. If she can figure it out, she can protect herself from uncertainty or rejection.

Why It Works (On You)

- You believe awareness = control
- You think you can prevent things from going wrong
- You're trying to feel safe
- You mistake thinking more for understanding more

Long-Term Effects

- Anxiety and mental exhaustion
- Overdependence on external validation
- Loss of presence in the relationship
- Self-doubt
- Emotional burnout

How to Recognize It Early

- You're thinking more than experiencing
- Small things feel big quickly
- You're constantly seeking reassurance
- Your mood shifts based on their behavior

The Trap: You think if you analyze enough, you'll feel secure.

The Reality Check: Overthinking doesn't create clarity. It creates anxiety.

Your Dating UnExpert Truth: "If you're confused, it's not your job to decode — it's your job to observe."

Your Dating UnExpert Move

- Stop filling in gaps with assumptions
- Let actions speak before reacting
- Ground yourself in what's actually happening

THE AVOIDANT WOMAN

Desires connection but instinctively pulls away when things become emotionally real or vulnerable.

What It Sounds Like

- "I just don't want anything serious right now."
- "I like my space."
- "I'm just really independent."
- "I don't need a relationship."
- "I get bored easily."

What It Looks Like

- Strong initial interest, then emotional distance
- Pulls back when things deepen
- Avoids vulnerability or difficult conversations
- Keeps people at arm's length
- Prioritizes independence over connection

The Psychological Play: Distance = safety. If she doesn't get too close, she can't get hurt.

Why It Works (On You)

- Independence is attractive
- She feels low-pressure and easy at first
- You want to "earn" closeness
- The distance creates intrigue

Long-Term Effects

- Inconsistent connection
- Emotional distance
- Frustration and confusion
- Difficulty building something stable

How to Recognize It Early

- Pulls away when things get deeper
- Avoids emotional conversations
- Keeps things casual even when it feels like more
- You feel closer than she acts

The Trap: You think time will make her open up.

The Reality Check: If she wanted closeness, she wouldn't be avoiding it.

Your Dating UnExpert Truth: "Unavailable isn't mysterious. It's unavailable."

Your Dating UnExpert Move

- Don't chase distance
- Match energy, not potential
- Choose someone who meets you emotionally

BOUNDARY BENDER

Knows her boundaries... but consistently compromises or abandons them to keep someone, avoid conflict, or maintain connection.

What It Sounds Like

- "It's not a big deal."
- "I'm fine with it." *(she's not)*
- "I don't want to make it awkward."
- "I'll just let it go this time."
- "I don't want to lose him over this."

What It Looks Like

- Says yes when she means no
- Lets things slide repeatedly
- Prioritizes keeping the connection over self-respect
- Adjusts her standards to match his behavior
- Avoids enforcing consequences

The Psychological Play: Connection over self-protection. She bends to keep the relationship intact, even if it costs her peace.

Why It Works (On You)

- You don't want to seem difficult
- You fear losing the connection
- You believe flexibility makes you "easy to love"
- You hope things will improve without confrontation

Long-Term Effects

- Loss of self-respect
- Resentment
- Blurred boundaries
- Emotional exhaustion
- Accepting less over time

How to Recognize It Early

- You ignore your own discomfort
- You say yes when you want to say no
- You justify behavior you don't like
- You feel uneasy but stay anyway

The Trap: You think bending keeps the relationship.

The Reality Check: What you tolerate teaches people how to treat you.

Your Dating UnExpert Truth: "Every time you bend your boundary, you break your own trust."

Your Dating UnExpert Move

- Say what you actually mean
- Follow through with consequences
- Choose self-respect over temporary connection

THE BUILDER

Sees a man's potential and invests time, energy, and emotional labor into helping him become who she believes he could be.

What It Sounds Like

- "He just needs the right support."
- "I see who he *could* be."
- "He has so much potential."
- "He's just going through a phase."
- "I can help him get there."

What It Looks Like

- Encourages, guides, and emotionally supports him constantly
- Invests in his growth more than he does
- Stays for who he *could become*, not who he is
- Excuses current behavior for future potential
- Takes on the role of motivator, therapist, and cheerleader

The Psychological Play: Hope-driven attachment. She bonds to the future version of him... instead of the present reality.

Why It Works (On You)

- You're nurturing and supportive
- You believe in growth
- You feel purposeful helping someone
- You want to be part of his "success story"

Long-Term Effects

- Emotional exhaustion
- One-sided investment
- Delayed realization of reality
- Feeling unappreciated
- Wasted time on potential

How to Recognize It Early

- You're giving more than you're receiving
- You're focused on who he *could be*
- You're explaining or defending his behavior
- You feel responsible for his growth

The Trap: You think your love can build him.

The Reality Check: You can't build someone who isn't building themselves.

Your Dating UnExpert Truth: "Potential is not a relationship."

Your Dating UnExpert Move

- Date who he is, not who he could be
- Match effort, not intention
- Stop investing where there's no return

CHILL GIRL COMPLEX

Pridefully low-maintenance, unbothered, and "easygoing"... while suppressing real needs, standards, and emotions.

What It Sounds Like

- "I'm not like other girls."
- "I'm super chill, I don't care."
- "I'm not needy."
- "It's fine, really." *(it's not)*
- "I don't need anything."

What It Looks Like

- Downplays needs to seem low-maintenance
- Accepts behavior she doesn't actually like
- Avoids expressing emotions or expectations
- Performs "coolness" instead of authenticity
- Internalizes everything to keep the vibe easy

The Psychological Play: Approval through suppression. She becomes what she thinks is easier to love… instead of being real.

Why It Works (On You)

- You want to be chosen
- You fear being "too much"
- You think being easygoing keeps him around
- You associate low needs with desirability

Long-Term Effects

- Resentment
- Emotional suppression
- Loss of authenticity
- Feeling unseen and unmet
- Burnout from pretending

How to Recognize It Early

- You say "it's fine" when it's not
- You avoid expressing needs
- You downplay your feelings
- You feel easy… but not fulfilled

The Trap: You think being low-maintenance makes you more lovable.

The Reality Check: The right person doesn't need you to minimize yourself.

Your Dating UnExpert Truth: "Being chill shouldn't cost you your standards."

Your Dating UnExpert Move

- Say what you actually feel
- Stop performing "low maintenance"
- Let someone meet your real needs

THE CLINGER

Attaches quickly and tightly, seeking constant closeness, reassurance, and connection to feel secure.

What It Sounds Like

- "Why haven't you texted me back?"
- "Do you still like me?"
- "I just want to see you all the time."
- "I miss you." *(constantly)*
- "Are we okay?"

What It Looks Like

- Needs frequent communication and reassurance
- Becomes emotionally attached very quickly
- Prioritizes the relationship over everything else
- Feels anxious when there's distance
- Struggles to maintain independence

The Psychological Play: Security through closeness. The more connected she feels, the safer she feels.

Why It Works (On You)

- You crave connection and reassurance
- You fear losing the person
- You equate closeness with stability
- You feel relief when they respond

Long-Term Effects

- Anxiety and dependency
- Loss of independence
- Emotional overwhelm
- Pushing people away unintentionally
- Instability in relationships

How to Recognize It Early

- You feel anxious when they're not responding
- You prioritize them over yourself

- You seek constant reassurance
- Your mood depends on their attention

The Trap: You think more closeness will create more security.

The Reality Check: Closeness without stability creates anxiety, not security.

Your Dating UnExpert Truth: "Attachment isn't connection if it costs you your peace."

Your Dating UnExpert Move

- Build emotional security within yourself
- Maintain your independence
- Let connection grow instead of forcing it

THE COOL GIRL

Performs as low-maintenance, agreeable, and "effortless" to be liked... while suppressing real needs, feelings, and standards.

What It Sounds Like

- "I'm not like other girls."
- "I don't care what you do."
- "I'm super chill."
- "It's really not a big deal."
- "I don't need much."

What It Looks Like

- Pretends to be okay with things she's not
- Downplays needs to seem easygoing
- Avoids conflict to keep the vibe "fun"
- Adapts herself to what he wants
- Prioritizes being liked over being real

The Psychological Play: Approval through performance. She becomes who she thinks is easiest to love... instead of who she actually is.

Why It Works (On You)

- You want to be chosen
- You fear being "too much"

- You've seen what happens when women ask for more
- You think being easy keeps him around

Long-Term Effects

- Resentment
- Emotional suppression
- Loss of identity
- Feeling unseen and unmet
- Burnout from pretending

How to Recognize It Early

- You say "it's fine" when it's not
- You avoid expressing needs
- You adjust yourself to match him
- You feel easy... but not fulfilled

The Trap: You think being chill makes you more lovable.

The Reality Check: The right person doesn't need a watered-down version of you.

Your Dating UnExpert Truth: "If you have to perform to be loved, it's not love."

Your Dating UnExpert Move

- Be honest about your needs early
- Stop editing yourself for approval
- Let someone choose the real you

DELUSION LOYALIST

Stays loyal to someone who isn't showing up, committing, or choosing her... based on hope, potential, or emotional attachment.

What It Sounds Like

- "He'll come around."
- "I just know he cares."
- "He's just going through something."
- "It's complicated."
- "He's not like this with me."

What It Looks Like

- Stays committed without receiving commitment
- Defends his behavior to others
- Holds onto rare good moments
- Ignores consistent patterns
- Waits instead of walking away

The Psychological Play: Hope over reality. She chooses belief in what *could be* over what is clearly happening.

Why It Works (On You)

- You're emotionally invested
- You've seen glimpses of potential
- You don't want to "give up too soon"
- You believe loyalty will be rewarded

Long-Term Effects

- Wasted time
- Emotional exhaustion
- Lowered self-worth
- Staying stuck in cycles
- Delayed healing

How to Recognize It Early

- You're loyal without being chosen
- You justify behavior you wouldn't accept from others
- You're waiting more than you're receiving
- You feel stuck but hopeful

The Trap: You think loyalty will make him choose you.

The Reality Check: Loyalty to the wrong person is self-abandonment.

Your Dating UnExpert Truth: "Staying isn't strength if it's costing you yourself."

Your Dating UnExpert Move

- Look at patterns, not moments
- Stop defending behavior that hurts you
- Choose yourself before he doesn't

EMOTIONAL LABORER

Carries the emotional weight of the relationship... managing communication, feelings, and effort while the other person coasts.

What It Sounds Like

- "I just want to talk this through."
- "I think we can work on this."
- "Let me explain how I feel."
- "I'm trying to understand you."
- "I'll fix it."

What It Looks Like

- Initiates all emotional conversations
- Tries to resolve every issue
- Explains, processes, and holds space constantly
- Carries communication and connection
- Stays engaged even when effort isn't matched

The Psychological Play: Responsibility for connection. She takes on the role of maintaining the relationship... even when it's not mutual.

Why It Works (On You)

- You value communication
- You believe effort can fix things
- You want to make it work
- You feel responsible for the outcome

Long-Term Effects

- Emotional burnout
- One-sided relationship
- Resentment
- Feeling unappreciated
- Loss of emotional energy

How to Recognize It Early

- You're always the one bringing things up
- You're doing the emotional work alone

- You feel responsible for fixing issues
- You're exhausted from trying

The Trap: You think if you work harder emotionally, the relationship will improve.

The Reality Check: You can't carry a relationship alone.

Your Dating UnExpert Truth: "If you're the only one doing the work, it's not a partnership."

Your Dating UnExpert Move

- Stop over-functioning emotionally
- Notice what's not being reciprocated
- Let the relationship reflect reality, not effort

THE FIXER

Takes responsibility for improving, healing, or stabilizing the other person... often at the expense of herself.

What It Sounds Like

- "He just needs support."
- "I can help him through this."
- "He's been through a lot."
- "I understand him."
- "I just need to be patient."

What It Looks Like

- Tries to solve his problems
- Gives advice, guidance, and emotional support constantly
- Stays through behavior that needs fixing
- Prioritizes his growth over her own needs
- Feels responsible for his progress

The Psychological Play: Control through care. If she can fix the problem, she can fix the relationship.

Why It Works (On You)

- You're empathetic and nurturing
- You feel needed

- You believe love means helping
- You want to be the one who "gets him"

Long-Term Effects

- Emotional exhaustion
- One-sided relationship
- Resentment
- Loss of personal focus
- Staying longer than you should

How to Recognize It Early

- You're doing more for him than he is for himself
- You feel responsible for his behavior
- You stay because of what he *could become*
- You're constantly trying to improve things

The Trap: You think helping him will make him love you better.

The Reality Check: You can't fix someone into being the partner you need.

Your Dating UnExpert Truth: "Love is not a renovation project."

Your Dating UnExpert Move

- Step out of the fixer role
- Let people show you who they are
- Choose partners, not projects

THE GHOSTED-BUT-STILL-LOYAL GIRL

Continues to emotionally hold space for someone who has disappeared... staying loyal to a connection that no longer exists.

What It Sounds Like

- "He'll come back."
- "I don't think it's over."
- "I just want to give him space."
- "He wouldn't just disappear for no reason."
- "I'm not talking to anyone else."

What It Looks Like

- Waits after being ghosted
- Avoids moving on "just in case"
- Keeps emotional attachment alive
- Doesn't fully accept the ending
- Stays mentally connected to someone absent

The Psychological Play: Attachment without closure. She holds onto the connection because letting go feels more painful than waiting.

Why It Works (On You)

- You want answers
- You believe there must be a reason
- You hold onto the good moments
- You're not ready to accept the ending

Long-Term Effects

- Delayed healing
- Emotional stagnation
- Difficulty moving forward
- Continued attachment to someone unavailable

How to Recognize It Early

- You're waiting instead of moving on
- You're loyal to someone not showing up
- You avoid new connections
- You're mentally stuck in the past

The Trap: You think waiting will bring clarity.

The Reality Check: Silence is clarity.

Your Dating UnExpert Truth: "You can't stay loyal to someone who left."

Your Dating UnExpert Move

- Accept the ending as it is
- Stop holding space for absence
- Choose forward movement

THE "I CAN CHANGE HIM" GIRL

Believes her love, patience, or influence can transform a man into the partner she wants him to be.

What It Sounds Like

- "He's different with me."
- "I just need to give him time."
- "He's never had someone like me."
- "I know he can be better."
- "I see something in him."

What It Looks Like

- Stays for potential instead of reality
- Excuses behavior as temporary
- Invests heavily in his growth
- Ignores clear patterns
- Believes she's the exception

The Psychological Play: Hope as control. If she believes she can change him, she doesn't have to accept what is.

Why It Works (On You)

- You believe in growth
- You want to feel special or chosen
- You've seen glimpses of who he *could be*
- You don't want to give up too soon

Long-Term Effects

- Wasted time
- Emotional exhaustion
- Repeated disappointment
- Loss of self-worth
- Staying stuck in cycles

How to Recognize It Early

- You're focused on potential
- You're explaining away behavior

- You believe you're the exception
- You're investing more than you're receiving

The Trap: You think you'll be the one who changes him.

The Reality Check: If he wanted to change, he would.

Your Dating UnExpert Truth: "You're not the exception. You're the experience."

Your Dating UnExpert Move

- Accept who he is now
- Stop investing in potential
- Choose someone who's already ready

THE INVESTIGATOR

Uses intense observation, research, and pattern-tracking to uncover the truth... often driven by anxiety, inconsistency, or lack of clarity.

What It Sounds Like

- "Something feels off."
- "I just want to be sure."
- "That doesn't add up."
- "I need to check something."
- "I'm not crazy."

What It Looks Like

- Deep dives social media, follows, likes, timestamps
- Cross-references stories, timelines, behavior
- Notices small inconsistencies quickly
- Screenshots, re-reads, analyzes patterns
- Looks for proof instead of asking directly

The Psychological Play: Control through information. If she can find the truth herself, she doesn't have to rely on someone who feels unreliable.

Why It Works (On You)

- Your intuition is actually picking up on something
- You don't trust what you're being told

- You want certainty
- You're trying to protect yourself

Long-Term Effects

- Anxiety and obsession
- Loss of peace
- Distrust in relationships
- Emotional exhaustion
- Hypervigilance

How to Recognize It Early

- You're researching more than communicating
- You feel the need to "confirm" everything
- You're gathering evidence instead of asking questions
- You feel uneasy even when nothing is confirmed

The Trap: You think finding proof will give you peace.

The Reality Check: If you feel the need to investigate, something is already wrong.

Your Dating UnExpert Truth: "You shouldn't have to go detective to feel secure."

Your Dating UnExpert Move

- Address inconsistencies directly
- Trust patterns over proof
- Choose clarity over investigation

THE LOYALTY QUEEN

Pridefully loyal, committed, and ride-or-die... even when the person she's loyal to isn't showing up, choosing her, or deserving it.

What It Sounds Like

- "I'm not giving up on him."
- "I'm just loyal like that."
- "I don't leave when things get hard."
- "He'll realize what he has."
- "I'm not like other girls."

What It Looks Like

- Stays through inconsistency, disrespect, or absence
- Defends him to others
- Prioritizes loyalty over self-respect
- Holds on longer than necessary
- Sees leaving as failure instead of clarity

The Psychological Play: Identity through loyalty. She defines herself by how much she can endure… instead of what she deserves.

Why It Works (On You)

- Loyalty feels like strength
- You don't want to be seen as someone who gives up
- You believe commitment should be unconditional
- You want to be valued for staying

Long-Term Effects

- Loss of self-worth
- Emotional burnout
- Staying in unhealthy dynamics
- Delayed growth
- Resentment

How to Recognize It Early

- You're loyal without reciprocity
- You're staying out of principle, not happiness
- You defend behavior you shouldn't accept
- You feel stuck but committed

The Trap: You think loyalty makes you valuable to the wrong person.

The Reality Check: Loyalty to the wrong person is self-betrayal.

Your Dating UnExpert Truth: "Loyalty isn't strength when it's misplaced."

Your Dating UnExpert Move

- Redirect loyalty toward yourself
- Stop proving your worth through endurance
- Choose reciprocity, not suffering

THE PICK-ME

Seeks validation and selection by prioritizing male approval over her own standards, often by minimizing herself or competing with other women.

What It Sounds Like

- "I'm not like other girls."
- "I don't cause drama."
- "I'm so easygoing."
- "Girls are just too much."
- "I get along better with guys."

What It Looks Like

- Downplays her needs to be chosen
- Competes with other women for attention
- Seeks male approval as validation
- Accepts less to stay desirable
- Adjusts personality to match what he wants

The Psychological Play: Validation through selection. Being chosen becomes more important than choosing correctly.

Why It Works (On You)

- You want to feel special
- You fear not being chosen
- You associate approval with worth
- You've been conditioned to compete

Long-Term Effects

- Loss of authenticity
- Low standards
- Dependence on external validation
- Insecurity
- Unfulfilling relationships

How to Recognize It Early

- You're focused on being chosen
- You minimize your needs
- You compare yourself to other women
- You adjust yourself for approval

The Trap: You think being chosen equals being valued.

The Reality Check: Being chosen means nothing if you chose wrong.

Your Dating UnExpert Truth: "You don't win by being picked. You win by picking right."

Your Dating UnExpert Move

- Shift from seeking approval to setting standards
- Stop competing — start choosing
- Let your value stand without performance

POTENTIAL WIFE SYNDROME

Acts like a committed partner before being chosen as one... giving loyalty, effort, and emotional investment without reciprocity.

What It Sounds Like

- "I just treat people how I'd want to be treated."
- "I don't play games."
- "I'm just naturally giving."
- "I don't see the point in holding back."
- "I'd make such a good partner."

What It Looks Like

- Gives girlfriend-level effort early
- Prioritizes him quickly
- Invests emotionally before commitment
- Shows loyalty without being chosen
- Treats potential like a relationship

The Psychological Play: Earned love. She believes showing she's "wife material" will make him choose her.

Why It Works (On You)

- You value genuine connection
- You don't want to play games
- You believe effort should be met with effort
- You think being "good enough" will secure the relationship

Long-Term Effects

- Overinvestment
- Feeling unappreciated
- Being taken for granted
- Emotional burnout
- Confusion when effort isn't matched

How to Recognize It Early

- You're giving more than the relationship has earned
- You're emotionally invested quickly
- You're showing loyalty without clarity
- You feel like you're proving your value

The Trap: You think showing your worth will make him choose you.

The Reality Check: The right person doesn't need to be convinced.

Your Dating UnExpert Truth: "You don't audition for a role you already qualify for."

Your Dating UnExpert Move

- Let investment build mutually
- Match effort, don't lead with it
- Let someone choose you without proving

THE OVER-ANALYZER

Dissects every detail of the relationship... trying to find meaning, predict outcomes, and avoid uncertainty.

What It Sounds Like

- "What did that mean?"
- "Why would he say that?"
- "I feel like something shifted."
- "Do you think this is a sign?"
- "I just want to understand."

What It Looks Like

- Replays conversations repeatedly
- Searches for hidden meaning in small actions

- Seeks constant clarity or reassurance
- Overthinks tone, timing, and behavior
- Struggles to stay present

The Psychological Play: Control through understanding. If she can figure everything out, she can protect herself from getting hurt.

Why It Works (On You)

- You're intuitive and observant
- You want clarity
- You don't trust inconsistency
- You believe awareness will prevent mistakes

Long-Term Effects

- Anxiety
- Mental exhaustion
- Loss of peace
- Difficulty enjoying the relationship
- Emotional instability

How to Recognize It Early

- You're thinking more than experiencing
- Small things feel bigger than they are
- You're constantly seeking meaning
- You feel mentally drained

The Trap: You think more thinking will give you more clarity.

The Reality Check: Clarity comes from patterns, not overthinking.

Your Dating UnExpert Truth: "If you need to analyze it this much, it's already off."

Your Dating UnExpert Move

- Focus on consistent behavior
- Stop filling in gaps
- Stay grounded in what's actually happening

OVEREXPLAINER

Feels the need to over-justify, clarify, and explain thoughts, feelings, and actions... often to be understood, accepted, or avoid conflict.

What It Sounds Like

- "I just want to explain what I meant..."
- "I didn't mean it like that, I meant..."
- "I'm not trying to upset you, I just..."
- "Let me clarify..."
- "I just want to make sure you understand..."

What It Looks Like

- Sends long messages explaining feelings
- Clarifies intentions repeatedly
- Tries to prevent misunderstanding at all costs
- Over-communicates to avoid conflict
- Feels responsible for how she's perceived

The Psychological Play: Approval through clarity. If she explains enough, she can avoid rejection, conflict, or misinterpretation.

Why It Works (On You)

- You want to be understood
- You fear being misread
- You value communication
- You're trying to keep things smooth

Long-Term Effects

- Emotional exhaustion
- Feeling unheard despite explaining more
- Over-responsibility in communication
- Loss of confidence
- Frustration

How to Recognize It Early

- You feel the need to explain everything
- You send long messages to clarify yourself
- You're trying to control how you're perceived
- You feel misunderstood often

The Trap: You think explaining more will make them understand you better.

The Reality Check: The right person doesn't need a paragraph to understand you.

Your Dating UnExpert Truth: "If they misunderstand you after clarity, it's not confusion — it's misalignment."

Your Dating UnExpert Move

- Say it once, clearly
- Stop over-justifying
- Let people meet you where you are

RED FLAG COLLECTOR

Sees, names, and even jokes about red flags... but continues dating the person anyway.

What It Sounds Like

- "He's such a red flag, I know."
- "I should probably run."
- "This is so toxic lol."
- "I know better, don't judge me."
- "It's fine, I can handle it."

What It Looks Like

- Identifies problematic behavior immediately
- Talks about it openly... but doesn't act on it
- Stays entertained or intrigued by dysfunction
- Normalizes red flags as part of the experience
- Continues despite clear warning signs

The Psychological Play: Awareness without boundaries. She sees the truth... but doesn't trust herself enough to act on it.

Why It Works (On You)

- You think awareness protects you
- You're entertained by the chaos
- You believe you can handle it
- You don't want to leave too soon

Long-Term Effects

- Repeated unhealthy patterns
- Emotional burnout
- Loss of self-trust
- Normalizing dysfunction
- Delayed growth

How to Recognize It Early

- You call out red flags but stay anyway
- You joke about behavior that bothers you
- You feel uneasy but continue
- You know… but you're not acting

The Trap: You think knowing better is enough.

The Reality Check: Awareness without action changes nothing.

Your Dating UnExpert Truth: "If you see the red flag and stay, it's no longer a warning — it's a choice."

Your Dating UnExpert Move

- Act on what you already know
- Stop normalizing what doesn't feel right
- Trust your instincts the first time

THE REWRITER

Alters the reality of the relationship in her mind… softening, justifying, or reframing behavior to make it easier to stay.

What It Sounds Like

- "He didn't mean it like that."
- "He's just stressed."
- "It's not as bad as it sounds."
- "He's actually really sweet sometimes."
- "I think I'm just overthinking it."

What It Looks Like

- Minimizes behavior that hurt her
- Focuses on good moments over consistent patterns
- Reframes actions to make them more acceptable
- Talks herself out of leaving
- Holds onto a "nicer" version of reality

The Psychological Play: Protection through distortion. If she softens the truth, she doesn't have to face the pain of what it actually is.

Why It Works (On You)

- You're emotionally attached
- You don't want to be wrong

- You want it to work
- You're avoiding the discomfort of leaving

Long-Term Effects

- Self-betrayal
- Confusion
- Staying in unhealthy situations longer
- Loss of clarity and confidence
- Emotional exhaustion

How to Recognize It Early

- You're constantly justifying behavior
- You downplay what actually happened
- You focus on exceptions, not patterns
- You feel conflicted but stay

The Trap: You think reframing reality will make it better.

The Reality Check: Changing the story doesn't change the behavior.

Your Dating UnExpert Truth: "If you have to rewrite it to accept it, it's not right."

Your Dating UnExpert Move

- Look at patterns, not moments
- Say things exactly as they are
- Choose truth over comfort

THE RIDE-OR-DIE

Pridefully loyal, all-in, and committed... even when the relationship is unhealthy, unreciprocated, or damaging.

What It Sounds Like

- "I'm not leaving him."
- "I stay when things get hard."
- "I'm just built different."
- "I'm loyal no matter what."
- "I don't give up on people."

What It Looks Like

- Stays through clear mistreatment or inconsistency
- Sees leaving as weakness
- Endures more than she should
- Ties identity to loyalty and endurance
- Confuses suffering with strength

The Psychological Play: Identity through endurance. She proves her value by how much she can withstand.

Why It Works (On You)

- Loyalty feels like strength
- You don't want to "fail" at the relationship
- You believe love means staying
- You take pride in being different

Long-Term Effects

- Loss of self-respect
- Emotional burnout
- Staying in unhealthy dynamics
- Resentment
- Delayed healing

How to Recognize It Early

- You stay even when you're unhappy
- You equate leaving with failure
- You endure more than you should
- You feel stuck but committed

The Trap: You think staying proves your strength.

The Reality Check: Walking away is often the stronger choice.

Your Dating UnExpert Truth: "Loyalty without self-respect is self-abandonment."

Your Dating UnExpert Move

- Redefine what strength looks like
- Choose yourself over endurance
- Leave what's costing you your peace

THE ROMANTICIZER

Sees ordinary or inconsistent behavior through a romantic, idealized lens... turning moments into meaning and potential into reality.

What It Sounds Like

- "It just feels different with him."
- "I can't explain it, it's just a vibe."
- "That moment meant something."
- "I think there's something real here."
- "It's not like anything I've had before."

What It Looks Like

- Assigns deep meaning to small actions
- Builds emotional narratives quickly
- Focuses on chemistry over consistency
- Ignores red flags in favor of "the feeling"
- Creates a story that feels bigger than reality

The Psychological Play: Fantasy over facts. She fills in the gaps with meaning, turning moments into a relationship that doesn't actually exist.

Why It Works (On You)

- You're intuitive and emotionally aware
- You crave depth and connection
- You trust how something feels
- You believe in rare, meaningful bonds

Long-Term Effects

- Attachment to imagined potential
- Disappointment when reality doesn't match
- Difficulty letting go
- Emotional confusion
- Repeating fantasy-based patterns

How to Recognize It Early

- You're creating meaning without consistency
- You feel deeply connected very quickly
- You're building a story in your head

- You're prioritizing feelings over facts

The Trap: You think the feeling means it's real.

The Reality Check: Feelings can be real... without the relationship being real.

Your Dating UnExpert Truth: "Chemistry creates a spark. Consistency creates a relationship."

Your Dating UnExpert Move

- Slow down the narrative in your head
- Look for patterns, not moments
- Let reality build before meaning

THE SITUATIONSHIP THERAPIST

Analyzes, understands, and emotionally supports a man in an undefined relationship... doing the emotional work while he stays unchanged.

What It Sounds Like

- "I understand why he's like this."
- "He has a lot of trauma."
- "He just needs someone patient."
- "I see what he's going through."
- "I can help him work through it."

What It Looks Like

- Breaks down his behavior instead of reacting to it
- Offers emotional support without receiving it
- Stays in undefined dynamics to "help him grow"
- Prioritizes understanding over boundaries
- Becomes his emotional safe space... without commitment

The Psychological Play: Connection through understanding. She bonds by analyzing and supporting him... instead of requiring him to show up.

Why It Works (On You)

- You're empathetic and emotionally intelligent
- You value understanding people deeply
- You believe patience leads to growth
- You feel connected through emotional depth

Long-Term Effects

- Emotional burnout
- One-sided investment
- Staying in situationships too long
- Feeling drained and unfulfilled
- Delayed clarity

How to Recognize It Early

- You're analyzing him more than evaluating him
- You're giving emotional support without reciprocity
- You're staying to "help" instead of being chosen
- You feel like his therapist, not his partner

The Trap: You think understanding him will change him.

The Reality Check: Understanding someone doesn't obligate them to change.

Your Dating UnExpert Truth: "You're not his therapist. And this isn't your case study."

Your Dating UnExpert Move

- Stop over-analyzing and start evaluating
- Require action, not insight
- Choose mutual effort, not emotional labor

NEUTRAL / CROSSOVER ARCHETYPES

THE CHAOS ADDICT

Feels most alive in unpredictability, drama, and emotional highs and lows… often mistaking instability for passion.

What It Sounds Like

- "It's never boring with him."
- "I like a little chaos."
- "It's just intense between us."
- "Normal relationships feel boring."
- "We have a lot of ups and downs."

What It Looks Like

- Attracted to inconsistent or unavailable partners
- Thrives in push-pull dynamics
- Feels drawn to drama or emotional extremes
- Gets bored in stable, healthy relationships
- Repeats toxic cycles

The Psychological Play: Familiar dysfunction. Chaos feels like connection because it mirrors emotional patterns they're used to.

Why It Works (On You)

- Intensity feels like passion
- Emotional highs create attachment
- Calm feels unfamiliar or "off"
- You associate unpredictability with excitement

Long-Term Effects

- Emotional instability
- Burnout
- Difficulty sustaining healthy relationships
- Addiction to toxic patterns
- Confusion between peace and boredom

How to Recognize It Early

- You're drawn to inconsistency
- Calm feels uncomfortable
- You mistake drama for depth
- Your relationships feel like rollercoasters

The Trap: You think stable means boring.

The Reality Check: Peace doesn't feel like chaos... and that's the point.

Your Dating UnExpert Truth: "If it feels like a rollercoaster, it's not love — it's adrenaline."

Your Dating UnExpert Move

- Learn to tolerate stability
- Redefine what "exciting" means
- Choose peace, even if it feels unfamiliar

THE ESCAPE ARTIST

Disappears, withdraws, or creates distance the moment things become emotionally real, serious, or require accountability.

What It Sounds Like

- "I just need space."
- "This is moving too fast."
- "I've got a lot going on right now."
- "I'm not ready for this."
- "I don't want to mess this up."

What It Looks Like

- Strong start, then sudden retreat
- Pulls away after emotional or physical closeness
- Avoids deeper conversations
- Creates distance when expectations arise
- Disappears when things get real

The Psychological Play: Avoidance of vulnerability. When things shift from casual to real, they exit instead of engaging.

Why It Works (On You)

- You try to give space and be understanding
- You believe they're overwhelmed, not unavailable
- You hold onto how it started
- You think they'll come back when ready

Long-Term Effects

- Emotional confusion
- Push-pull cycles
- Anxiety and overthinking
- Difficulty trusting stability

How to Recognize It Early

- Pulls back when things deepen
- Avoids emotional conversations
- Inconsistent presence
- You feel the shift clearly

The Trap: You think giving space will bring them back stronger.

The Reality Check: People who want connection don't run from it.

Your Dating UnExpert Truth: "If they disappear when it gets real, they're not ready for real."

Your Dating UnExpert Move

- Don't chase distance
- Observe how they handle depth
- Choose someone who leans in, not out

THE FANTASY BUILDER

Creates an idealized version of the relationship through words, plans, and emotional projection... without grounding it in real, consistent action.

What It Sounds Like

- "We'd be so good together."
- "I can see us doing this..."
- "You're exactly what I've been looking for."
- "This just feels right."
- "I've thought about us a lot."

What It Looks Like

- Talks about a future early on
- Creates emotional intimacy through vision, not action
- Paints a picture of what "could be"
- Uses words to deepen connection quickly
- Doesn't follow through consistently

The Psychological Play: Emotional projection. They build the relationship in theory... instead of in reality.

Why It Works (On You)

- It feels meaningful and intentional
- You get pulled into the vision
- You feel chosen and seen
- You start imagining the future too

Long-Term Effects

- Attachment to something that never existed
- Disappointment
- Confusion between words and reality
- Difficulty trusting future connections

How to Recognize It Early

- Big talk, little follow-through
- Future-focused without present effort
- Emotional connection builds faster than behavior supports
- You feel invested quickly

The Trap: You fall in love with the idea of what it could be.

The Reality Check: A future isn't real unless it's being built now.

Your Dating UnExpert Truth: "Words build dreams. Actions build relationships."

Your Dating UnExpert Move

- Watch what they do, not what they say
- Don't attach to future talk
- Require consistency before belief

THE LOVE ADDICT

Craves the feeling of being in love — the intensity, the closeness, the emotional high — more than the actual stability of a relationship.

What It Sounds Like

- "I just love love."
- "I fall hard."
- "I've never felt this way before." (every time)
- "When it's right, you just know."
- "I want something real... so badly."

What It Looks Like

- Falls quickly and intensely
- Jumps from one relationship to the next
- Prioritizes emotional highs over compatibility
- Becomes deeply attached early
- Struggles to be alone

The Psychological Play: Addiction to intensity. The feeling of love becomes the reward... not the person or the relationship itself.

Why It Works (On You)

- It feels passionate and exciting
- You feel deeply chosen
- The intensity mimics real connection
- It moves quickly, so it feels "certain"

Long-Term Effects

- Repeated emotional highs and crashes
- Poor partner selection
- Dependency on relationships
- Difficulty sustaining healthy love
- Burnout from cycles

How to Recognize It Early

- Intensity builds very quickly
- Strong emotions before real foundation
- History of fast relationships
- Struggles with being alone

The Trap: You think intensity means it's real.

The Reality Check: Love isn't proven by how fast it starts... but how steady it stays.

Your Dating UnExpert Truth: "Addiction to love will keep you from real love."

Your Dating UnExpert Move

- Slow down emotional investment
- Look for consistency, not intensity
- Get comfortable with neutral, not just highs

THE SERIAL DATER

Continuously dates, talks to, or entertains multiple people... rarely pausing to process, reflect, or build something meaningful.

What It Sounds Like

- "I just like meeting new people."
- "I'm seeing what's out there."
- "I'm not putting pressure on anything."
- "I don't like being tied down."
- "I just go with the flow."

What It Looks Like

- Always talking to someone new
- Rarely single for long (but not deeply committed either)
- Keeps multiple options open
- Moves on quickly from one person to the next
- Avoids emotional depth or reflection

The Psychological Play: Avoidance through motion. As long as they keep moving, they don't have to sit with discomfort, rejection, or self-reflection.

Why It Works (On You)

- They're charming and engaging
- It feels exciting and new
- You think you might be the one they choose
- Their attention feels intentional (even if it's not exclusive)

Long-Term Effects

- Lack of meaningful connection
- Emotional shallowness
- Burnout from constant dating
- Difficulty forming deep bonds
- Repetitive cycles

How to Recognize It Early

- Always has multiple options
- Rarely slows down or focuses on one person
- Moves on quickly
- Avoids deeper conversations about intention

The Trap: You think you'll be the one who makes them stop.

The Reality Check: People who don't pause don't process.

Your Dating UnExpert Truth: "If they're always looking, they're not building."

Your Dating UnExpert Move

- Ask direct questions about intention
- Don't compete with options
- Choose someone who's ready to focus

THE TIME WASTER

Engages just enough to keep things going... while never intending to build anything real or lasting.

What It Sounds Like

- "I'm just seeing where things go."
- "I'm not in a rush."
- "I like taking things slow."
- "Let's just enjoy it."
- "I'm open to whatever happens."

What It Looks Like

- Consistent communication with no progression
- Avoids defining anything over time
- Keeps you engaged but not advancing
- Doesn't invest in building a future
- Months pass with no real change

The Psychological Play: Passive delay. They don't end it… but they don't build it either.

Why It Works (On You)

- It feels steady, not chaotic
- You think progress just takes time
- You don't want to rush something good
- You believe it's naturally unfolding

Long-Term Effects

- Wasted time
- Emotional attachment without outcome
- Frustration and confusion
- Delayed opportunity for real connection

How to Recognize It Early

- Time is passing with no clarity
- Conversations don't evolve into action
- No forward movement
- You feel stuck in "almost"

The Trap: You think patience will create progress.

The Reality Check: Time doesn't build a relationship. Effort does.

Your Dating UnExpert Truth: "If it's not growing, it's stalling."

Your Dating UnExpert Move

- Set a timeline for clarity
- Look for progression, not just presence
- Walk away from stagnation

Seduction & Power Terms

The Aging Baby

An adult who seeks constant nurturing, reassurance, and emotional caretaking while quietly avoiding responsibility, growth, or independence. They don't want a partner. They want a regulator, a fixer, a steady source of comfort they never have to become for themselves.

Behavior Pattern (How They Operate)

- Hooks you with vulnerability or "softness"
- Quickly positions you as their emotional support system
- Leans on you for decisions, validation, stability
- Avoids accountability by playing overwhelmed, confused, or fragile
- Becomes dependent… then resentful when you burn out

Archetypes Through History

- The eternal "man-child" trope in literature and film
- Characters who never leave home emotionally, even if they do physically
- The charming but incapable partner seen in modern rom-coms

Modern-Day Version

- Needs constant texting reassurance
- "I don't know what I'd do without you" energy by week two
- Can't handle basic life logistics without outsourcing it to you
- Turns you into therapist, assistant, and emotional support human

Signature Phrases

- "I just need you right now"
- "You're the only one who understands me"
- "I'm just going through a lot"
- "Can you help me figure this out?"

Why People Fall For It

- Because it feels like being needed.
- Because nurturing feels like love.
- Because being chosen as "the safe place" feels intimate... until it becomes a responsibility you never signed up for.

The Damage

- Emotional exhaustion
- Loss of attraction
- Quiet resentment
- You stop being a partner and become a caretaker

Spot It Fast

- Needs constant reassurance
- Avoids decisions
- Plays overwhelmed often
- Leans on you for emotional regulation
- Little to no personal accountability

Avoid / Counter

- Stop over-functioning
- Don't reward helplessness
- Watch what they do without your support

Your Dating UnExpert Take: Support is part of love. Dependency is not. If they can't stand on their own, they will eventually lean on you until you collapse.

The Anti-Seducer

A person who unknowingly destroys attraction through behaviors rooted in insecurity, control, or miscalibrated effort. They don't lose people by accident. They repel them through pressure, neediness, arrogance, or emotional blindness.

Behavior Pattern (How They Operate)

- Tries too hard or not at all
- Overcompensates with intensity, control, or ego
- Misreads signals and doubles down
- Creates discomfort instead of attraction
- Pushes people away while trying to pull them closer

Archetypes Through History

- The overbearing suitor in classic literature

- The jealous, controlling lover
- The self-absorbed figure who mistakes dominance for magnetism

Modern-Day Version

- Double texts into oblivion
- Comes on too strong too fast
- Tries to impress instead of connect
- Talks at you, not with you
- Creates pressure where there should be ease

Signature Phrases

- "Why didn't you respond?"
- "I just want something real" (after 2 days)
- "I'm not like other guys/girls"
- "Be honest with me" (but can't handle the truth)

Why People Fall For It: They don't, long-term. But early on, effort can look like interest. Confidence can be faked. And intensity can be mistaken for depth... until it becomes overwhelming.

The Damage

- Attraction dies quickly
- Emotional pressure replaces chemistry
- The other person pulls away... fast

Spot It Fast

- Overeager or overcontrolling
- Poor emotional awareness
- Creates pressure early
- Doesn't read the room
- Tries to force connection

Avoid / Counter

- Don't reward intensity over compatibility
- Watch how they handle space
- Attraction should feel natural, not managed

Your Dating UnExpert Take: Attraction isn't just about what to do. It's about what to stop doing. Most people don't need more effort. They need less desperation.

The Beauty

Someone whose physical attractiveness shapes how the world responds to them, often leaving them seen, desired, and pursued... but rarely understood. They are valued for how they look, not who they are.

Behavior Pattern (How They Operate)

- Receives attention easily
- Becomes accustomed to surface-level validation
- Struggles to filter genuine interest from projection
- May lean into appearance because it's what "works"
- Quietly craves depth but attracts surface

Archetypes Through History

- Helen of Troy — desired, fought over, rarely known
- The "it girl" figure across decades
- The muse who inspires obsession but lacks agency

Modern-Day Version

- High engagement on social media, low emotional fulfillment
- Constant attention, minimal real connection
- People assume personality based on appearance
- Struggles to be taken seriously beyond looks

Signature Phrases

- "People always assume..."
- "They only like me for..."
- "No one actually knows me"

Why People Fall For It: Projection. Fantasy. Aesthetic attraction. People fall in love with what they see... not who is actually there.

The Damage

- Objectification
- Lack of emotional depth in relationships
- Feeling unseen despite constant attention

Spot It Fast

- Gets attention easily but struggles with depth
- People idealize them quickly
- Relationships stay surface-level
- Feels unseen despite being desired

Avoid / Counter

- Prioritize people who ask real questions

- Watch who engages beyond appearance
- Don't mistake attention for connection

Your Dating UnExpert Take: Attraction gets attention. Depth keeps it. If someone never goes beyond your surface, they were never there for you.

The Coquette

A master of attraction through emotional rhythm. They create desire not by giving fully, but by controlling presence and absence. They pull you in, then disappear just enough to make you chase the feeling they created.

Behavior Pattern (How They Operate)

- Engages with charm and intrigue
- Creates emotional highs
- Withdraws at peak interest
- Reappears just enough to reignite desire
- Keeps you slightly off balance

Archetypes Through History

- Classic seductresses in literature
- The unattainable muse
- Figures who inspire obsession through distance and mystery

Modern-Day Version

- Hot-and-cold texting patterns
- Disappears right when things feel close
- Gives just enough to keep you hooked
- Leaves conversations slightly unresolved

Signature Phrases

- "I've just been busy"
- "I like to go with the flow"
- "I don't want to rush anything"
- "I miss you" (right when you start moving on)

Why People Fall For It

- Because uncertainty creates obsession.
- Because inconsistency mimics emotional highs and lows.
- Because the brain gets addicted to the chase.

The Damage

- Anxiety
- Obsessive thinking
- Emotional dependency on unpredictability

Spot It Fast

- Hot and cold behavior
- Disappears at peak connection
- Keeps things undefined
- Reappears just in time

Avoid / Counter

- Don't reward inconsistency
- Watch patterns, not moments
- Choose clarity over chemistry

Your Dating UnExpert Take: Mystery creates attraction. Inconsistency creates anxiety. If you're confused, that's not chemistry. That's instability.

The Charmer

Someone who creates instant emotional connection through attention, flattery, and hyper-attunement... without ever revealing anything real about themselves. They don't bond. They mirror, perform, and adapt until you feel seen.

Behavior Pattern (How They Operate)

- Reads you quickly
- Reflects your interests, humor, and energy back to you
- Makes you feel uniquely chosen
- Keeps the focus on you while staying slightly vague themselves
- Builds comfort fast... without depth

Archetypes Through History

- Don Juan — adored by many, known by none
- Social manipulators who thrive on likability over authenticity
- The smooth operator in every era who never quite gets pinned down

Modern-Day Version

- Asks all the right questions early
- Mirrors your texting style, humor, and values

- Feels "so easy" to talk to
- Weeks later... you realize you know almost nothing about them

Signature Phrases

- "That's exactly how I feel too"
- "You're different"
- "I've never met anyone like you"
- "I just get you"

Why People Fall For It

- Because it feels like connection.
- Because being understood is intoxicating.
- Because they reflect your best self back to you... and it feels like intimacy.

The Damage

- False intimacy
- Emotional confusion
- Realization that the connection was one-sided

Spot It Fast

- Feels instantly aligned with you
- Asks a lot, shares little
- Adapts quickly to your personality
- Hard to define who they actually are

Avoid / Counter

- Ask direct questions
- Watch for consistency in identity
- Don't confuse ease with intimacy

Your Dating UnExpert Take: Charm is not depth. If they feel perfect too quickly, it's probably because they're performing, not revealing.

The Charismatic

A naturally magnetic presence fueled by confidence, clarity, and purpose. They don't chase attention. They generate it. People are drawn to their energy, often before they even understand why.

Behavior Pattern (How They Operate)

- Commands attention without forcing it
- Speaks with certainty and direction
- Creates emotional momentum in groups
- Inspires belief, excitement, or admiration

- Moves people… sometimes without grounding them

Archetypes Through History

- Visionary leaders, performers, and influencers
- Figures who could move crowds with presence alone
- The captivating personality people orbit around

Modern-Day Version

- The person everyone watches in the room
- Strong social presence, high engagement
- Feels exciting, alive, and larger-than-life
- People get swept up in their energy quickly

Signature Phrases

- "Trust me"
- "We're going to do something big"
- "Just come with me"
- "I see things differently"

Why People Fall For It

- Because certainty is attractive.
- Because direction feels safe.
- Because confidence can feel like truth… even when it isn't.

The Damage

- Losing your own voice in their momentum
- Idealizing them without truly knowing them
- Following energy instead of evaluating substance

Spot It Fast

- Strong presence immediately
- People gravitate toward them
- Speaks with confidence and certainty
- Creates fast emotional momentum

Avoid / Counter

- Slow yourself down
- Separate energy from character
- Ask: who are they when no one's watching

Your Dating UnExpert Take: Magnetism is powerful. Just make sure it's attached to something real. Energy without integrity is just influence.

The Conqueror

A pursuit-driven personality motivated by challenge, ego, and the thrill of "winning." Their interest is highest when you are hardest to get… and lowest once you're secured.

Behavior Pattern (How They Operate)

- Targets what feels just out of reach
- Applies pressure, effort, and pursuit
- Escalates quickly during the chase
- Gains validation once they "win"
- Withdraws or loses interest after

Archetypes Through History

- Casanova — driven by conquest, not commitment
- The classic hunter mentality in romantic lore
- Characters who value pursuit over partnership

Modern-Day Version

- Obsessed in the beginning
- Loves the chase, the tension, the game
- Becomes distant once you're emotionally available
- Reappears when you pull away

Signature Phrases

- "I love a challenge"
- "I don't usually do this"
- "You're hard to read"
- "I had to have you"

Why People Fall For It

- Because pursuit feels like value.
- Because effort feels like intention.
- Because being "chosen" after a chase feels earned.

The Damage

- Sudden emotional drop-off
- Confusion about what changed
- Feeling like a prize, not a partner

Spot It Fast

- High effort early, low effort later
- Interest spikes when you pull away
- Gets bored with consistency

- Treats connection like competition

Avoid / Counter

- Don't reward chase dynamics
- Stay consistent instead of reactive
- Watch what happens after they "get" you

Your Dating UnExpert Take: If they only show up when it's a challenge, they're not built for something real. They're built for the game.

The Crushed Star

Someone who once felt admired, important, or desired... and now chases external validation to reclaim that identity. They aren't connecting with you. They're trying to feel like themselves again.

Behavior Pattern (How They Operate)

- Seeks admiration and reassurance
- Talks about who they "used to be"
- Needs consistent validation to feel stable
- Leans on you to rebuild their identity
- Becomes dependent on your perception of them

Archetypes Through History

- The fallen celebrity
- The former "it person" chasing relevance
- Characters defined by past glory rather than present identity

Modern-Day Version

- Constantly referencing their peak era
- Needs reassurance about attractiveness, success, worth
- Performs confidence but seeks validation underneath
- Uses relationships as proof they still "have it"

Signature Phrases

- "I used to..."
- "People always loved me for..."
- "I just want to feel like myself again"
- "Do you still think I'm..."

Why People Fall For It

- Because it feels like helping.
- Because restoring someone feels meaningful.
- Because you believe your love can rebuild them.

The Damage

- Emotional drain
- One-sided validation loop
- You become responsible for their self-worth

Spot It Fast

- Needs frequent reassurance
- Lives in past validation
- Seeks admiration over connection
- Identity feels unstable

Avoid / Counter

- Don't become their mirror
- Watch for self-generated confidence
- Support, don't carry

Your Dating UnExpert Take: You can support someone. You cannot restore their identity. That's an inside job.

The Dandy

A figure of intrigue who uses style, aesthetic, and identity fluidity to disrupt expectations and create attraction. They draw people in through uniqueness, not conformity… often remaining just out of reach emotionally.

Behavior Pattern (How They Operate)

- Uses appearance and presence as expression
- Breaks traditional norms intentionally
- Creates intrigue through ambiguity
- Attracts attention without seeking approval
- May use mystery to avoid emotional clarity

Archetypes Through History

- Oscar Wilde — wit, style, and rebellion as identity
- The artistic provocateur
- The figure who turns self-expression into magnetism

Modern-Day Version

- Distinct aesthetic, highly curated identity
- Feels different from everyone else
- Draws people in through originality
- Hard to categorize… sometimes hard to connect with

Signature Phrases

- "I don't really fit into labels"
- "I just do my own thing"
- "People don't always get me"
- "I like being different"

Why People Fall For It

- Because difference is magnetic.
- Because mystery feels deep.
- Because uniqueness feels rare and exciting.

The Damage

- Confusion between depth and ambiguity
- Emotional distance masked as intrigue
- Difficulty forming grounded connection

Spot It Fast

- Strong aesthetic identity
- Hard to categorize emotionally
- Feels intriguing but unclear
- Keeps a level of distance

Avoid / Counter

- Appreciate without idealizing
- Separate mystery from avoidance
- Ask for clarity and watch the response

Your Dating UnExpert Take: Not everyone is meant to be defined. But if they can't be known, they can't be loved in a real way either.

The Disappointed Dreamer

Someone quietly unfulfilled by their life who projects fantasy, romance, and possibility onto people as a form of escape. They're not falling in love with you. They're falling in love with what you represent.

Behavior Pattern (How They Operate)

- Feels stuck or uninspired in their current life
- Craves excitement, novelty, emotional highs
- Projects fantasy onto new people quickly
- Builds a future in their head before reality catches up
- Becomes disillusioned when reality doesn't match the dream

Archetypes Through History

- Jay Gatsby — obsessed with an ideal, not the real person

- Romantic idealists in literature chasing “something more”
- The dreamer who confuses longing with love

Modern-Day Version

- Falls fast because they’re bored, not because it’s real
- Builds entire future scenarios after a few dates
- Sees you as their “way out” of their current life
- Loses interest when the fantasy fades

Signature Phrases

- “I just want something more”
- “I feel like you could change everything for me”
- “I’ve been waiting for something like this”
- “This feels different”

Why People Fall For It

- Because it feels romantic.
- Because being someone’s “escape” feels powerful.
- Because intensity gets mistaken for meaning.

The Damage

- Unrealistic expectations
- Emotional projection
- Disappointment when reality sets in

Spot It Fast

- Talks about the future too soon
- Romanticizes everything quickly
- Feels intense without real foundation
- Seems more excited about possibility than reality

Avoid / Counter

- Slow the pace
- Stay grounded in what’s actually happening
- Watch consistency over imagination

Your Dating UnExpert Take: Boredom is loud. It will convince you anything new is meaningful. It’s not. It’s just different.

The Drama Queen / King

Someone addicted to emotional intensity, conflict, and chaos. They don’t feel alive in peace. They feel alive in reaction, escalation, and emotional turbulence.

Behavior Pattern (How They Operate)

- Creates emotional highs and lows
- Escalates small issues into big conflicts
- Feels uncomfortable in calm or stability
- Picks fights, tests boundaries, or stirs tension
- Reconnects through intensity, not resolution

Archetypes Through History

- Volatile lovers in tragic romances
- Characters who equate passion with conflict
- The chaos-driven partner in countless stories

Modern-Day Version

- Starts arguments over minor things
- Needs constant emotional stimulation
- Confuses toxicity with chemistry
- Says "we're just passionate" to justify dysfunction

Signature Phrases

- "I just feel things deeply"
- "Why are you being so calm?"
- "You don't care enough"
- "I need more from you" (but can't define it)

Why People Fall For It

- Because intensity feels like passion.
- Because highs feel addictive.
- Because calm can feel unfamiliar if chaos is what you're used to.

The Damage

- Emotional exhaustion
- Constant instability
- Loss of peace and clarity

Spot It Fast

- Frequent emotional swings
- Escalates quickly
- Creates problems out of nothing
- Feels uncomfortable in calm moments

Avoid / Counter

- Don't engage in escalation
- Stay grounded and steady

- If everything is always intense, it's not healthy

Your Dating UnExpert Take: Peace is not boring. It's unfamiliar to people who are addicted to dysfunction.

The Exotic Fetishist

Someone drawn to novelty, difference, or "otherness," often reducing people to what makes them unique rather than who they are. They are attracted to the idea of you, not the reality of you.

Behavior Pattern (How They Operate)

- Focuses heavily on what makes you "different"
- Idealizes your background, culture, or traits
- Sees you as an experience, not a person
- Struggles to connect beyond surface-level fascination
- Moves on once the novelty fades

Archetypes Through History

- Colonial-era fascination with the "exotic"
- Characters obsessed with the unfamiliar
- The outsider who becomes a symbol rather than a person

Modern-Day Version

- "I've always wanted to date someone like you"
- Over-focuses on your background or identity
- Treats you like a new experience to explore
- Loses interest once the novelty wears off

Signature Phrases

- "You're so different"
- "I've never been with someone like you"
- "That's so interesting about you"
- "I love your vibe" (but can't go deeper)

Why People Fall For It

- Because it feels like admiration.
- Because being seen as unique feels validating.
- Because attention can mask objectification.

The Damage

- Feeling reduced to a trait
- Lack of real emotional connection
- Being "interesting" instead of valued

Spot It Fast

- Over-focus on what makes you "different"
- Shallow curiosity
- Lack of deeper emotional interest
- Interest fades quickly

Avoid / Counter

- Look for depth of questions
- Watch if they engage beyond surface traits
- Don't mistake fascination for connection

Your Dating UnExpert Take: If they're attracted to your difference but don't respect your depth, they're not seeing you. They're consuming you.

The Ideal Lover

A person who reflects your deepest desires, fantasies, and emotional needs so precisely that it feels like fate. They don't just connect with you. They become what you've always wanted.

Behavior Pattern (How They Operate)

- Studies your desires, values, and emotional gaps
- Mirrors your ideal relationship dynamic
- Feels perfectly aligned early on
- Creates emotional intensity through precision
- Often cannot sustain the performance long-term

Archetypes Through History

- Jay Gatsby (again, but from the other side) — creating an ideal to be loved
- The "perfect partner" illusion in romantic narratives
- Figures who embody fantasy more than reality

Modern-Day Version

- Shares all your values instantly
- Feels like they "just get you" on every level
- Says exactly what you've always wanted to hear
- Becomes inconsistent once the mask slips

Signature Phrases

- "I've been looking for someone like you"
- "This is exactly what I want too"
- "You're everything I've been waiting for"

- "I feel like this is meant to be"

Why People Fall For It

- Because it feels like alignment.
- Because it feels rare.
- Because it feels like finally being chosen correctly.

The Damage

- Emotional whiplash when consistency breaks
- Confusion between real connection and performance
- Difficulty trusting future connections

Spot It Fast

- Feels perfect too quickly
- Matches everything you say
- No friction, no difference, no individuality
- Intensity without time

Avoid / Counter

- Look for differences, not just similarities
- Slow things down
- Pay attention to consistency over time

Your Dating UnExpert Take: Real connection builds. It doesn't arrive fully formed in week one.

The Idol Worshiper

Someone who places their partner on a pedestal, idealizing them to the point of distortion. They don't see you clearly. They see a version of you they've created.

Behavior Pattern (How They Operate)

- Idealizes quickly
- Overpraises and elevates you
- Ignores flaws or red flags
- Builds unrealistic expectations
- Eventually becomes disappointed when reality shows up

Archetypes Through History

- Devoted followers in mythology and romance
- Characters who fall in love with an illusion
- The admirer who confuses projection with devotion

Modern-Day Version

- "You're perfect" energy early on

- Over-the-top admiration
- Puts you on a pedestal quickly
- Becomes disillusioned when you show normal human flaws

Signature Phrases

- "You can do no wrong"
- "You're everything"
- "I've never met anyone like you"
- "You're perfect"

Why People Fall For It

- Because it feels amazing at first.
- Because being adored feels validating.
- Because it feels like finally being fully appreciated.

The Damage

- Pressure to maintain perfection
- Sudden shift from admiration to disappointment
- Feeling misunderstood when reality hits

Spot It Fast

- Overpraise early
- Unrealistic admiration
- Ignores flaws
- Moves too fast emotionally

Avoid / Counter

- Stay grounded in reality
- Don't perform perfection
- Let them see the real you early

Your Dating UnExpert Take: Being idealized is not the same as being known. And what's built on illusion will always collapse under reality.

The Natural

Someone who embodies spontaneity, openness, and emotional ease in a way that disarms others instantly. They don't perform connection. They create an environment where it happens naturally.

Behavior Pattern (How They Operate)

- Moves through interactions with ease and authenticity
- Makes others feel comfortable quickly
- Doesn't overthink or overperform
- Creates lightness without trying

- Builds connection through presence, not effort

Archetypes Through History

- The carefree spirit in literature and storytelling
- Characters who disarm others through innocence and openness
- The "effortless one" who makes connection feel simple

Modern-Day Version

- Easy to talk to from the start
- No games, no pressure, no performance
- Feels refreshing compared to typical dating dynamics
- People feel like themselves around them quickly

Signature Phrases

- "Just be yourself"
- "It's not that serious"
- "Let's just enjoy it"
- "Go with it"

Why People Fall For It

- Because it feels safe.
- Because it feels easy.
- Because it removes the pressure most people are used to.

The Damage

- Can be taken for granted
- May lack intentional depth if not balanced
- Others may project more meaning than is actually there

Spot It Fast

- Feels effortless to be around
- No pressure, no games
- Naturally engaging
- Doesn't overcomplicate connection

Avoid / Counter

- Appreciate it, don't idealize it
- Look for depth alongside ease
- Don't mistake comfort for long-term compatibility

Your Dating UnExpert Take: Real ease is rare. But make sure it's not just comfort without direction.

The New Prude

Someone who presents as controlled, reserved, or "proper," while internally wrestling with suppressed desire, curiosity, or rebellion. Their restraint creates tension that eventually demands release.

Behavior Pattern (How They Operate)

- Maintains a composed, controlled exterior
- Avoids vulnerability or exploration
- Suppresses desires instead of integrating them
- Experiences internal tension and frustration
- May swing between restraint and sudden release

Archetypes Through History

- The repressed figure in classic literature
- Characters torn between duty and desire
- The "proper" persona hiding inner conflict

Modern-Day Version

- Appears put-together, controlled, "low drama"
- Avoids emotional or physical expression
- Secretly craves more but doesn't act on it
- May have sudden, unexpected shifts in behavior

Signature Phrases

- "That's not really my thing"
- "I'm just more reserved"
- "I don't do that"
- "I like to keep things simple"

Why People Fall For It

- Because restraint can feel intriguing.
- Because mystery can feel deep.
- Because control can look like stability.

The Damage

- Internal frustration
- Emotional disconnection
- Sudden, confusing behavioral shifts

Spot It Fast

- Highly controlled behavior
- Avoids vulnerability
- Feels emotionally restricted

- Subtle tension beneath the surface

Avoid / Counter

- Look for alignment, not suppression
- Watch for consistency
- Don't try to "unlock" someone who won't open

Your Dating UnExpert Take: Repression doesn't remove desire. It builds pressure behind it.

The Novice

An inexperienced or naive individual who approaches relationships with curiosity, openness, and limited awareness of risk. Their innocence attracts... but also leaves them vulnerable.

Behavior Pattern (How They Operate)

- Eager to learn and experience
- Trusts quickly
- Seeks guidance or direction
- Lacks pattern recognition
- May overlook red flags due to inexperience

Archetypes Through History

- The innocent entering a complex world
- Characters guided, shaped, or misled by others
- The beginner navigating unfamiliar emotional terrain

Modern-Day Version

- New to dating or certain relationship dynamics
- Asks questions, seeks reassurance
- Easily influenced by stronger personalities
- Learns through experience, sometimes the hard way

Signature Phrases

- "I've never done this before"
- "Is this normal?"
- "I just want to see where it goes"
- "I trust you"

Why People Fall For It

- Because innocence feels refreshing.
- Because it feels genuine.
- Because it allows others to feel knowledgeable or needed.

The Damage

- Vulnerability to manipulation
- Poor boundaries
- Emotional confusion from lack of experience

Spot It Fast

- Inexperienced in relationships
- Trusts quickly
- Looks for guidance
- Misses obvious red flags

Avoid / Counter

- Encourage awareness, not dependence
- Let experience build naturally
- Watch how others treat their innocence

Your Dating UnExpert Take: Curiosity is powerful. Just don't outsource your judgment while you're learning.

The Pampered Royal

Someone who expects to be pursued, prioritized, and indulged without offering equal effort in return. They view relationships as something to receive from, not build together.

Behavior Pattern (How They Operate)

- Expects attention and effort
- Offers minimal reciprocity
- Positions themselves as the prize
- Tests how much you'll give
- Becomes dissatisfied even when receiving

Archetypes Through History

- Royal figures accustomed to being served
- The "high-value" persona taken to imbalance
- Characters who expect devotion without contribution

Modern-Day Version

- Expects constant effort, planning, and attention
- Rarely initiates or reciprocates
- Believes they are the "catch" without question
- Leaves others feeling like they're trying to earn them

Signature Phrases

- "I like to be treated well"

- "You should want to do that for me"
- "I deserve that"
- "Effort matters" (but only yours)

Why People Fall For It

- Because exclusivity feels valuable.
- Because earning someone's attention feels rewarding.
- Because people confuse effort with worth.

The Damage

- One-sided relationships
- Emotional imbalance
- Constant feeling of not doing enough

Spot It Fast

- Low effort, high expectations
- Rarely initiates
- Expects to be pursued
- Doesn't reciprocate energy

Avoid / Counter

- Match effort, don't exceed it
- Watch what they give without prompting
- Don't chase someone who isn't moving toward you

Your Dating UnExpert Take: If effort only flows one way, it's not attraction. It's imbalance.

The Professor

An intellectually driven type who connects through ideas, analysis, and mental stimulation—often prioritizing thought over emotional depth. They can make connection feel deep... without actually being emotionally available.

Behavior Pattern (How They Operate)

- Engages through conversation and ideas
- Values intelligence and mental challenge
- Analyzes rather than feels
- Creates connection through discussion, not vulnerability
- May avoid emotional intimacy through intellectualization

Archetypes Through History

- The intellectual thinker detached from emotion
- Scholars and philosophers prioritizing logic over feeling

- Characters who "understand everything" but struggle to connect

Modern-Day Version

- Deep conversations early on
- Talks about psychology, philosophy, life meaning
- Feels mentally stimulating
- Emotionally… harder to access

Signature Phrases

- "Let's think about this logically"
- "That's interesting from a psychological standpoint"
- "I've been reading about…"
- "Here's how I see it"

Why People Fall For It

- Because it feels deep.
- Because mental stimulation feels like connection.
- Because intelligence is attractive.

The Damage

- Emotional needs go unmet
- Overthinking replaces feeling
- Connection feels deep but lacks intimacy

Spot It Fast

- Highly intellectual conversations
- Avoids emotional vulnerability
- Analyzes instead of expresses
- Feels deep but distant

Avoid / Counter

- Look for emotional availability
- Don't confuse intellect with intimacy
- Ask how they feel, not just what they think

Your Dating UnExpert Take: Mental connection is powerful. But if they can explain feelings better than they can feel them, you'll always be slightly alone.

The Rake

A highly passionate, desire-driven pursuer who overwhelms with intensity, attention, and urgency. They don't just like you. They consume you. And in that consumption, you feel chosen above everyone else.

Behavior Pattern (How They Operate)

- Locks in quickly with intense focus
- Floods you with attention, desire, and urgency
- Creates emotional and physical intensity early
- Makes you feel singular, unmatched, irreplaceable
- Pulls back once the intensity peaks or fades

Archetypes Through History

- Casanova — passion as conquest, not permanence
- The obsessive romantic figure in literature
- Lovers defined by intensity, not consistency

Modern-Day Version

- Fast, intense texting and attention
- Feels obsessed with you early on
- Talks in extremes
- Disappears or cools off once things stabilize

Signature Phrases

- "I've never felt this way before"
- "I need you"
- "You're everything"
- "I can't get enough of you"

Why People Fall For It

- Because intensity feels real.
- Because desire feels validating.
- Because being chosen that strongly feels rare.

The Damage

- Emotional crash after the high
- Confusion when intensity fades
- Attachment built on adrenaline, not stability

Spot It Fast

- Overwhelming attention early
- Speaks in extremes

- Moves fast emotionally and physically
- Energy drops suddenly

Avoid / Counter

- Slow the pace
- Don't match intensity blindly
- Watch what remains when the high fades

Your Dating UnExpert Take: Intensity creates attachment fast. That doesn't mean it can sustain anything real.

The Reformed Rake / Siren

A once wild, passionate, or pleasure-driven individual now living a more restrained life... but still internally pulled toward the intensity they left behind. They haven't transformed. They've contained.

Behavior Pattern (How They Operate)

- Presents as stable, grounded, "past that phase"
- Avoids fully engaging with desire or chaos
- Feels internal tension between who they were and who they are
- Occasionally slips into old patterns
- Carries quiet dissatisfaction

Archetypes Through History

- The retired libertine
- The reformed seductress trying to live "correctly"
- Figures torn between freedom and structure

Modern-Day Version

- "I've done all that, I'm over it" energy
- Lives more controlled, structured life
- Still drawn to intensity behind the scenes
- May relapse into old dynamics under pressure or temptation

Signature Phrases

- "That's not me anymore"
- "I've grown out of that"
- "I just want something calm now"
- "I've changed"

Why People Fall For It

- Because transformation is attractive.
- Because stability feels safe.

- Because people believe the past is fully resolved.

The Damage

- Internal conflict leaks into the relationship
- Sudden shifts in behavior
- Feeling like something is always slightly… off

Spot It Fast

- Strong past, overly controlled present
- Avoids discussing old patterns deeply
- Feels restrained rather than aligned
- Subtle tension beneath calm

Avoid / Counter

- Look for true integration, not suppression
- Ask how they've changed, not just if they have
- Watch for consistency under pressure

Your Dating UnExpert Take: If desire is suppressed instead of integrated, it doesn't disappear. It waits.

The Rescuer /ˈre-skyü-ər/

Someone who derives identity and worth from helping, fixing, or saving others. They don't just love people. They take responsibility for them.

Behavior Pattern (How They Operate)

- Drawn to people who need support
- Steps in quickly to help, guide, or fix
- Overextends emotionally and practically
- Feels needed, therefore valuable
- Burns out or becomes resentful

Archetypes Through History

- The savior figure in romantic and tragic narratives
- The martyr who gives everything
- Characters who confuse sacrifice with love

Modern-Day Version

- Attracted to "projects" or struggling partners
- Over-gives early
- Takes on emotional labor automatically
- Struggles to set boundaries

Signature Phrases

- "I just want to help"
- "They've been through a lot"
- "I can fix this"
- "They just need someone to show up"

Why People Fall For It

- Because it feels like love.
- Because being cared for feels safe.
- Because giving feels meaningful.

The Damage

- Burnout
- Imbalance
- Loss of self in the process

Spot It Fast

- Over-giving early
- Drawn to struggling partners
- Avoids boundaries
- Feels responsible for others' emotions

Avoid / Counter

- Don't over-function
- Let people show up for themselves
- Watch for mutual effort

Your Dating UnExpert Take: Support is healthy. Responsibility for someone else's life is not.

The Roué /rü-ˈā/

A seasoned pleasure-seeker who has experienced it all and now feels under-stimulated by what once excited them. They chase novelty not out of curiosity… but out of boredom.

Behavior Pattern (How They Operate)

- Seeks stimulation and variety
- Becomes quickly bored with consistency
- Pursues newness over depth
- Has high tolerance for intensity
- Moves on when things feel familiar

Archetypes Through History

- The jaded aristocrat

- The indulgent libertine
- Figures who exhaust pleasure until nothing satisfies

Modern-Day Version

- Always chasing something new
- Gets bored in stable relationships
- Has "seen it all" energy
- Moves on when excitement dips

Signature Phrases

- "I've already done that"
- "I just need something different"
- "I get bored easily"
- "I like variety"

Why People Fall For It

- Because experience feels attractive.
- Because confidence comes with familiarity.
- Because novelty feels exciting.

The Damage

- Lack of stability
- Constant chasing
- Inability to sustain connection

Spot It Fast

- Easily bored
- Constant need for stimulation
- Avoids routine
- Moves on quickly

Avoid / Counter

- Don't try to "be enough"
- Watch their history
- Choose consistency over excitement

Your Dating UnExpert Take: If they're chasing new, they're not built to stay. Depth requires repetition. They avoid it.

The Siren /ˈsī-rən/

A deeply sensual, magnetic presence that draws others in through energy, allure, and emotional intoxication. They don't pursue. They pull.

Behavior Pattern (How They Operate)

- Radiates confidence and sensuality
- Uses presence more than words
- Creates strong emotional and physical pull
- Keeps a layer of mystery
- Leaves others slightly disoriented

Archetypes Through History

- Mythological sirens luring sailors
- The seductive muse
- Figures whose power lies in presence alone

Modern-Day Version

- Magnetic energy in person
- Strong physical or emotional pull
- People feel drawn without clear reason
- Leaves a lasting impression

Signature Phrases

- "Come here"
- "Relax"
- "Don't overthink it"
- "Just feel it"

Why People Fall For It

- Because attraction bypasses logic.
- Because desire feels primal.
- Because energy can override clarity.

The Damage

- Loss of perspective
- Acting on feeling over reality
- Confusing chemistry with compatibility

Spot It Fast

- Strong physical/emotional pull
- Hard to explain attraction
- Feels intoxicating

- Leaves you slightly off-balance

Avoid / Counter

- Stay grounded
- Separate feeling from fact
- Don't abandon logic

Your Dating UnExpert Take: Attraction is powerful. But if it overrides your judgment, it's not connection. It's influence.

THE STAR

An elusive, elevated presence that creates desire through distance, mystique, and what they represent. They are admired, idealized, and pursued... but rarely truly known.

Behavior Pattern (How They Operate)

- Maintains emotional or physical distance
- Reveals just enough to intrigue
- Creates curiosity and projection
- Avoids full accessibility
- Builds desire through absence

Archetypes Through History

- Marilyn Monroe — adored, projected onto, rarely fully known
- The untouchable icon
- Figures defined by image more than intimacy

Modern-Day Version

- Highly curated presence
- Slightly out of reach emotionally
- People become obsessed from a distance
- Hard to fully connect with

Signature Phrases

- "I like my space"
- "You don't need to know everything"
- "I keep things private"
- "You'll see"

Why People Fall For It

- Because distance creates desire.
- Because mystery invites projection.
- Because what we don't have feels more valuable.

The Damage

- Falling for an idea, not a person
- Emotional distance
- Lack of real connection

Spot It Fast

- Feels slightly out of reach
- Limited emotional access
- Highly curated presence
- Creates intrigue, not clarity

Avoid / Counter

- Look for accessibility
- Don't chase distance
- Choose presence over mystery

Your Dating UnExpert Take: Mystery creates attraction. But relationships require access. If they stay distant, they stay fantasy.

Movies that Exhibit Trash Behavior

Sometimes the fastest way to understand your love life isn't another conversation, it's a pattern you've already watched play out. The confusion, the almosts, the intensity that feels like something... until it doesn't. These stories aren't new. They've been written, performed, and replayed for years just with different faces and better lighting. What changes is your ability to recognize them.

This section breaks down those patterns through the lens of familiar narratives, pairing them with the exact behaviors defined in the *Dictionary of Trash Behavior*. Not to analyze the movies, but to help you see your own situation more clearly. Because once you can name the pattern, you stop personalizing it... and that's where everything starts to shift.

Situationships, Almosts & Emotional Chaos

1. He's Just Not That Into You

- **Terms:** Breadcrumbing, Back Burner, Clarity Starvation
- **Why it hits:** Mixed signals decoded... brutally.

2. 500 Days of Summer

- **Terms:** Delusionship, Attachment Hallucination, Almost Guy
- **Why it hits:** One person in reality, one in fantasy.

3. Someone Great

- **Terms:** Almost Griever, Emotional Recycling, Boxoflies Syndrome
- **Why it hits:** Mourning something that never fully chose you.

4. Friends with Benefits

- **Terms:** Attentionship, Emotional Booty Call, Commitmency
- **Why it hits:** "Casual" doing a lot of emotional heavy lifting.

5. No Strings Attached

- **Terms:** Emotional Slot Machine, Confusionship, Cannonballing
- **Why it hits:** Hookup → feelings → denial → chaos loop.

6. La La Land

- **Terms:** Almost Guy, Convenience Chemistry, Emotional Recycling
- **Why it hits:** Right connection, wrong life timing.

7. One Day

- **Terms:** Back Burner, Emotional Placeholder, Attachmencycle
- **Why it hits:** Years of "almost choosing each other."

8. Before Sunrise (Trilogy)

- **Terms:** Convenience Chemistry, Almost Griever, Delusionship
- **Why it hits:** Deep connection... with no structural follow-through.

9. Before We Go

- **Terms:** Convenience Chemistry, Emotional Placeholder, Almost Guy
- **Why it hits:** One night intimacy that can't exist in real life.

10. Call Me By Your Name

- **Terms:** Cannonballing, Almost Griever, Attachment Hallucination
- **Why it hits:** Intensity without permanence.

11. Love & Other Drugs

- **Terms:** Emotional Booty Call, Commitmency, Emotional Self-Betrayal
- **Why it hits:** Avoidance disguised as independence.

12. The Spectacular Now

- **Terms:** Effort Sponge, Emotional Airbnb, Almost Guy

- **Why it hits:** One grows… the other stays emotionally unavailable.

13. Like Crazy

- **Terms:** Clarity Starvation, Attachmencycle, Delusionship
- **Why it hits:** Distance + inconsistency = emotional torture.

14. The Last Song

- **Terms:** Cannonballing, Emotional Slot Machine, Almost Griever
- **Why it hits:** Fast attachment, fragile foundation.

15. How to Be Single

- **Terms:** Attention Leasing, Delulu Dating, Convenience Chemistry
- **Why it hits:** Entertaining chaos while pretending it's exploration.

16. Sleeping with Other People

- **Terms:** Confusionship, Attentionship, Commitmency
- **Why it hits:** "We're just friends"… doing relationship things.

17. To All the Boys I've Loved Before

- **Terms:** Delusionship, Convenience Chemistry, Almost Guy
- **Why it hits:** Fake relationship… real feelings… unclear intentions.

18. The Half of It

- **Terms:** Emotional Placeholder, Delusionship, Attachment Hallucination
- **Why it hits:** Loving someone who emotionally lives somewhere else.

19. Begin Again

- **Terms:** Convenience Chemistry, Almost Griever, Emotional Recycling
- **Why it hits:** Healing connection… not a forever one.

20. Before Midnight

- **Terms:** Emotional Overdraft, Effort Reversal, Clarity Starvation

- **Why it hits:** What happens when "almost perfect" meets real life.

Toxic Men, Narc Energy & Manipulation

1. **Gone Girl**
   - **Terms:** Ego Preservation Mode, Emotional Blackmail, Double Life
   - **Why it hits:** When control matters more than truth.
2. **The Wolf of Wall Street**
   - **Terms:** Ego-nomics, Attention Leasing, Audacity Syndrome
   - **Why it hits:** Chaos, ego, and zero accountability packaged as charisma.
3. **American Psycho**
   - **Terms:** Algorithmic Validation Addiction, Egoverload, Emotionally Bankrupt
   - **Why it hits:** A man built entirely on image... with nothing underneath.
4. **The Other Woman**
   - **Terms:** Adultery, Affair, Double Life, Deluluvictim
   - **Why it hits:** Lies collapse the second women compare reality.
5. **You (Series, but culturally required)**
   - **Terms:** Emotional Hoovering, Ego-sexual, Double Life
   - **Why it hits:** Obsession disguised as love... with a narration to justify it.
6. **Fatal Attraction**
   - **Terms:** Emotional Blackmail, Deluluvictim, Confusionbond
   - **Why it hits:** When obsession escalates into control and consequences.
7. **Cruel Intentions**
   - **Terms:** Ego Farming, Emotional Manipulation, Clownfidence
   - **Why it hits:** Seduction used as a power game, not connection.

8. Dirty John

- **Terms:** Emotional Parasitic, Ego Preservation Mode, Double Life
- **Why it hits:** The charming man with a past… that keeps repeating.

9. The Talented Mr. Ripley

- **Terms:** Identity Manipulation, Egoverload, Emotionalillusionism
- **Why it hits:** Becoming whoever he needs to be to gain access.

10. Basic Instinct

- **Terms:** Emotional Control, Ego-nomics, Power Seduction
- **Why it hits:** When attraction becomes psychological dominance.

11. Fifty Shades of Grey

- **Terms:** Emotional Control, Ego Preservation Mode, Commitmency
- **Why it hits:** Control framed as romance… without emotional safety.

12. The Great Gatsby

- **Terms:** Delusiondependence, Ego-sexual, Emotional Recycling
- **Why it hits:** Obsession with an idea… not the actual person.

13. Match Point

- **Terms:** Double Life, Ego Preservation Mode, Emotional Self-Betrayal
- **Why it hits:** When protecting status matters more than human life.

14. Closer

- **Terms:** Emotional Blackmail, Confusionship, Ego Preservation Mode
- **Why it hits:** Brutal honesty weaponized to hurt, not heal.

15. The Social Network

- **Terms:** Algorithmic Validation Addiction, Ego Farming, Emotionally Bankrupt
- **Why it hits:** Builds an empire… loses every real connection.

16. Silver Linings Playbook

- **Terms:** Emotional Ping-Pong, Emotional Instability, Confusionbond
- **Why it hits:** When dysfunction feels like chemistry.

17. Obsessed

- **Terms:** Emotional Blackmail, Deluluvictim, Boundary Violation
- **Why it hits:** Refusal to accept reality turns into fixation.

18. The Perfect Guy

- **Terms:** Ego Preservation Mode, Emotional Hoovering, Control Tactics
- **Why it hits:** The "perfect" man who turns the second control is threatened.

19. Unfaithful

- **Terms:** Adultery, Emotional Self-Betrayal, Delusionloophole
- **Why it hits:** One decision fueled by fantasy... destroys everything real.

20. The Devil Wears Prada

- **Terms:** Ego-nomics, Audacity Syndrome, Emotional Overdraft (on others)
- **Why it hits:** Power without empathy... and the cost of staying too long.

Bare Minimum Men & Delusion

1. Failure to Launch

- **Terms:** Bare Minimum Bandit, Effortphobic, Emotionallygoner
- **Why it hits:** Fully grown man... allergic to effort.

2. Knocked Up

- **Terms:** Affordating, Effort Sponge, Convenience King
- **Why it hits:** She builds the life. He shows up... occasionally.

3. The Break-Up

- **Terms:** Effort Reversal, Emotional Overdraft, Clarity Avoidance Addiction

- **Why it hits:** Effort disappears and resentment takes over.

4. Forgetting Sarah Marshall

- **Terms:** Emotionallygoner, Effortlesshole, Bare Minimum Love Language
- **Why it hits:** He only grows after she leaves. Classic.

5. Bridesmaids

- **Terms:** Bare Minimum Bandit, Convenience King, Emotional Unavailability
- **Why it hits:** The "casual guy" who keeps you exactly where he wants you.

6. How to Lose a Guy in 10 Days

- **Terms:** Consistency Cosplay, Ego-nomics, Effort Inflation
- **Why it hits:** Both playing games… neither offering anything real.

7. He's All That

- **Terms:** Delulunarc, Effortlesshole, Clownfidence
- **Why it hits:** Confidence with absolutely nothing to back it up.

8. She's All That

- **Terms:** Bareminimumism, Effort Inflation, Delusionloophole
- **Why it hits:** One decent act suddenly makes him "worthy."

9. Crazy, Stupid, Love

- **Terms:** Egoverload, Effort Reversal, Clownfidence
- **Why it hits:** Men doing the most externally… and the least emotionally.

10. Just Go With It

- **Terms:** Effort Sponge, Convenience King, Attention Leasing
- **Why it hits:** She carries the entire situation while he benefits.

11. The Ugly Truth

- **Terms:** Ego-nomics, Bare Minimum Bandit, Audacity Syndrome
- **Why it hits:** Loud opinions, low emotional intelligence.

12. Two Night Stand

- **Terms:** Cannonballing, Effortphobic, Bare Minimum Love Language
- **Why it hits:** Forced proximity doesn't fix lack of effort.

13. **What Happens in Vegas**
    - **Terms:** Convenience King, Effort Reversal, Bareminimumism
    - **Why it hits:** Commitment only when legally forced... yikes.
14. **Along Came Polly**
    - **Terms:** Emotional Chaos + Effortphobic, Clownfidence
    - **Why it hits:** Unstable man, zero planning, somehow still centered.
15. **The Heartbreak Kid**
    - **Terms:** Delusiondependence, Effort Reversal, Bare Minimum Bandit
    - **Why it hits:** Realizes too late... after doing the least the entire time.
16. **My Best Friend's Girl**
    - **Terms:** Effortlesshole, Ego-nomics, Emotional Immaturity
    - **Why it hits:** Weaponized bad behavior disguised as personality.
17. **That Awkward Moment**
    - **Terms:** Commitmency, Attentionship, Effortphobic
    - **Why it hits:** Wants access... refuses definition.
18. **The Internship**
    - **Terms:** Clownfidence, Delulunarc, Effort Inflation
    - **Why it hits:** Overconfidence carrying men further than competence.
19. **Hitch**
    - **Terms:** Consistency Cosplay, Effort Inflation, Ego Preservation Mode
    - **Why it hits:** Teaching men how to perform effort... not sustain it.
20. **Friends (Ross, respectfully...)**

- **Terms:** Emotional Overdraft, Ego Preservation Mode, Effort Reversal
- **Why it hits:** Wants you... but only on his terms and timeline.

Toxic Patterns, Trauma Bonds & Spirals

1. Twilight

- **Terms:** Chokehold, Emotional Self-Harm, Attachmencycle
- **Why it hits:** You know it's bad... but you're still obsessed.

2. The Notebook

- **Terms:** Emotional Ping-Pong, Cannonballing, Chemistry Confusion
- **Why it hits:** Romanticized instability. Exhausting in real life.

3. Eat Pray Love

- **Terms:** Emotional Recycling, Closure Addiction, Almost Griever
- **Why it hits:** Leaving the life... not the pattern (at first).

4. Blue Valentine

- **Terms:** Delayed Disrespect, Emotional Overdraft, Effort Reversal
- **Why it hits:** Love fades when growth doesn't happen.

5. 6 Years

- **Terms:** Emotional Self-Harm, Confusionbond, Emotional Ping-Pong
- **Why it hits:** Staying long after it stopped being healthy.

6. Malcolm & Marie

- **Terms:** Emotional Blackmail, Ego Preservation Mode, Emotional Ping-Pong
- **Why it hits:** One argument... exposing the entire relationship.

7. Revolutionary Road

- **Terms:** Emotional Overdraft, Delayed Disrespect, Emotionalillusionism
- **Why it hits:** The dream life becomes the trap.

8. Candy (2006)

- **Terms:** Emotional Self-Harm, Emotional Overdraft, Attachmencycle
- **Why it hits:** Addiction + love = a cycle you can't win.

9. Endless Love

- **Terms:** Chokehold, Delusiondependence, Emotional Self-Harm
- **Why it hits:** Intensity overriding reality.

10. Wicker Park

- **Terms:** Attachment Hallucination, Delusionloophole, Emotional Recycling
- **Why it hits:** Chasing a version of someone that isn't real.

11. The Best of Me

- **Terms:** Emotional Recycling, Attachmencycle, Delusiondependence
- **Why it hits:** Going back to what already didn't work.

12. Dear John

- **Terms:** Clarity Starvation, Emotional Recycling, Almost Griever
- **Why it hits:** Love lost through silence and distance.

13. The Choice

- **Terms:** Delusionloophole, Emotional Recycling, Attachment Conflict
- **Why it hits:** Holding onto one moment to justify everything.

14. Remember Me

- **Terms:** Cannonballing, Emotional Self-Harm, Almost Griever
- **Why it hits:** Fast love, lasting emotional damage.

15. If I Stay

- **Terms:** Emotional Recycling, Almost Griever, Attachment Conflict
- **Why it hits:** Torn between past love and future self.

16. Adrift

- **Terms:** Emotionalillusionism, Attachment Hallucination, Trauma Bonding
- **Why it hits:** Survival distorts connection.

17. The Light Between Oceans

- **Terms:** Emotional Self-Betrayal, Delusiondependence, Moral Spiral
- **Why it hits:** One choice becomes a lifetime loop.

18. Safe Haven

- **Terms:** Trauma Bonding, Emotional Protection Loop, Delusiondependence
- **Why it hits:** Safety mistaken for compatibility.

19. Like Sunday, Like Rain

- **Terms:** Emotional Overdraft, Quiet Detachment, Almost Griever
- **Why it hits:** The spiral isn't always loud... sometimes it's slow.

20. One Day (Anne Hathaway)

- **Terms:** Attachmencycle, Emotional Recycling, Almost Griever
- **Why it hits:** Years of repeating the same emotional timing issue.

Modern Dating, Apps & Digital Behavior

1. The Social Network

- **Terms:** Algorithmic Validation Addiction, Ego Farming, Clout Chasing
- **Why it hits:** Built connection for the world... lost it in real life.

2. Don Jon

- **Terms:** Algorithmic Validation Addiction, Ego-sexual, Attentionorexic
- **Why it hits:** Addicted to fantasy, disconnected from real intimacy.

3. Easy A

- **Terms:** Reputation Clout Chasing, Delusionloophole, Social Narrative Control
- **Why it hits:** Your dating life becomes a storyline... whether it's true or not.

4. Ingrid Goes West

- **Terms:** Algorithmic Validation Addiction, Clout Chasing, Emotionalillusionism
- **Why it hits:** Social media obsession turns into identity loss.

5. Catfish (Documentary)

- **Terms:** Catfishing, Attachment Hallucination, Delusionship
- **Why it hits:** Falling for someone who never existed.

6. Nerve

- **Terms:** Clout Chasing, Ego-nomics, Digital Validation Loop
- **Why it hits:** Attention becomes currency... and addiction.

7. Disconnect

- **Terms:** Digital Boyfriend, Emotional Detachment, Online Illusion Bond
- **Why it hits:** Lives intertwined online... disconnected in reality.

8. You've Got Mail

- **Terms:** Digital Boyfriend, Attachment Hallucination, Delusionship
- **Why it hits:** Falling in love through words... before reality hits.

9. Her

- **Terms:** Digital Boyfriend, Emotionalillusionism, Attachment Hallucination
- **Why it hits:** Emotional intimacy with something that can't fully exist.

10. Trust (2010)

- **Terms:** Catfishing, Emotional Manipulation, Digital Grooming
- **Why it hits:** Online connection hides dangerous reality.

11. Unfriended

- **Terms:** Digital Reputation Spiral, Social Narrative Control, Online Fallout
- **Why it hits:** Your entire social identity can collapse online.

12. Assassination Nation

- **Terms:** Clout Chasing, Social Exposure Spiral, Digital Chaos
- **Why it hits:** Private lives weaponized publicly.

13. Mainstream

- **Terms:** Clout Chasing, Ego Farming, Algorithmic Validation Addiction
- **Why it hits:** Fame becomes more important than identity.

14. Hard Candy

- **Terms:** Online Persona Manipulation, Catfishing, Power Reversal
- **Why it hits:** Digital identities aren't always what they seem.

15. Cam

- **Terms:** Algorithmic Validation Addiction, Identity Fragmentation, Ego-sexual
- **Why it hits:** When your online persona takes over your reality.

16. Not Okay

- **Terms:** Clout Chasing, Delusiondependence, Social Narrative Control
- **Why it hits:** Faking a life online... and getting trapped in it.

17. Spree

- **Terms:** Algorithmic Validation Addiction, Egoverload, Clout Obsession
- **Why it hits:** Attention at any cost becomes the goal.

18. The Circle

- **Terms:** Surveillance Culture, Validation Addiction, Digital Persona Control
- **Why it hits:** When privacy disappears, performance takes over.

19. Searching

- **Terms:** Digital Identity Layers, Hidden Reality, Online Persona Gaps
- **Why it hits:** You never fully know someone through a screen.

20. Love, Guaranteed

- **Terms:** Dating App Burnout, False Promises, Clarity Starvation
- **Why it hits:** Apps promise connection... deliver confusion.

Affairs, Cheating & Messy Truths

1. Unfaithful

- **Terms:** Adultery, Affair, Emotional Self-Betrayal
- **Why it hits:** One decision... irreversible consequences.

2. Closer

- **Terms:** Emotional Blackmail, Ego Preservation Mode, Confusionbond
- **Why it hits:** Brutal honesty mixed with even worse behavior.

3. The Last Letter From Your Lover

- **Terms:** Affair, Delusionship, Emotional Hoarding
- **Why it hits:** Romanticizing something that required betrayal to exist.

4. Fatal Attraction

- **Terms:** Affair, Emotional Blackmail, Deluluvictim
- **Why it hits:** When a "casual" affair refuses to stay casual.

5. The Bridges of Madison County

- **Terms:** Affair, Emotional Self-Betrayal, Almost Griever
- **Why it hits:** Deep love... built on impossible timing and betrayal.

6. Match Point

- **Terms:** Double Life, Ego Preservation Mode, Adultery
- **Why it hits:** Protecting status at any cost.

7. Little Children

- **Terms:** Adultery, Delusiondependence, Emotional Escape Loop
- **Why it hits:** Affairs as an escape from unfulfilled lives.

8. Chloe

- **Terms:** Suspicion Spiral, Emotional Manipulation, Affair Setup
- **Why it hits:** When insecurity creates the very betrayal you feared.

9. Notes on a Scandal

- **Terms:** Power Imbalance Affair, Emotional Blackmail, Control
- **Why it hits:** Obsession hiding behind "connection."

10. Indecent Proposal

- **Terms:** Transactional Betrayal, Ego-nomics, Emotional Fallout
- **Why it hits:** What happens when love is put up for negotiation.

11. Original Sin

- **Terms:** Deception, Double Life, Emotionalillusionism
- **Why it hits:** Desire built on lies.

12. The Painted Veil

- **Terms:** Adultery, Emotional Self-Betrayal, Redemption Arc
- **Why it hits:** Betrayal followed by forced growth.

13. Diary of a Mad Black Woman

- **Terms:** Adultery, Egoverload, Emotional Overdraft
- **Why it hits:** When a man upgrades his life and discards you… until consequences hit.

14. Addicted

- **Terms:** Affair Addiction, Emotional Self-Harm, Delusiondependence
- **Why it hits:** Knowing it's wrong… and still going back.

15. Two Lovers

- **Terms:** Emotional Cheating, Confusionbond, Delusionship
- **Why it hits:** Torn between stability and desire.

16. Derailed

- **Terms:** Affair, Deception Spiral, Consequence Explosion
- **Why it hits:** One "small" mistake turns into a life collapse.

17. The Good Girl

- **Terms:** Emotional Affair, Escape Fantasy, Delusiondependence
- **Why it hits:** Boredom turns into bad decisions.

18. Disobedience

- **Terms:** Forbidden Affair, Emotional Suppression, Identity Conflict
- **Why it hits:** Desire colliding with societal expectations.

19. A Perfect Murder

- **Terms:** Double Life, Ego-nomics, Betrayal Strategy

- **Why it hits:** Love becomes leverage.

20. Take This Waltz

- **Terms:** Emotional Cheating, Delusionloophole, Affair Escalation
- **Why it hits:** Crossing the line slowly… until you're fully over it.

Other Dating Books by Sarah Melland

I didn't write these books to tell women what to do. I wrote them because I watched too many brilliant women blame themselves for systems that were never built for them to win. Every book I've written exists for a different moment in a woman's life not to fix her, but to remind her who she already is when she's not apologizing, bargaining, or shrinking to survive. If this book helped you see more clearly, the others are here to meet you wherever you are next.

THE BREAKUP BAND-AID

(The one that started it all)

This was written for the woman in acute emotional pain. The one who can't sleep, can't eat, can't stop replaying the ending. It doesn't rush healing or romanticize strength. It simply holds you steady while the bleeding slows and reminds you that heartbreak is not a personal failure, it's a human one. This book exists to keep you company in the dark so you don't confuse pain with truth.

THE DATING SURVIVAL BIBLE

This is the field guide. The pattern decoder. The moment you stop asking *"What's wrong with me?"* and start asking *"What keeps repeating and why?"* It's designed to take women out of emotional free-fall and into clarity, discernment, and self-trust. Not rules. Not games. Just reality, clearly labeled.

RED FLAG TRANSLATOR

This book exists for the moment your intuition starts whispering but you don't yet trust it. It puts language to what you feel but can't quite articulate: the subtle tells, the phrases that sound harmless but aren't, the behaviors that always lead to the same ending. It's not about suspicion. It's about fluency.

THE ART OF WAR & DATING

Dating isn't failing because women care too much—it's failing because they're moving without strategy. *The Art of War & Dating* reframes modern romance as what it actually is: decision-making under uncertainty. It teaches you how to observe, time, and exit cleanly instead of overexplaining, overinvesting, and overhoping. This isn't about playing games or "winning" someone—it's about self-command, clarity, and knowing when to stop fighting battles that were never worth your energy in the first place.

MEDITATIONS & DATING

If *The Art of War & Dating* is strategy, *Meditations & Dating* is mastery of self. Inspired by Marcus Aurelius, it brings stoic clarity into the emotional chaos of modern dating—teaching you how to stay grounded when everything around you is inconsistent, unclear, or triggering. It's not about detaching from love, but about becoming so steady within yourself that no situation, text, or person gets to destabilize you again. Calm, clear, and quietly powerful—that's the energy.

1001 DATING IDEAS

Not every book needs to be heavy. This one is about joy, curiosity, creativity, and remembering that dating doesn't have to feel like a job interview or a trauma reenactment. It's here to reintroduce play, intention, and choice back into connection without abandoning your standards.

BECOMING HER

This book is not about dating at all. It's about identity. It's for the woman who is done centering her life around being chosen and ready to return to herself: her voice, her intuition, her power, her inner coherence. This is the book women read when they stop asking for permission and start living from alignment.

THE ULTIMATE WOMAN'S GUIDE TO LETTING GO

This one is for the season after survival when the noise fades and something quieter, deeper, and more honest begins to emerge. It doesn't force closure. It doesn't rush forgiveness. It teaches release without erasure and helps women put down what they were never meant to carry.

A SINGLE GIRL'S GUIDE SERIES

(Including IVF, sex, and the bucket list)

These books exist to normalize the full, complex, joyful reality of modern womanhood. Desire. Choice. Biology. Humor. Autonomy. They are reminders that there is no single timeline, no single script, and no single way to build a meaningful life. You get to choose and you don't owe anyone an explanation.

AND IF YOU LEARN BEST BY PLAYING...

I've also created games, worksheets, prompts, and tools designed to help you integrate this work into real life not just understand it intellectually. These are for women building businesses, rebuilding confidence, redefining love, or simply learning how to trust themselves again.

You'll find all of that at **yourdatingunexpert.etsy.com**

FINAL WORD

You don't need all of these books.
You don't need to become someone else.
You just need the right words at the right moment.

Take what helps. Leave what doesn't. And trust that the version of you this work is pointing toward has been there all along waiting patiently for you to stop abandoning her.

With love,
Your Dating UnExpert

www.ingramcontent.com/pod-product-compliance
Lightning Source LLC
Chambersburg PA
CBHW051501030726
47592CB00006B/2033

9781969137242